Love the SAT Test Prep presents

SAT & ACT Grammar Mastery

ACT English & SAT Writing Rules

2nd Edition

A Guide & Workbook for the 17 Most Crucial

English Grammar Topics on the SAT & ACT Tests.

By Christian Heath

Founder of Love the SAT Test Prep

www.LovetheSAT.com

Also by Christian Heath

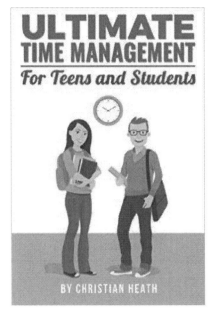

Ultimate Time Management for Teens and Students

If there's one thing that unites every high school student, it's that they never have enough time or energy to get everything done. It's time for that to change.

This book contains an arsenal of tips, tricks, and strategies from a veteran SAT & ACT tutor and elite-college graduate that will work for every high school student at any point in their high school career.

Get better grades, have more fun, reduce your anxiety, enjoy life more, win more scholarships, and get into a better college! Available on Amazon at https://amzn.to/2SxWPj8.

Personalized SAT & ACT Tutoring

Get higher SAT & ACT scores with a fun & friendly 1-on-1 personal tutor! Our staff of experienced SAT & ACT prep tutors can work with any high school student to reach new high scores, build confidence, eliminate testing anxiety, and have fun along the way. Contact us today by emailing **Help@LovetheSAT.com** or call **1-800-653-8994** for a FREE, personalized consultation and lesson plans custom-tailored to your needs, goals, and busy schedule.

Table of Contents

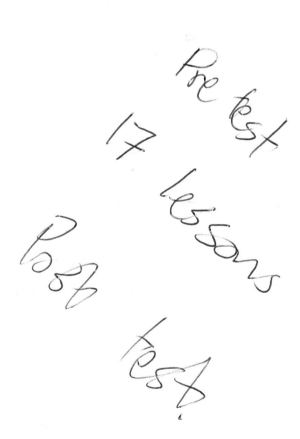

How to Use This Book in 10 Easy Steps

Here are the ten steps I recommend to get the most out of this book in the shortest time:

1) If you have an eBook copy, I recommend printing yourself a paper copy - at least for the Pretest and any chapters you study from. Please recycle when you're done!

2) Read the introduction, my personal note, and the three Prelessons on Parts of Speech, Eliminating Details and Rearranging Sentences.

3) Take the Pretest. You don't need a timer.

4) Check the Pretest. Make a list of topics you get wrong and keep it somewhere safe.

5) Study one Lesson at a time. Focus first on the Pretest topics you got wrong. Read the lesson and study it until you feel ready for the practice questions at the end of the chapter.

6) Do the practice questions on the topic. You can either go from start to finish in one sitting, or do half of the practice questions and leave the rest for review later.

7) Check your practice problems. Study the explanations of any you got wrong until you understand them.

8) After you've mastered each topic that you missed on the Pretest, take the Posttest.

9) Check the Posttest. Make a second list of any topics you got wrong; these still need your attention. Rinse and repeat steps 5-8 for these remaining topics.

10) If you answer all the questions in the book, I highly recommend waiting a few weeks and then doing steps 1-9 again. It might seem like overkill to do the whole book twice, but this will expose any lessons that you failed to learn. If you can get a question right once, you should be able to get it right again, even weeks or months later.

If you have questions at any time, please email us at **Help@LovetheSAT.com** or call **1-800-653-8994** for a free personalized consultation. We also offer 1-on-1 personalized private tutoring on SAT & ACT Grammar - and every other part of the SAT & ACT tests.

Timers & Official Study Guides

No timer is necessary to improve your SAT & ACT Grammar skills (and scores) at first. This book is focused on understanding and mastering the fundamentals. Speed comes with clarity about the basic rules, so focus on understanding the basics and I promise, speed and accuracy on the SAT & ACT will follow close behind.

However, once you understand the material, it is important to do at least three timed practice sections from The Official SAT Study Guide (https://amzn.to/2LYGZvH) and/or The Official ACT Prep Guide (https://amzn.to/2Aw7Avj).

Practicing with the Official Study Guide(s)

I highly recommend picking up a copy of the Official Study Guide for whichever test you are taking (see the links above to get them on Amazon.com).

However, you should study from this book first before moving onto the Official Study Guides. It's important to understand the fundamentals first; otherwise, it will be difficult to improve even with continuous practice. It's hard to learn from your mistakes in the Official Study Guides, because there aren't good explanations provided; my book is designed to counteract this lack of explanations and prepare you with a deeper understanding and greater confidence.

Introduction

Thank you for reading my SAT & ACT Grammar book! As the founder of an independent SAT & ACT prep tutoring company, it means a lot to me to have your trust - for you to trust that I really know what's on the SAT & ACT tests, and how to teach it to you.

I promise that this book will reward your trust. I have spent hundreds of hours planning, writing, and revising it; I've tested these concepts with hundreds of my private tutoring students, and gotten the thumbs-up. Personally, I'm confident this the best book in the world to help you prepare for both the SAT and ACT grammar tests.

In my private SAT & ACT tutoring lessons, I teach that speed comes with solid fundamentals and practice. This book is designed to help you nail down the grammar fundamentals tested on the SAT & ACT. It will teach you the Eight Parts of Speech and the Seventeen Grammar Rules that you need to know. In my years of experience, and across multiple perfect scores, I have found that these seventeen rules cover 99% of the entire SAT & ACT grammar tests. You should master these seventeen topics before you do anything else for SAT & ACT grammar.

This book gives you a wide variety of resources at your fingertips: a Pretest to immediately let you know where you need to focus; twenty lessons that explain each topic; over three hundred practice questions; a Posttest to check yourself after you've studied up. You might only need to review two grammar topics, or you might need to learn all seventeen from scratch. In either situation, this book will be a practical and invaluable learning resource for higher scores.

I should mention that the "facts" provided in the example sentences and practice questions are not all true; many are made up. It's difficult to make up hundreds of meaningful sentences out of nowhere, so I let my imagination run wild! I only mention this so that you don't quote one of my practice questions on some history paper you're writing and get in trouble for using incorrect "factual" evidence!

This book may not be the greatest history and trivia book of all time, but it's not meant to be. I set out to write a highly-focused grammar book that would be incredibly useful to students with a broad range of SAT & ACT English and grammar scores. As I type this, many months after beginning this project, I feel that I have succeeded. I hope that you will feel the same way after reading and applying the lessons contained within.

Get started on your Pretest right away - practice makes perfect!

- Christian, founder of Love the SAT Test Prep

A Personal Note

Look, I'm 31 years old and life is good. I have a lot of fun stuff I like to do. I play guitar, ride my motorcycle, write music, hang out with my friends, and keep myself from working a "real job" (I've been self-employed for years now). I love to travel when I can, I play my music way too loud, and am happiest when I'm outside in the sun.

I think my life is pretty exciting and cool, but I still think that knowing the proper rules of grammar for yourself is awesome!

What I'm trying to say here is that good grammar is not just for dorks. Being able to speak and write properly - to express myself clearly and accurately - is something that I take pride in. It doesn't mean that I have to sound like a nerd all the time!

There are some tremendous benefits to understanding proper grammar that I've noticed throughout my life.

Studying grammar will help you in the immediate future with your SAT & ACT scores, getting into a better college, scholarship money, bragging rights, sure...

But take it from someone who's been through the whole process and seen a little bit of life on the other side: knowing the commonly-used rules of English is essential for success in many aspects of life.

You can earn more money...

Explain yourself more clearly...

Learn new languages faster...

Read more good books... and spend less time on reading boring ones for school...

You'll appreciate good slang more (it's a lot more interesting when you know what rules it's breaking!)...

And you can always break the rules when you feel like it!

You don't have to sound geeky all the time just because you've mastered the rules of the English language.

Far from it – proper grammar will be something you can "turn on" and really impress the right people at the right time... admissions officers, your English teacher, a potential investor, a TV interviewer... who knows!

But I promise you that people - that includes you! - are evaluated and judged for their strength (or weakness) in grammar, every single day, even if they don't realize it.

If your grammar is weak, you may be missing opportunities that you don't even know are there. If your grammar is strong, it's just one more way to impress the people around you and get the most out of life.

Study now – don't sacrifice your whole life to school, but do take it seriously – and you will be reaping the rewards for the rest of your life. Being smart will always be cool.

Best of luck,
- Christian at Love the SAT Test Prep

Prelesson A: What Are Parts of Speech?

Let's start these SAT & ACT grammar lessons off with a fundamental question: What are "Parts of Speech"?

Well, Parts of Speech are "types of words." Every word in English has a "type."

Let me give you a well-known example: Nouns. A "noun" is a type of word representing a person, place, thing, or idea. A noun is one of the fundamental Parts of Speech in English - for example, "cat" is a noun, because a cat is a *thing*.

In the entire English language - all the books, movies, and plays ever written; all the speeches ever given; every English-language conversation in history, put together - how many different Parts of Speech do you think there are in total?

I mean it - stop for a second and think. How many different Parts of Speech are there in the entire English language?

Take a guess. Write the number down. Don't worry, no one ever gets this question right anyway.

I'll be waiting with the answer when you're ready.

...

...Ready? You've got your best guess written down for the total number of different Parts of Speech?

OK, here comes the answer...

There are eight of them.

Yes, just eight Parts of Speech - for the entire English language.

It's absolutely remarkable when you think about it. There are only eight types of words in our entire language!

These SAT & ACT grammar tests might be easier than you thought...

Now it's time to get a list going. What are the names of all eight Parts of Speech?

The 8 Parts of Speech: A Crucial List

It's very, very important to memorize the names and meanings of the eight Parts of Speech. Soon we'll cover the specific details of each one, but let's start getting familiar with their names right away.

Note: Memorize the list in the exact order it is presented here!

The 8 Parts of Speech

1. Nouns
2. Verbs
3. Adjectives
4. Adverbs
5. Pronouns
6. Prepositions
7. Conjunctions
8. Interjections

Note that the last 3 all have names ending in "-tion", which helps me remember them.

Practice writing this list down from memory on a spare sheet of paper. You need to be quick, confident, and *natural* with the names of all eight Parts of Speech.

Now let's go on to an individual breakdown of each of the eight, so you can define and recognize them one-by-one.

Nouns

A noun is a person, place, thing, or idea. These can be capitalized ("proper" nouns like *America*, *Mr. Jarvis*, or *Netflix*) or uncapitalized ("common" nouns like *tree*, *arrow*, or *bucket*.)

Examples of Nouns:

- *fireman* (a person)
- *bedroom* (a place)
- *mop* (a thing)
- *honesty* (an idea)

Note: An "idea" could be an intangible concept like *honesty*, *love*, or *patriotism*.

Verbs

A verb is a "doing" or "being" word.

> "The dog *runs* towards the ball."

Notice that the word "runs" shows what the dog is *doing.* That's what makes "runs" a verb.

Most students think verbs are only "action words," but what about this example?

> "The cat *is* happy."

Notice that in this case, the cat isn't *doing* any *action* - it's just being happy!
Good kitty! :)

Adjectives

Most students, when asked, will say that adjectives "describe nouns." But, here's a question for you. If I say "I have *three* cats," would you say that I have "described" my cats?

Take a moment to think about that and decide. I'm not trying to lead you in any direction, I just want to know what you think.

...

OK, got your response ready? Well, most students say emphatically no, I have not *described* my cats. And I agree with them, personally. However, the word "three" actually *is* an adjective!

That's why I find it more useful to say:

"Adjectives *modify* nouns."

This can include colors, numbers, qualities, and many other modifications.

> The *purple* cat yowls. (The adjective "purple" modifies the noun "cat.")
>
> I ride a *loud* motorcycle. (The adjective "loud" modifies the noun "motorcycle.")
>
> There are *fourteen* butterflies in the yard. (The adjective "fourteen" modifies the noun "yard.")

Adverbs

Ad*verbs* are close cousins of adjec*tives*. So, let's start by borrowing part of the same definition: "Ad*verbs* modify ..."

If you're anything like most students, you'll know that adverbs can modify *verbs*:

"The cat ran *quickly*"

This shows the adverb "quickly" modifying the verb "ran."

A few students also know that adverbs can modify *adjectives*, as well:

"The *extremely* fast cat ran across the street"

This shows the adverb "extremely" modifying the adjective "fast."

Very few students get all three functions of the adverb. The third is to modify *other adverbs*:

"The fast cat ran *extremely* quickly across the street"

This shows the adverb "quickly" being modified by another adverb, "extremely."

Note that the vast majority of adverbs in English end in "-ly," but not all of them. For the SAT & ACT tests, you should mostly focus on the ones that *do* end in "-ly."

To sum up adverbs: they modify verbs, adjectives, and other adverbs, and usually end in "-ly."

Pronouns

Pronouns are the short, "anonymous" words like *it*, *he*, *them*, and *I*. They act just like nouns in many ways. However, they have some important special rules. A complete mastery of pronouns is worth many points on the SAT & ACT tests.

Take a second to ask yourself this question: Why do we like having these pronoun words in our language? How are they helpful?

... Have you thought about it?...

Most of us will agree these words - words like *it* and *them* - are useful for shortening our sentences and not having to say the same names, objects, and places over and over again.

Indeed, that is their most valuable asset - pronouns save us time and repetition.

Now ask yourself this: What is the potential *downside* of using pronouns like "it" and "they" in our conversations? How can these words cause problems?

... Have you thought about it? ...

Well, the best answer would probably be that pronouns are potentially confusing because of how vague and non-specific they are.

That's why I call pronouns "anonymous nouns" that replace *specific* nouns.

For example:

"My dog is running around. *She* is very excited."

This shows the noun "dog" being replaced by the anonymous pronoun "she."

Important: There is a special term - the *antecedent* - for the specific noun that is being replaced by a given pronoun. In the example above, we would refer to the noun "dog" as the *antecedent* of the pronoun "she."

If you understand these important fundamental concepts about pronouns, you're well on your way to a higher SAT and ACT grammar score.

Prepositions

Prepositions are words that show *positional relationship* between two nouns. You can remember by the word "position," which is hidden inside the name "pre*position.*"

The ultimate way to instantly understand prepositions is with "THE SQUIRREL TEST." Here's how it works:

> The squirrel ran *up* the tree.
> The squirrel jumped *over* the tree.
> The squirrel tunneled *through* the tree.
> The squirrel is *under* the tree.

All those italicized words are prepositions. Easy, right? Notice now how their definition makes more sense: prepositions are words that show *positional relationship* between two nouns, such as a squirrel and a tree.

Another interesting fact is that all prepositions create "prepositional phrases," which can be completely ignored without hurting the sentence. Prepositional phrases begin at the preposition and continue until the "object of the preposition." In all our examples above, the "object of the preposition" is the word "tree."

This helps enormously when **Eliminating Details** (Prelesson B). For example, in the gray box above, you can ignore the prepositional phrase "up the tree" and still read the complete sentence "The squirrel ran." Try it; this works on all four examples!

Conjunctions

"Conjunction Junction" is the famous Schoolhouse Rock train station where sentences and ideas hook up together. A conjunction conjoins (which just means "joins or combines") two ideas A and B with a logical transition word of some kind.

> James was hungry, *so* he made a sandwich.

Common examples of conjunctions are *and, however, but, or, so, because* and many similar "joining" or "transitioning" words. Try to think of three other conjunctions on your own, right now (search your words on the internet to make sure they are actually conjunctions.)

Interjections

Interjections are "interrupting" words such as *Ow, Hey, Yo,* and so forth.

These words are not an important part of speech for the SAT & ACT Tests, but I thought I should tell you about them. Covering only 7 out of the 8 Parts of Speech seemed weird!

Prelesson B: Eliminating Details

Before we get into the main grammar lessons, I have two important strategies to teach you.

I use this upcoming technique on almost every grammar question on the SAT & ACT. I also can get a perfect score on the SAT & ACT English sections every time I take them. There is *definitely* a connection here.

Here's my surprising claim: I propose that most of the sentences in the SAT & ACT verbal sections are based on a very basic, very simple grammatical structure, and that you can learn to see it for yourself.

"Wait, wait!" I can hear you saying. "I saw some *really messed-up sentences* the last time I looked at the SAT / ACT grammar test. I don't believe you."

OK, it's true that the sentences *look* bad. Specifically, they look overly complicated. Too many words. Too many details clouding the air. All the choices sound wrong, or maybe they all sound right.

That's because the SAT and ACT's #1 method of making grammar questions more difficult is by distracting you with details. These unnecessary details blind your eyes, trip up your "inner ear," and fog your mind.

Luckily, now that you know this, you'll be able to untie many of the knots that the SAT & ACT have tied for you.

A simple sentence might look like this:

"Robert read a book."

The test-writers need this sentence to fill a couple of lines, so that it has plenty of room to add extra details to this simple sentence and make it appear more complex.

First, they might add info and tell us a little more about Robert as a sort of "side note":

"Robert, *who was my roommate*, read a book."

Then they might tell us more about *where* Robert was reading the book:

"Robert, who was my roommate, read a book *at the wooden picnic table*."

Then, they might tell us more about *how* Robert was reading the book:

"Robert, who was my roommate, read a book *with his feet up and his easy chair reclined* at the wooden picnic table."

Everything I've added, step by step, has been *unnecessary detail* and can be removed again, piece by piece, to return the sentence to its original, uncomplicated basics.

NOW – visualize the uses this could have on the SAT & ACT Grammar sections:

What if our original sentence, "Robert read a book," actually had an error in it – like:

"Robert reading a book"?

It's easy to spot the error (it's a Sentence Fragment, from Lesson 9 on **Sentence Structure**) when there are no details complicating matters. That's good.

BUT – what if that same error was buried deep inside the extra-complicated version of the same sentence?

Would you still notice the error? Here's the sentence:

"Robert, who was my roommate, reading a book with his feet up and his easy chair reclined at the wooden picnic table."

Certainly, some of you *will* catch this error. But just as certainly, many of you will not, once it has been buried in a long-winded sentence.

Besides, even if you caught this one error instinctively, how are you going to guarantee that you catch the errors *every single time* – even on other grammar topics that come less naturally to you?

Can you see why I would use this mindset and strategy to eliminate details on virtually every single grammar question on the SAT and ACT?

If you agree about the potential usefulness of applying this method to every grammar question, keep reading for more tips on how to spot and remove unnecessary details.

Common Types of Extra "Distracting" Details

- **Details about *location* are not essential to the sentence structure:** The words in italics can be eliminated:"I ran *around outside* as thunder boomed *above my head*."

- **Details placed *between two commas* are almost never essential to the sentence:** The acrobat*, who originally appeared to be quite talented upon the tightrope,* fell."

- **Adjectives and Adverbs are never essential to the sentence:** descriptive words simply add color to the sentence. "The *blue* dog barked *loudly*." "The *tall telephone* pole leaned *dangerously*."See also **Parts of Speech** (Prelesson A) and **Adjectives & Adverbs** (Lesson 3).

- **Modifying phrases are never essential to the sentence:** a "modifying phrase," such as "*Leaning against the tree*, the giraffe ate some leaves," is something you must learn to recognize. These can also be called "Parenthetical Clauses," as you will learn in Lesson 9 on **Sentence Structure**

  We should already be wary of these phrases because of Lesson 11 on **Misplaced Modifiers**, because modifying phrases are frequently incorrect for reasons you will learn within that chapter. However, if a modifying phrase has been *correctly* used, it may be eliminated as extra detail, in this case leaving: "The giraffe ate some leaves."

As a final example, let's put ourselves in the test-maker's shoes again and write a question together.

We'll start with a basic sentence containing an error. Then, we'll add a ton of details to make things look more confusing.

Here's the simple sentence I propose to begin with – it contains a **Subject-Verb Agreement** error (Lesson 1):

"John and his friend races cars on weekends."

The italics contain the error: "John and his friend" is plural, but "races" is singular (read up on **Subject-Verb Agreement** if you don't understand what I mean).

Now let's try to hide that error with details. First, let's add something about *where* they race their cars:

"John and his friend races cars *at the Santa Monica Racetrack* on weekends."

Now let's add some detail about John:

> "John, *who concerns himself with nothing besides automobiles*, and his friend races cars at the Santa Monica Racetrack on weekends."

Next, let's be more specific about *when* they race cars:

> "John, who concerns himself with nothing besides automobiles, and his friend races cars at the Santa Monica Racetrack on weekends *when the sun is shining*."

OK, let's add something more about John's friend:

> "John, who concerns himself with nothing besides automobiles, and his friend Henry, *a man of some importance*, races cars at the Santa Monica Racetrack on weekends when the sun is shining."

Finally, let's include a little more details about the "automobiles":

> "John, who concerns himself with nothing besides *classic* automobiles *built by hand*, and his friend Henry, a man of some importance, races cars at the Santa Monica Racetrack on weekends when the sun is shining."

The original Subject-Verb error doesn't exactly leap out at you anymore, does it?

Here's our final sentence, SAT/ACT-style:

> "John, who concerns himself with nothing besides classic automobiles built by hand, and his friend Henry, a man of some importance, races cars at the Santa Monica Racetrack on weekends when the sun is shining."

Simply attacking the sentence in reverse and eliminating all of the unnecessary details we just added would make life seem so much simpler. Once the details are taken out, the basic Subject-Verb error will pop right out again.

We will continue to refer to this method throughout the book as "Eliminating Details." Practice it well. It will make the grammar sections *infinitely easier* when you make it a habit on every question.

Prelesson C: Rearranging Word Order

OK, let me start this Prelesson off with a gripe that I think you'll sympathize with.

The SAT & ACT claim to be all about "clarity" in grammar – in general, they penalize unclear sentences or consider them incorrect, and are really picky about small mistakes even when everyone knows "what they mean."

Yet there's this one thing that's "technically" correct even though it makes a clear sentence more confusing, and the SAT & ACT usually use this trick a few times per test.

Let me give you an example:

> If you would normally say "My house is cold in the winters," the SAT & ACT can change that to "Cold in the winters is my house."

They've placed the verb, "is," before the *subject* of that verb, which is "my house."

Again, no one actually talks like this, but it's "technically" correct.So, the SAT & ACT can use it to cover a bigger problem. Our original sentence could contain a **Subject-Verb Error** (Lesson 1):

> "My *house are* cold in the winters."

Now the SAT or ACT could rearrange it, which helps cover the error:

> "Cold in the winters *are* my *house.*"

If you're not attentive, you might slip up and think that "winters are" sounds pretty good, so the subject-verb pair is fine. It's not.

Here's another sentence with a similar mistake. Can you dig it out before continuing?

> "Eating peanuts were the elephant."

Rearrange this sentence:

> "The elephant were eating peanuts."

Now the sentence order sounds more normal - except for the error!

"Elephant" is singular, but "were" is plural. That's a **Subject-Verb Agreement** Error (Lesson 1)!

The authors of the SAT & ACT can combine this rearranged-sentence technique with unnecessary details to come up with some truly horrifying-looking sentences, but simply by using the two simple strategies of **Eliminating Details** and **Rearranging Word Order**, you can turn these sentences back into something resembling human speech, and you will catch *many* more hidden errors.

One final tip: Eliminate details BEFORE rearranging the sentence. Here's an example of a complicated sentence that needs both detail-elimination and word-order-rearranging:

> "Under the polka-dotted umbrella hid the child, while fell the cold rain all around her."

Eliminate details: "Under the polka-dotted umbrella" is detail about *where* something happened. So is "all around her." "Cold" is also extra descriptive detail.

Here's what we have left:

> "Hid the child, while fell the rain."

Rearrange both halves to get a simpler sentence:

> "The child hid, while the rain fell."

Pretest

37 Questions
17 Grammar Topics

Answers follow the Pretest.
Explanations within Lessons 1-17.

1. Joseph <u>Wharton, along with his many</u> <u>successful business ventures, has</u> helped shape the history of American industry.

(A) [NO CHANGE]

(B) Wharton, including his many successful business ventures, have

(C) Wharton, along with his many successful business ventures, have

(D) Wharton and his many successful business ventures has

2. Project SCORE was the first communications satellite ever put into Earth's orbit, and <u>it will</u> <u>be launched</u> on December 18, 1958.

(A) [NO CHANGE]

(B) it was launched

(C) they were launched

(D) it is launched

3. Despite the group's many musical successes, <u>they are struggling</u> to afford new instruments and gas money for the van.

(A) [NO CHANGE]

(B) they struggle

(C) it is struggling

(D) he and she are struggling

4. An ocean mammal, such as the blue whale, <u>behaves quite differently</u> than mammals that live on land.

(A) [NO CHANGE]

(B) behave quite differently

(C) behaves quite different

(D) has behaviors quite differently

5. The "desert rally," an endurance race by dune buggies across hostile terrain, <u>that only the</u> <u>fiercest competitors qualify for.</u>

(A) [NO CHANGE]

(B) which only the fiercest competitors can qualify for.

(C) and only the fiercest competitors qualify for it.

(D) is a contest that only the fiercest competitors qualify for.

6. <u>While it panted and strained at its leash, the</u> <u>dog's owner attempted to restrain the puppy</u> when it saw a squirrel at the dog park.

(A) [NO CHANGE]

(B) The dog's owner attempted to restrain the puppy while it panted and strained at its leash

(C) While it panted and strained at its leash, the puppy's owner attempted to restrain it

(D) The dog's owner, while it panted and strained at its leash, attempted to restrain the puppy

7. The small house built in the field used the <u>average</u> building materials that were available in the region: wood, stone, brick, and glass.

(A) [NO CHANGE]

(B) arbitrary

(C) stereotypical

(D) characteristic

8. Beethoven's music is known for being logical, yet emotive; challenging, yet occasionally simple; and unique, yet <u>derived from previous styles.</u>

(A) [NO CHANGE]

(B) previous styles influenced it.

(C) was derived from previous styles.

(D) it was derived from previous styles.

9. The intrepid explorers of the wilderness discovered a new <u>river, they also found</u> a pair of mountains they named "Dipyramid."

(A) [NO CHANGE]

(B) river, found

(C) river; they also find

(D) river and found

10. Cyclone Althea devastated portions of northern Australia in December 1971; the strong winds ripped roofs off houses, hail damaged vehicles and windows, <u>and it cost</u> the Australian federal government close to a billion dollars in modern-day adjusted values.

(A) [NO CHANGE]

(B) and they cost

(C) and those cost

(D) and the storm cost

11. There are several activities that I like to practice <u>every day; motorcycling</u>, running, and songwriting.

(A) [NO CHANGE]

(B) every day: motorcycling,

(C) every day, motorcycling,

(D) every day. Motorcycling,

12. During his college interview, Jose was <u>confused by</u> several questions, including one about his favorite types of animals, and another that asked, "if you were a flavor of ice cream, what flavor would you be?"

(A) [NO CHANGE]

(B) confused at

(C) confused with

(D) confused for

Consider the sentence below as you answer the following question, Question 13.

"The Cloisters" is a museum in New York City that is constructed of four covered walkways from Europe - named the Cuxa, Bonnefont, Trie, and Saint-Guilhem, respectively - that were disassembled and transported to American soil between 1934 and 1939.

13. Which of the following choices provides the most relevant and useful supporting details for the sentence above?

(A) [NO CHANGE]

(B) a continent located in the Northern Hemisphere of the globe

(C) "cloisters" is another word for "covered walkways"

(D) moved from their places of origin

14. The use of robots on farms is growing rapidly, since it is often more cost-effective than human farm workers.

(A) [NO CHANGE]

(B) more cost-effective than the use of

(C) more cost-effective than using

(D) less costly than

Consider the paragraph below as you answer the following question, Question 15:

[1] The Japanese battleship *Nagato* was built in 1920 as the most powerful capital ship in the Imperial Japanese Navy. [2] Her earliest noteworthy service was carrying supplies for the survivors of the Great Kanto earthquake in 1923. [3] *Nagato* then participated in the Second Sino-Japanese War of 1937. [4] Now, the wreck of the *Nagato* is considered one of the top ten shipwreck-diving spots in the world. [5] She remained in service during World War 2 and was involved in the surprise attack on Pearl Harbor as the flagship of Admiral Isoroku Yamamoto. [6] Impressively, *Nagato* was the only Japanese battleship to survive the entirety of World War 2. [7] In 1946, the massive vessel was destroyed (with no sailors on board) in the American nuclear weapons tests named "Operation Crossroads" held at Bikini Atoll.

15. To make this paragraph most logical, sentence 4 should be placed

(A) where it is now.

(B) before sentence 1.

(C) after sentence 5.

(D) after sentence 7.

16. The soldier successfully pulled his ally from the <u>helicopter wreck, and since the</u> flames engulfed their craft, he was unable to repair the vehicle.

   (A) [NO CHANGE]

   (B) helicopter wreck, the

   (C) wreck of the helicopter, with the consequence that

   (D) helicopter wreck, but because

18. Is it right that <u>us workers must suffer due to</u> incompetent management?

   (A) [NO CHANGE]

   (B) we workers must suffer despite

   (C) us workers must suffer despite

   (D) we workers must suffer due to

17. The Vauxhall <u>automobile, being designed</u> to be economical, has recently regained popularity among car collectors.

   (A) [NO CHANGE]

   (B) automobile being designed

   (C) automobile, designed

   (D) automobile, a car designed

Consider the paragraph below as you answer the following two questions, Questions 19 and 20.

Of these, polyethylene is the most common type of plastic, accounting for 34% of the world's total plastics market. It has a startlingly-wide range of applications; for example, ultra-high-density polyethylene is used in hip joint replacements, industrial shipping, and ice-skating rinks. [A] <u>On the other end of the spectrum, low-density polyethylene is often used for plastic wraps, tubing, and food storage.</u> In between these "high-density" and "low-density" uses, polyethylene can also be found in film applications, water plumbing, milk jugs, garbage containers, and children's toys.

19. The writer is considering adding the following sentence as an introduction to the paragraph above.

    Plastics are one of the most common and useful construction materials in modern global industry, and are produced in a wide range of varieties.

    Should the writer make this addition here?

    (A) Yes, because the sentence provides an essential supporting example to the paragraph.

    (B) Yes, because the sentence effectively introduces the main topic of the paragraph.

    (C) No, because the sentence contradicts a central point made within the paragraph.

    (D) No, because the following sentence ("Of these, polyethylene is…") already provides a more effective introduction to the paragraph.

20. At Point [A], the writer is considering deleting the underlined sentence. Should the writer make this change?

    (A) Yes, because it provides an excessive list of examples for a term that has already been defined.

    (B) Yes, because it interrupts the overall flow of the paragraph.

    (C) No, because it provides effective support for an essential counterargument within the paragraph.

    (D) No, because it provides examples that are used as a key point for a comparison within the paragraph.

21. Our football team, currently in the running for the championship, and our school tennis star, who has dominated her recent <u>matches, is putting us</u> in the running for a record season this year.

    (A) [NO CHANGE]
    (B) matches, was putting us
    (C) matches, are putting us
    (D) matches, were putting us

22. <u>The pine tree, known for its majestic appearance and sweet scent, and its needles can be used to brew tea.</u>

   (A) [NO CHANGE]
   (B) The pine tree, known for its majestic appearance and sweet scent, has needles that can be used to brew tea.
   (C) Known for its majestic appearance and sweet scent, the pine tree's needles can be used to brew tea.
   (D) The pine tree, its needles can be used to brew tea, is known for its majestic appearance and sweet scent.

23. Neither the duck <u>nor the goose is able to</u> enjoy long periods of time without a nearby body of water.

   (A) [NO CHANGE]
   (B) nor the goose
   (C) or the goose is able to
   (D) nor the goose are able to

24. I think that most Japanese manufacturers' cars get better mileage and are more reliable than <u>American automakers.</u>

   (A) [NO CHANGE]
   (B) making cars in America
   (C) American automakers' cars
   (D) what they make in America

25. Darla's apartment was often difficult to fall asleep in, because it was <u>adjacent with</u> a room of rowdy party animals who loved to stay up late and blast their stereo system at maximum volume.

   (A) [NO CHANGE]
   (B) adjacent to
   (C) adjacent at
   (D) adjacent into

26. Authors selected for the philosophy journal must be respected in <u>their field, and</u> should hold advanced degrees and have a great deal of practical experience.

   (A) [NO CHANGE]
   (B) his or her field, and
   (C) their field, they
   (D) their field, such authors

27. <u>Bursting with color, the pale hospital patient appreciated her friend's gift of flowers.</u>

   (A) [NO CHANGE]
   (B) Bursting with color, the pale hospital patient's friend's gift of flowers was appreciated.
   (C) The pale hospital patient, bursting with color, appreciated her friend's gift of flowers.
   (D) The pale hospital patient appreciated her friend's gift of flowers, which was bursting with color.

28. Plymouth was once a brand of automobiles produced in the United States, but it was dissolved and absorbed into other brands in 2001; however, some investors <u>would like to revive</u> the marque, leaving the future of the Plymouth name in question.

(A) [NO CHANGE]

(B) will revive

(C) revived

(D) reviving

29. Although deforestation is extremely detrimental to the planet's delicate ecology, <u>yet</u> many timber companies continue to harvest lumber for large corporate profits.

(A) [NO CHANGE]

(B) and

(C) but

(D) [DELETE the underlined portion]

30. The bass guitar differs from standard guitars in that the bass <u>has fewer strings, a longer neck, and the ability to produce lower notes.</u>

(A) [NO CHANGE]

(B) has fewer strings, a longer neck, and can produce lower notes.

(C) having fewer strings, a longer neck, and can produce notes more low.

(D) with lower strings, a longer neck, and lower notes.

31. <u>Charles and me love</u> to play dodgeball, and we have spent many an hour engaged in this exciting pastime.

(A) [NO CHANGE]

(B) Charles and I love

(C) Charles and me loves

(D) Charles and I loves

32. Christina Wahlberg <u>can handle a foil quite deft</u>; in fact, she has competed in Olympic fencing.

(A) [NO CHANGE]

(B) can deft handle a foil

(C) can handle a foil quite deftly

(D) being a deft foil-handler

33. <u>Unethical political decisions are able to be protested by concerned American citizens.</u>

(A) [NO CHANGE]

(B) Unethical political decisions have the ability to be protested by concerned American citizens.

(C) Concerned American citizens are able to protest unethical political decisions made by politicians.

(D) Concerned American citizens are able to protest unethical political decisions.

34. Historical wolf hunts would include noblemen, conscripted peasant farmers, and trained wolfhounds, though they were often injured as the wolves attempted to defend themselves with teeth and claws.

    (A) [NO CHANGE]

    (B) it was

    (C) the wolfhounds were

    (D) these were

Consider the sentence below as you answer the following question, Question 35.

James Scawen was a British politician in the mid-1700s who was once pressured by a large mob to reveal how he had voted in an important election, and his father inherited a large estate near London.

35. Which of the following choices provides the most relevant conclusion to the preceding sentence?

    (A) [NO CHANGE]

    (B) but he declined to share this information, stating that he must keep his vote secret in order to remain "an independent man."

    (C) and in his later years, he developed Carshalton Park with improvements like canals, mills, and grottoes.

    (D) and he lived from 1734 to 1801.

36. There are many kinds of dogs, but mine - a golden retriever, is my favorite, he is very loyal and friendly.

    (A) [NO CHANGE]

    (B) retriever - is my favorite; he

    (C) retriever - is my favorite, he

    (D) retriever) is my favorite; he

37. I prefer modern boat designs, and although my cousins enjoyed the interior styling of the old steamship, I considered the decor fairly primordial.

    (A) [NO CHANGE]

    (B) elderly

    (C) old-fashioned

    (D) ancient

STOP.

Pretest Answers

Note: After each answer, I've named the grammar topic of the question. Start by focusing on the chapters that cover topics that you got incorrect.

Detailed explanations for each Pretest question are given in its Lesson. Go the appropriate Lesson for a complete breakdown of any question you missed.

1. A, Subject-Verb Agreement (Lesson 1)
2. B, Verb Tense & Form (Lesson 2)
3. C, Pronoun-Antecedent Agreement (Lesson 5)
4. A, Adjectives & Adverbs (Lesson 3)
5. D, Sentence Structure (Lesson 9)
6. B, Misplaced Modifiers (Lesson 11)
7. D, Vocab Word Choice (Lesson 12)
8. A, Parallelism & Comparisons (Lesson 10)
9. D, Sentence Structure (Lesson 9)
10. D, Pronoun-Antecedent Clarity (Lesson 4)
11. B, Punctuation Marks (Lesson 8)
12. A, Idioms & Prepositions (Lesson 17)
13. A, Objective Questions (Lesson 14)
14. B, Parallelism & Comparisons (Lesson 10)
15. D, Moving Sentences & Paragraphs (Lesson 16)
16. D, Conjunctions & Transitions (Lesson 7)
17. C, Redundancy & Wordiness (Lesson 13)
18. D, Pronoun Case (Lesson 6)
19. B, Adding or Removing Information (Lesson 15)
20. D, Adding or Removing Information (Lesson 15)
21. C, Subject-Verb Agreement (Lesson 1)
22. B, Sentence Structure (Lesson 9)
23. A, Pronoun-Antecedent Agreement (Lesson 5)
24. C, Parallelism & Comparison (Lesson 10)
25. B, Idioms & Prepositions (Lesson 17)
26. A, Sentence Structure (Lesson 9)
27. D, Misplaced Modifiers (Lesson 11)
28. A, Verb Tense & Form (Lesson 2)
29. D, Conjunctions & Transitions (Lesson 7)
30. A, Parallelism & Comparison (Lesson 10)
31. B, Pronoun Case (Lesson 6)
32. C, Adjectives & Adverbs (Lesson 3)
33. D, Redundancy & Wordiness (Lesson 13)
34. C, Pronoun-Antecedent Clarity (Lesson 4)
35. B, Objective Questions (Lesson 14)
36. B, Punctuation Marks (Lesson 8)
37. C, Vocab Word Choice (Lesson 12)

LESSON 1
Subject-Verb Agreement (Singular-Plural)

If I was only allowed to teach ONE grammar rule to any SAT or ACT prep student, this is the one I would pick.

The name may be long, but it's also perfect: "Subject-Verb Agreement (Singular-Plural)" - which I will often abbreviate as "**Subject-Verb Agreement**" for the rest of this book. This rule is about *agreement* between an essential pair of words that every sentence needs: **a subject** and **a main verb.**

Every single sentence in English contains a subject and a main verb, so you can imagine why this rule is so important.

What do the Subject and Main Verb have to "agree" on? That's whether they are *singular* or *plural* - "one" or "many". The subject and main verb must both agree upon this.

A singular subject needs a singular verb. Plural subject, plural verb. It's a very basic concept that can be dressed up in all sorts of creative and challenging ways.

Let's look at a simple sentence:

"Sam walks to the beach."

The "Subject" is the main character; in this case, "Sam." The main verb is "walks," which is the primary action that the subject is doing.

This sentence sounds fine, but what if we alter our sentence to:

"Sam *walk* to the beach."

Sounds pretty terrible, doesn't it?

Your ears know that a singular/plural error has happened. They just *know!*

In grammar-speak, here's what went wrong. "Sam" is singular noun – *one* person. However, "*walk*" is a plural verb, so they don't match up. "*Walks,*" on the other hand, was singular, which is why the original sentence sounded perfectly fine.

A Helpful Test

If you can't tell the difference between singular and plural verbs, use "He blanks, they blank.":

Test the sentence in your mind with both "he/she" and "they." You'd say "he *walks*, they *walk*." Your inner ear *will* know which way is correct.

Is "swims" a singular or plural word? Try the test: "he *swims*, they *swim*." Since "swims" sounds right when matched with the singular "he," we know that "swims" is a singular verb.

Is "jump" a singular or plural verb? "He jumps, they jump": it's plural, because it sounds right when matched with the plural "they."

Is "falls" singular or plural? How about "whistle"? (singular: "he falls," then plural: "they whistle.")

I use this simple test throughout the SAT & ACT to help me figure out if a word is singular or plural.

Telling the Difference Between Singular & Plural Nouns

You shouldn't have much trouble determining if most nouns are singular or plural. However, there are some "tricky" nouns that the SAT & ACT use to trap unwary students. Here are some examples:

Tricky words that may sound plural, but are actually singular:

- Everyone
- Team
- Country
- The whole business

- The group
- The team
- Pack (of dogs)
- School (of fish)

All of these words are SINGULAR – just one team, just one school of fish, etc. – *even though we know that they are made up of many people or animals.* The SAT will try to trick you like this:

> "The entire team are packing their bags and going back home."

In the above example, the question is trying to exploit confusion you may have about whether "team" is singular or plural. Remember that we're talking about just *one* team, even though it's made up of many players. Therefore the main verb should use the singular, and read:

> "The entire team *is* packing its bags and going back home."

Identifying "Compound" Plural Subjects

Sentences can include what I call "compound" plural subjects. This is when multiple singular nouns combine to form one plural subject. For example:

"Sam and Bally walk to the beach."

Now, even though both "Sam" and "Bally" are singular, they have been glued together with the conjunction "and." From now on, the sentence will be talking about both of these people *together*, and two people make a *plural* subject. That's why this sentence uses the plural verb "walk," not the singular "walks."

If you didn't pay attention to the "*Sam and*" at the beginning of the sentence, you would only focus on "*Bally walk* to the beach." That would sound wrong to you, and you'd probably change "walk" to the singular verb form, like so:

"...Bally *walks* to the beach."

Now this *small section* of the sentence sounds good, but if you plugged it back in and suddenly noticed "Sam and" at the beginning of the sentence, you'd realize the Subject-Verb Agreement was now wrong!

The SAT & ACT exploit this compound-subject trick by inserting giant piles of steaming distraction in the middle of sentences (that's why you apply Prelesson B on **Eliminating Details**!)

Here's an example, based on our previous sentence. My alterations won't change anything about the basic structure of the sentence "Sam and Bally walk to the beach." I'm just adding bunch of junk details to distract you from the compound plural subject "Sam and Bally":

"Sam, who had kept in touch with her old friend for some time (even after leaving Florida), and, alongside her, her friend Bally, walk amidst the butterflies to the isolated beach."

WHEW. Now that sentence looks *awful.*

Doesn't it sound wrong if you only focus narrowly on the portion "alongside her, her friend Bally, walk amidst the butterflies"? Your ear will prefer the singular form "Bally *walks* amidst the butterflies." Resist that temptation, because really, there's still a compound plural subject and verb: "Sam and Bally (compound plural) *walk*."

This is a sentence where **Eliminating Detail** will really bust through the fog. We can safely ignore everything except a small portion of our original sentence: "Sam and Bally walk."

Catching Compound Plural Subjects: Imagine the Action

Another tactic that helps me catch these mistakes is to actually visualize the sentence taking place in my head. Is *one* thing doing the action (singular), or are *two or more* nouns involved (plural)? Mentally picturing the sentence will often help answer this question.

A few more examples of compound plural subjects:

- "They and I"

- "The seagull, the raven, and the dove"

- "The cat, sitting in the meadow, and the dog, jumping at the gate" (There are two animals. Get rid of details and you have "The cat and the dog.")

- My brother, who is often found designing video games, my father, who loves his classic cars, and my mother, who enjoys reading about philosophy" (There are three people. Get rid of the details and you have "My brother, my father, and my mother")

Identifying "Trick" Compound Subjects

Occasionally, a sentence may appear to you at first to be a compound plural subject, but when you eliminate unessential details, it turns out to be singular, not compound. Here's an example:

The dog, along with his many canine friends, jumps in the water.

Looking at this sentence, it would seem that "many" dogs (plural) are jumping in the water. That is, in fact, what is being described, but *grammatically*, the subject and verb of this sentence are still singular.

That's because "along with his many canine friends" is a nonessential modifying phrase (you'll learn to call this a "Parenthetical Clause" in Lesson 9 on **Sentence Structure**). It's attached to "the dog," but this phrase is not essential to the structure of the sentence. You can eliminate details and reduce the sentence to "The dog jumps in the water," which is entirely singular.

It's not part of a compound subject in the same way that "The dog *and his many friends* jump in the water" would be. In this latter case, it would most definitely be a compound plural subject and plural verb.

Continually use elimination of details to discover the essential structure of each sentence, then properly match singular and plural to ensure that Subjects and Verbs can agree.

Subject-Verb Agreement Quick Reference

- Singular subjects go with singular verbs. Plural subjects go with plural verbs. This is the among the most common topics on the SAT & ACT Grammar sections.

- Use the test "he blanks / they blank" (e.g. "he *runs* / they *run*") and trust your ear to determine if a verb is singular or plural.

- Eliminate details and use your logic to decide if the subject is singular or plural.

- Remember that some words might sound plural, but are really *singular collective groups*, like "the entire company" or "the whole country."

- Compound plural subjects are plural because they are made of multiple singular subjects.

- Sometimes, a nonessential descriptive clause can seem like part of a compound plural subject at first - but nonessential clauses will never count towards the main subject, so exclude them. Study Parenthetical Clauses in Lesson 9 on **Sentence Structure**.

OK, let's look at some questions from the Pretest:

Our football team, currently in the running for the championship, and our school tennis star, who has dominated her recent <u>matches, is putting us</u> in the running for a record season this year.

(A) [NO CHANGE]

(B) matches, was putting us

(C) matches, are putting us

(D) matches, were putting us

OK – You should see the main verb "*is*" underlined and already be thinking, "what could go wrong here?" Well, one common possibility is a Subject-Verb Disagreement error...

So, ask yourself "*who* or *what* is putting the school in the running for a record season"? According to the sentence, that's *both* the football team *and* the school tennis star.

Since we're talking about *both* a team and a person, we have a *compound plural* subject, and our main verb needs to be plural as well. However, in the sentence, the main verb "is" is currently singular. That's our classic Subject-Verb Agreement mistake: a *plural* subject (football team *and* tennis star) mistakenly matched to a *singular* verb form ("*is*" instead of "*are*.") The subject and verb don't *agree* on whether they should be singular or plural.

This eliminates both "singular verb" answer choices, which are Choice A ("is") and Choice B ("was"). Looking at our remaining options, they are both plural verbs ("are" and "were") but they have different **Verb Tenses** (see the next Lesson for more info). Looking at the timeframe of the sentence, it's more likely that we should stay with present tense (notice the clue words "currently," "recent," and "this year"). **Choice C is the correct answer**, because it's both *plural* and *present tense*.

Here's another example from the Pretest:

> Joseph <u>Wharton, along with his many successful business ventures, has</u> helped shape the history of American industry.
>
> (A) [NO CHANGE]
> (B) Wharton and his many successful business ventures has
> (C) Wharton, including his many successful business ventures, have
> (D) Wharton, along with his many successful business ventures, have

This is an example of a "trick" compound subject. It might look like "Joseph Wharton" *and* "his successful business ventures" are the subject of the original sentence, but it's *just Joseph Wharton* that counts. As usual, stuff set between two commas is just unimportant detail - a Parenthetical Clause (see Prelesson B on **Removing Details** and Lesson 9 on **Sentence Structure**). Take this portion out of the sentence to simplify it, and you'll be left with "Joseph Wharton *has* helped shape..."

Your ears should tell you that's correct, but you could also test like this: Is "Joseph Wharton" singular or plural? One person, so singular. But is the verb "*has*" singular or plural? Test by saying to yourself, "He *has*, he *have*." Which one sounds correct? The first, *singular* version.

"Has" is singular, so it's correctly matched with the singular subject "Joseph Wharton." That means Choice A, "No Change," is quite possibly correct.

Choice B drops the commas around "business ventures," making that middle section equal in importance to the subject "Joseph Wharton" - this creates the compound plural subject "Wharton *and* his ventures..." Now the subject really *is* plural, so the singular verb form "has" suddenly creates a singular-plural disagreement.

Choice C uses the plural verb "have," which disagrees with the singular subject "Joseph Wharton." It's also an example of a **Misplaced Modifier** error (Lesson 11). The descriptive phrase "including his business ventures" doesn't make sense here, because this phrase is modifying "Joseph Wharton," but a *person* can't contain or "include" business ventures. Read Lesson 11 on Misplaced Modifiers for more info and practice.

Choice D again puts the middle section back into commas, creating a Parenthetical Clause as in Choice A. This means the subject of the sentence remains Joseph Wharton (singular), but this answer choices uses the *plural* verb form "have," creating a Singular-Plural Disagreement error again.

After evaluating our options, **Choice A is correct** and all the other answer choices are wrong!

Subject-Verb Agreement
Practice Questions

1. The number of new bands from my hometown of Austin <u>are astonishing</u> when you consider that the city used to be much smaller than it is today.

   (A) [NO CHANGE]

   (B) were astonishing

   (C) is astonishing

   (D) astonish

2. Both the egg and the eggplant, which have little in common with one another, <u>is very</u> versatile when it comes to preparing a home-cooked meal for your family.

   (A) [NO CHANGE]

   (B) are very

   (C) they are very

   (D) was very

3. <u>Sitting on the couch and watching TV was</u> the best ways that Eric knew how to pass the time; unfortunately, he couldn't pass 11th grade.

   (A) NO CHANGE

   (B) Sitting on the couch, watching TV, were

   (C) Sitting on the couch and watching TV were

   (D) To sit on the couch and watching TV were

4. Arching their backs and <u>hissing is a behavior</u> common to many felines when they feel that their safety is threatened.

   (A) [NO CHANGE]

   (B) hissing are a behavior

   (C) hissing, behaviors

   (D) hissing are behaviors

5. According to my friend, a coin collector, <u>a number of people are seeking Liberty Head nickels</u> minted in 1883.

   (A) [NO CHANGE]

   (B) a number of people is seeking Liberty Head nickels

   (C) Liberty Head nickels are being sought by a number of people, they were

   (D) Liberty Head nickels are sought by a number of people

6. <u>There is</u> more than two decades left until the next major earthquake is expected to shake California.

   (A) [NO CHANGE]

   (B) There have been

   (C) There are

   (D) It has

7. Two writers in the USA, with unbelievable audacity, <u>were claiming</u> to write a thousand books a year by working as a team and barely sleeping.

(A) [NO CHANGE]
(B) is claiming
(C) was claiming
(D) has been claiming

8. Since news of the bankruptcy came suddenly, <u>the entire company are clearing out their desks</u> immediately.

(A) [NO CHANGE]
(B) everyone in the company are clearing out their desks
(C) everyone in the company is clearing out his or her desk
(D) the entire company is clearing out their desk

9. The school of fish, hiding among the jagged coral, <u>were easily seen</u> by the hammerhead shark, despite the gloomy camouflage of the surroundings.

(A) [NO CHANGE]
(B) seen
(C) are easily seen
(D) was easily seen

10. Philip Ferdinand's debt, which grew rapidly as he spent frivolously on extravagant luxuries, <u>were what ruined him in the end.</u>

(A) [NO CHANGE]
(B) was what ruined him in the end.
(C) and ruined him in the end.
(D) ruining him in the end.

11. The vote of the American people, who turned out in record <u>numbers, demonstrate</u> that our nation longs for more honest politicians to take office.

(A) [NO CHANGE]
(B) numbers, demonstrates
(C) numbers demonstrates
(D) numbers which demonstrate

12. Pham Tuyen's compositions, many of which praise Vietnamese <u>Communism, is proof that music can simultaneously be</u> art and propaganda.

(A) [NO CHANGE]
(B) Communism, are proof that music can at the same time simultaneously be
(C) Communism, and music can simultaneously be
(D) Communism, are proof that music can be both

13. The field of ceramics, which some laypeople simply call "pottery," <u>are wide and varied</u> in application.

   (A) [NO CHANGE]
   (B) is wide and varied
   (C) were wide and varied
   (D) and is wide and varied

14. The use of various drinking vessels for different <u>dining situations are</u> a commonly accepted practice across many world cultures.

   (A) [NO CHANGE]
   (B) dining situations were
   (C) dining situations is
   (D) dining situations being

15. My parents always told me that going to the horse races <u>are something to experience at least once in your life.</u>

   (A) [NO CHANGE]
   (B) are something that one should experience at least once in your life.
   (C) is something to experience at least once in your life.
   (D) is something one's life should experience at least once.

16. Neither <u>smoking nor drinking alcoholic beverages are</u> good for your long-term health.

   (A) [NO CHANGE]
   (B) to smoke nor drinking alcoholic beverages is
   (C) smoking nor to drink alcoholic beverages are
   (D) smoking nor drinking alcoholic beverages is

17. Down the wildflower-covered <u>mountain runs the trickle</u> of snowmelt and the roaring river that ends in a foaming waterfall.

   (A) [NO CHANGE]
   (B) mountain run the trickle
   (C) mountain, the trickle
   (D) mountain, runs the trickle

18. The condensation that forms on cold <u>glasses has</u> long been of interest to young scientists.

   (A) [NO CHANGE]
   (B) glasses have
   (C) glasses having
   (D) glasses are

19. Although both of the campers saw the mountain <u>lion, neither are going</u> to report the sighting to their counselors, since leaving the main trail is against camp rules.

(A) [NO CHANGE]

(B) lion but neither is going

(C) lion but neither are going

(D) lion, neither is going

20. Only one in <u>five doctors agrees</u> that health is more a matter of good genetics than of a balanced approach to eating and exercise.

(A) [NO CHANGE]

(B) five doctors agree

(C) five doctors have agreed

(D) five doctors are in agreement

21. <u>The collection of note shapes in written music from the 1400s are significantly different in appearance from the collection of note shapes in modern notation.</u>

(A) [NO CHANGE]

(B) The collection of note shapes in written music from the 1400s are, in appearance, significantly different from modern notation.

(C) The collection from the 1400s of note shapes in written music appearing significantly different from modern notation.

(D) Significantly different in appearance from the collection of note shapes in modern notation is the collection of note shapes in written music from the 1400s.

Subject-Verb Agreement Answers

1. C
2. B
3. C
4. D
5. A
6. C
7. A
8. C
9. D
10. B
11. B
12. D
13. B
14. C
15. C
16. D
17. B
18. A
19. D
20. A
21. D

Subject-Verb Agreement Explanations

1. C – What *exactly* "astonishes" in this sentence? It's not the bands, plural, but the *number* of them, singular. "*Are* astonishing" is a plural verb form, so it needs to change to the singular form ("*is* astonishing") in order to agree with its singular subject, "number."

2. B – "*Is* versatile" is a singular verb form, but "*both* the egg *and* the eggplant" forms a compound plural subject, so to the plural form, "*are* versatile."

3. C – The sentence is incorrect as written, because "sitting *and* watching" are two separate behaviors. That means they form a compound plural subject, but the verb "was" is singular, so it doesn't agree. Choice C resolves this problem with the plural verb form "were." Choice D contains a **Parallelism** error (Lesson 11).

4. D – Both arching their backs *and* hissing are named – two behaviors, plural! Our verb should also be plural: "Arching and hissing *are* behaviors."

5. A – NO CHANGE. "Number" is often a singular noun. In this case, it is actually plural, because it refers to a "number of *people*," which definitely means *more than one person* is looking for these coins – therefore the subject is plural, and already agrees properly with the verb "are seeking," which is also plural.Choice C has bad **Sentence Structure** (Lesson 9) and Choice D has a **Misplaced Modifier** (Lesson 11).

6. **Rearranging the sentence** (Prelesson C) yields "More than two decades *is* left until..." "*More than two decades*"is a plural subject, but "is" is a singular verb. Change "is" to "are" in order to achieve proper Subject-Verb Agreement.

7. A – NO CHANGE. Who "was claiming"? The "two writers," *plural*. But "was claiming" is a *singular* verb form, so change to the plural verb form "were claiming" in order to agree with the plural subject.

β 8. C – The original version makes the common mistake of assuming "company" is plural, when it's actually singular – just *one* company. That makes the *plural* verb "are" a bad Subject-Verb match. Choice C changes the subject from "company" to "everyone," which is still singular, and also uses the singular pronoun "his or her" to properly match (**Pronoun-Antecedent Agreement**, Lesson 5). This is a favorite trick of the SAT & ACT – we tend to think of companies, organizations, cities, countries, schools, etc. as being filled with people and therefore it's easy to imagine them as needing plural verbs, even though these nouns are actually singular.

9. What *exactly* was seen by the shark? It's the "school", *singular*, that was easily seen - not a bunch of individual fish. The verb "were" is plural, so it doesn't agree with the singular subject "school." Change the main verb "were" to the singular form, "was."

10. B – Philip's "debt," *singular*, was what ruined him in the end. However, "were" is a plural verb, so correct the Subject-Verb Agreement by changing to the singular verb form, "was."

11. B – What exactly does the "demonstrating" in this sentence? It's not "the American people," plural, but "the *vote*," singular, that demonstrates. "Demonstrate" is a plural verb form, so it doesn't currently agree with its singular subject, "the vote." Change to the singular verb "demonstrates" for successful agreement.

A 12. D – What exactly "is proof" in this sentence? "The compositions," *plural*, are the proof – so the singular verb "*is* proof" creates a Subject-Verb Disagreement error. Choice D correctly uses the plural verb form "are." Choice B is wrong because it is redundant: "simultaneously" and "at the same time" mean the same thing, and would be considered wrong on the SAT & ACT for reasons of **Redundancy** (Lesson 13).

13. B – Get rid of all the details and this sentence reads "The field are wide." Big singular/plural mistake: "*field*" is a singular subject noun, but the verb "are" is plural. Change to the singular verb form "is" to agree with the singular subject "field."

14. C – What exactly is a commonly-accepted practice? **Eliminate Details** (Prelesson B) to reduce to "The use *are* a practice." The subject noun "the use" is *singular*, but the verb "are" is plural, so there's a singular/plural agreement mistake trying to sneak past us, using unrelated plural words like "vessels" and "situations" as distracting camouflage. Another tip-off is the red flag "are *a* practice," which doesn't make much sense: "are" is a plural verb, so it almost never will be followed by any *singular* noun introduced with "a."

15. C – If all you saw was "the horse races *are…*" you might not catch the error. Really, the sentence is trying to say that "the act (*singular)* of going to the horse races" is something to do at least once. "*Going* to the horse races" is just *one* action, *singular,* so it needs a singular main verb like "is." Choice D is wrong because your *life* doesn't experience anything, *you* do.

If you're still puzzled by this question, here's a similar example that may help: "Going to the mall *are* fun." Sounds awful, right? It's the same deal as going to the horse races – we correctly would say: "Going to the mall *is* fun."

16. D – "Neither" and "neither/nor" can be singular *or* plural depending on the situation. These constructions follow the *second* noun in the list to decide if they are singular or plural. For example, "Neither the cat nor the *dogs*" is plural. "Neither the dogs nor the *cat*" is singular.

However, in this case, both of our nouns "smoking" and "drinking" are singular, but the main verb "are" is plural, so the Subject-Verb Agreement is wrong. Choice D properly matches a singular subject to a singular verb. Choice B also properly uses a singular verb, but commits a **Parallelism** error (see Lesson 10).

17. B – This might be one of the toughest questions in the book. In this case, the main verb "runs" is placed *before* its plural compound subject, which is very unusual in everyday speech, but not unacceptable grammatically. In fact, the SAT & ACT often exploit this loophole to create tough questions.

Take a closer look – *both* the "trickle of snowmelt" *and* "the roaring river" are running down the mountain. Since *two* bodies of water are running (plural), we need to use the plural verb form "run" instead of the singular form "runs."

One secret trick to deal with this "verb-before-subject" situation is to rearrange the order of the sentence without changing any of the words, like this: "The trickle of snowmelt *and* the roaring river that ends in a foaming waterfall <u>runs</u> down the wildflower-covered mountain." This is one major benefit of Prelesson C, **Rearranging Word Order**.

This trick can make Subject-Verb Agreement mistakes more obvious, because "subject-before-verb" is how most of us normally speak in everyday conversation, and our ear will do a better job of automatically recognizing any errors.

18. A –NO CHANGE. You might get tricked and only see "glasses have," which would seem to properly agree (plural noun + plural verb). However, look closer – actually, the subject is "condensation" *singular*, which has long been of interest to young scientists.

A 19. D – Remember, neither/nor follows the *second* noun in the list to decide if it acts singular or plural (review question 16). In this case, neither *one* of the campers will report the sighting – each of them, on their own, decides not to say anything. Seems pretty singular. So, we need to use a singular verb. Change the verb to the singular form, "*is* going."

B 20. A – NO CHANGE. Notice the somewhat-hidden subject: "only *one* doctor agrees with the following statement." "One" is a singular subject noun, but "agree" is a plural verb form ("they agree"). Keep the verb in the singular form, "agrees." Wouldn't it sound weird to say "Only one *agree*?" ☆ *verb for 1 doctor (sing) not the other five (plural)*

B 21. D – Choices A and B make the same singular/plural mistake: "The collection" is a singular subject noun, but "*are* different" uses a plural verb. It's easy to fall into the intentional trap of focusing on "note shapes" or "the 1400s," but those plural nouns are just parts of descriptive nonessential clauses (or "Parenthetical Clauses") that tell us more about "the collection." Review Prelesson B on **Eliminating Details** and also see Lesson 9 on **Sentence Structure**.

Choice C is a sentence fragment error (**Sentence Structure**, Lesson 9) or bad **Verb Form** (Lesson 2), depending on how you choose to look at it.

Choice D might *sound* weird and confusing, mainly because the main verb "is" comes before the subject "the collection," but it's acceptable. You can even **Rearrange Word Order** (Prelesson C) to get something that sounds a little more normal: "*The collection* of note shapes in written music from the 1400s *is* significantly different in appearance from the collection of note shapes in modern notation."

LESSON 2
Verb Tense & Form

The next grammar concept on the SAT & ACT is relatively simple for the majority of students. This is the concept of Verb *Tense* and *Form*.

First of all, I recommend reviewing Prelesson A on **Parts of Speech**, particularly the information on *verbs*. Remember that verbs are the "doing" or "being" words in English. They show actions (like "the dog *barks*") or "states of being" (like "the cat *is* happy").

Verbs are also the words in English responsible for showing *when* the action of the sentence is happening. This concept is called "Verb Tense." There are "future tense," "present tense," and "past tense" versions of every verb, and other more-advanced tense options as well.

Here are some simple examples of the most common verb tenses:

- I *run* (present tense)

- I *ran* (past tense)

- I *will run* (future tense)

The main source of Verb Tense questions on the SAT & ACT tests arise from an incorrect sequence of events, for example:

"*Once* I have my own car, I *had driven* to the movie theater."

In this example, the past-tense verb "had driven" is directly contradicting the timeline of the sentence - a timeline that shows the narrator does *not* have a car *yet*. So, it would be logically impossible to already have driven to the movie theater in the *past*. This is an example of a basic Verb Tense error: the timeline doesn't make sense, because a verb is in the wrong tense.

Let's fix the situation by changing the verb to future tense.

"*Once* I have my own car, I *will drive* to the movie theater."

Most Verb Tense errors are easy to find and explain - just stay on the lookout for any illogical timelines or sequences.

Verb *Form* is similar to Verb *Tense*, but slightly different. In fact, sometimes I just use "Verb Form" as my general name for other verb-based mistakes. Here's an example of what I call a "Verb Form" mistake:

"Please let me *to go* shopping!"

In this case, we should not use the infinitive verb form "to go", but rather the simple present tense form "go."

"Please let me *go* shopping!"

Note: Making the correct choice of Verb Tense & Form is often linked to the rule of **Parallelism** (see Lesson 10). Many questions that initially look like Verb Tense can turn out to actually be about Parallelism. Look for both of these rules to appear together often!

Now let's look at a simple example from the Pretest:

Project SCORE was the first communications satellite ever put into Earth's orbit, and <u>it will be launched</u> on December 18, 1958.

    (A) [NO CHANGE]

    (B) it was launched

    (C) they were launched

    (D) it is launched

Notice that the main underlined portion of this sentence focuses on a verb, "will be launched," and the four answer choices mainly make changes to the verb tense. We are given options for *past tense* ("was launched" and "were launched"), *present* tense ("is launched"), and *future tense* ("will be launched").

The timeline of the sentence makes clear that this satellite launch happened in the *past* (in "1958"), so we can remove all present (Choice D) and future (Choice A) options.

Between the remaining options, Choice B and C are both past tense (which we want), but Choice C commits a **Pronoun-Antecedent Agreement error** (read Lesson 5 for more information: the antecedent "satellite" must be replaced by the singular pronoun "it," not the plural pronoun "they").

That leaves only **Choice B as the correct answer**, because it matches the correct Verb Tense (the past tense) with a singular pronoun.

Verb Tense & Form Quick Reference

- Verb Tense primarily has to do with the order of events in a sentence or paragraph's timeline.

- When determining the timeline, context matters - find clues to the time periods and order of events within the sentence or paragraph.

- **Parallelism** (see Lesson 10) often has an influence on the correct choice of Verb Tense & Form. Be sure to study Parallelism carefully, and keep an eye out for it whenever you think you're looking at a Verb Tense and Form question.

Now let's look at one more example from the Pretest:

Plymouth was once a brand of automobiles produced in the United States, but it was dissolved and absorbed into other brands in 2001; however, some investors <u>would like to revive</u> the marque, leaving the future of the Plymouth name in question.

(A) [NO CHANGE]

(B) will revive

(C) revived

(D) reviving

Notice that the underlined portion and our possible answer choices are playing with the tenses and forms of the verb "revive." Take context clues from the rest of the sentence: the brand was dissolved in 2001 (in the past), but some investors *might* revive the brand (a future possibility). That eliminates Choice C, which is a past tense verb.

Choice D causes a **Sentence Structure** mistake (see Lesson 9) by removing the main verb "would like" and not replacing with another main verb, thus destroying the Independent Clause that must follow the semicolon (also see Lesson 8 on **Punctuation Marks**).

Between Choice A and B, these are both future tense forms. However, Choice B implies that this brand's revival is a *sure thing* ("*will* revive"), which conflicts with the meaning of the "future being in question" - while Choice A correctly leaves open the *possibility* of revival, without guaranteeing it ("*would like to* revive"). **Choice A** nails the correct verb tense and form, which makes it the right answer.

Verb Tense & Form
Practice Questions

1. While <u>you were</u> at the hotel eating lunch, I will be at the gym for my daily workout.

   (A) [NO CHANGE]
   (B) you are
   (C) you were being
   (D) you have been

2. It's a bad <u>idea to go to</u> an international airport without having your passport ready!

   (A) [NO CHANGE]
   (B) idea going to
   (C) idea will go to
   (D) idea went to

3. When your grandfather came to America two generations <u>ago, he runs a</u> small factory in New York.

   (A) [NO CHANGE]
   (B) ago, running a
   (C) ago, he will run a
   (D) ago, he ran a

4. This mountain began as a resort that <u>will attract</u> famous international visitors to its spa and hotel.

   (A) [NO CHANGE]
   (B) attracts
   (C) is attracting
   (D) once attracted

5. This wolf has not only learned to howl on cue, but also <u>will jump</u> over fences.

   (A) [NO CHANGE]
   (B) jumping
   (C) has jumped
   (D) to jump

6. <u>Lizards rustled</u> through the grass as we hiked up the hills of the wild island.

   (A) [NO CHANGE]
   (B) Lizards rustling
   (C) Lizards are rustling
   (D) Lizards will rustle

7. Someday <u>we went to the</u> North Pole to be like our favorite adventurers of olden days.

(A) [NO CHANGE]
(B) we will go to
(C) we had gone to
(D) we have gone

8. Having a computer <u>allowed you</u> to view more free entertainment than even a king and queen of a hundred years ago.

(A) [NO CHANGE]
(B) allows you
(C) allowing you
(D) is allowing you

9. Since I've studied hard for medical school for years, I <u>believed I would become</u> a doctor.

(A) [NO CHANGE]
(B) believed I will become
(C) believe I can become
(D) would become

10. The oceans <u>will have rose from</u> their ancient levels to their present-day levels because of powerful natural forces.

(A) [NO CHANGE]
(B) will be rising
(C) rose from
(D) will rise

Verb Tense & Form Answers

1. B
2. A
3. D
4. D
5. D
6. A
7. B
8. B
9. C
10. C

Verb Tense & Form Explanations

1. B - The future timeline clue "I *will be* at the gym" matches with "while you are at the gym". Both of these are talking about upcoming *future* events, so the timeline matches correctly.

2. A - NO CHANGE. This Verb Tense & Form question is fine the way it is.

3. D - Look at the timeline clue "when your grandfather came... two generations ago" which shows *past* tense. This is consistent with Choice D, which also uses "ran" to show an event in the past.

4. D - Check out the timeline clue "this mountain *began*," showing a timeframe in the *past tense*. That's why we want the past-tense Choice D, "once attracted."

5. D - The verb form "to howl" gives the clue that we will match with our choice, "to jump." This question also overlaps with **Parallelism** (Lesson 10) because the verbs in a list need to be the same tense and form as each other.

6. A - NO CHANGE. The timeline clue "as we hiked" shows that we are in the *past tense*. That matches correctly with "Lizards rustled," which is also in the past.

7. B - The timeline clue "someday" is your best hint that we're referencing the *future* tense, so let's use the future tense verb "we *will* go."

8. B - This sentence compares the *present* ("having a computer *allows* you") to the *past* ("a hundred years ago.") Therefore, use the present-tense verb "allows."

9. C - This timeline contrasts a past-tense event that's already occurred ("I *have studied*" already) - with a present-tense belief ("I *believe*" currently) - in a future possible (but uncertain) outcome ("I *can become* a doctor").

10. C - This statement about the changes from the earth's past up until the present day only makes sense with a past-tense verb form, like "*rose* from."

LESSON 3
Adjectives & Adverbs

As we know from Prelesson A on **Parts of Speech**, Adjectives are words that are used to *modify* nouns - to describe or add detail about nouns or pronouns. They tell us more about what something or someone is like. A few examples of Adjectives are "blue," "fast," "small," "important," and "complete."

We also learned that Ad*verbs* are words that modify *verbs, adjectives,* or *other adverbs*. Adverbs tell us more about *how* something is done or further clarify *other* modifiers. A few examples are "quickly," "fundamentally," "importantly," "completely," "extremely," and "very."

You can imagine adjectives and adverbs as twins separated at birth and raised in different ways. They have something in common: they both *modify* - describe and add details - to other words.

However, just like twins raised separately could have very different favorite foods, adjectives will only play nicely with one other type of words: Nouns. On the other hand, Adverbs are more omnivorous. They will play nicely with verbs, adjectives, and adverbs -but *never* with Nouns!

This may seem like a ridiculous distinction, but unfortunately, it's the way the grammar game is played in English. Therefore, for the SAT & ACT tests you need to be able to identify adjectives vs. adverbs and determine if they are "attached" to the right type of word – that is, are they modifying the correct types of words that each of these "twins" plays nicely with?

Let's take a closer look at the difference between Adjectives and Adverbs...

Telling the Difference Between Adjectives & Adverbs

The easiest common test for whether a modifying word is an adverb or an adjective is to look for an "-ly" at the end of the word. 99 times out of 100, an adverb will look like an adjective with "-ly" stuck on at the end of it.

Here are a few examples of regular, everyday Adjective / Adverb pairs:

The adjective "wise" becomes the adverb "wisely."

The adjective "sad" becomes the adverb "sadly."

The adjective "haughty" becomes the adverb "haughtily."

A very few adverbs are irregular: for example, the adjective "good" becomes the irregular adverb "well."

Here's the good news: the SAT & ACT virtually never test irregular adverbs!

Within the Adjectives & Adverbs topic, your job on the SAT or ACT is to identify these modifying words when they are underlined and make sure that adjectives and adverbs are each *only* modifying the types of words they're meant to play nicely with.

Adjectives & Adverbs Quick Reference

- Adjectives and adverbs both *modify* - add description and detail to other words - but they only "play nice" with their own favorite types of words.

- Adjectives only play with Nouns. Adverbs can play with Verbs, Adjectives, and other Adverbs but *not* Nouns. If you're confused, review Prelesson A on **Parts of Speech**!

- Any adverbs tested on the SAT & ACT are always regular and can be identified by the "-ly" at the end of the word.

- The SAT & ACT do not (or very, very rarely) test irregular adverbs.

- Most regular adverbs can be formed just by adding "-ly" to the end of an adjective.

- Be suspicious of descriptive or modifying words and double-check your common sense to identify what a given adjective or adverb is describing.

Let's look at a couple of examples from the Pretest:

> Christina Wahlberg <u>can handle a foil quite deft</u>; in fact, she has competed in Olympic fencing.
>
> (A) [NO CHANGE]
> (B) can deft handle a foil
> (C) can handle a foil quite deftly
> (D) being a deft foil-handler

In the underlined portion of this sentence, we see the adjective "deft" (meaning "skillful"). Should we leave it as-is, or must it be changed to its adverb form, "deftly"? To answer that question, we must identify the word within the sentence that "deft" is meant to modify.

First, apply some common sense – a "foil" is the type of sword used in fencing. Can an object, like a sword, be "skillful"? Nope! Swords just lie on the table until someone picks them up – it's the *person* using the sword who is skillful or "deft," not the sword itself.

However, in our sentence, "deft" is trying to modify *how* Christina *can handle* a foil. "Deft" isn't modifying a noun – the sentence does not say that "*Christina* is deft," but that she "*can handle a foil*" with skill. It's the action of "handling" that's being described. We're modifying a *verb*, not a noun. That means we need an adverb, not an adjective.

Therefore, Choice A is out, because it uses an adjective ("deft") to modify a verb ("can handle"). Choice B makes the same mistake, just with a different word order.

Choice D switches up the wording, and properly uses the adjective "deft" to modify the noun "foil-handler," but also results in **Wordiness** (see Lesson 13) and an incomplete sentence before the semicolon (see Lesson 9 on **Sentence Structure** and Lesson 10 on **Punctuation Marks**).

Choice C changes very little from the original sentence – it merely adds "-ly" to "deft" in order to transform it into the adverb "deftly" – but fortunately, that's all we need to fix this problem. Now the adverb "deftly" is being properly used to modify the action verb "can handle." **Choice C is correct!**

Here's another example from the Pretest:

An ocean mammal, such as the blue whale, <u>behaves quite differently</u> than mammals that live on land.

    (A) [NO CHANGE]

    (B) behave quite differently

    (C) behaves quite different

    (D) has behaviors quite differently

We can probably tell this is an Adjectives & Adverbs question because of the little "-ly" that is playing such a big role in the different answer choices.

First, look at Choice D. It's one of our worst options: the adverb "differently" is attempting to modify the noun "behaviors," and by now we know that adverbs *cannot* be used to modify nouns - only adjectives can modify nouns.

Now, take a look at Choice C. "Different" is an adjective, but the word is modifying how the whale "*behaves*," which is a *verb*! No way can we use an adjective to describe a verb – we would need an adverb instead.

We could repair this by changing "different" to its adverb form "differently." That leaves us with Choices A and B. One problem - Choice B commits a **Subject-Verb Agreement** error (see Lesson 1) by pairing a plural verb ("behave") with a singular subject ("an ocean mammal.)

That leaves **Choice A**, "No Change," as the correct answer. It uses an adverb, "differently" to modify a verb, "behaves," and also avoids any singular-plural mistakes.

Adjectives & Adverbs
Practice Questions

1. A well-trained team must practice <u>regular and diligently</u>, so that the members trust one another.

   (A) [NO CHANGE]
   (B) regular and diligent
   (C) regularly and diligent
   (D) regularly and diligently

2. After training for many years in the company of other well- disciplined soldiers, a sniper <u>shoots more accurately</u> than other marksmen.

   (A) [NO CHANGE]
   (B) shoots more accurate
   (C) can shoot more accurate
   (D) shoots accurately more

3. Though you may have training as a radiological technician, you can still <u>make a career change easy</u> to an executive role.

   (A) [NO CHANGE]
   (B) make a career change easier
   (C) make easy a career change
   (D) easily make a career change

4. You <u>must run quickly</u> to get first or second place in the highly competitive Olympic sprints.

   (A) [NO CHANGE]
   (B) must run quick
   (C) must run pretty quick
   (D) might run quickly

5. Kei Tari was a Japanese comedian and musician <u>who melded seamless jazz and humor</u>.

   (A) [NO CHANGE]
   (B) who seamlessly melded jazz and humor
   (C) who was known for his melding of seamless jazz and humor
   (D) who, with jazz and humor, seamlessly melded the two

6. Annual "Clean Your Computer Day" <u>is a keen-awaited holiday for</u> programmers around the world.

   (A) [NO CHANGE]
   (B) is keenly awaited by
   (C) is keenly awaiting for
   (D) is awaited with keenness by

7. Surprisingly, my anthropology professor says she <u>can speak easier</u> to a large crowd of people than to a small group of experts in her field.

(A) [NO CHANGE]
(B) can easily speak
(C) can speak more easy
(D) can speak more easily

8. The "Feaster Five" road race is known for <u>ending dramatically.</u>

(A) [NO CHANGE]
(B) ending dramatic.
(C) being dramatic and for ending.
(D) its having a dramatic ending.

9. Sir Erec is an Arthurian Knight of the Round Table, and as such, <u>he is required to fight valiant.</u>

(A) [NO CHANGE]
(B) he is valiantly required to fight.
(C) he is required to fight valiantly.
(D) requirements are that he must valiantly fight.

10. The champion lost all of our respect when she snatched the microphone and <u>gave a haughty</u> victory speech.

(A) [NO CHANGE]
(B) gave a haughtily
(C) gives a haughty·
(D) sounding haughtily, gave a

Adjectives & Adverbs Answers

1. D
2. A
3. D
4. A
5. B
6. B
7. D
8. A
9. C
10. A

Adjectives & Adverbs Explanations

1. D – "Regular" and "diligent" are supposed to be modifying how the team must practice. In this sentence, "practice" is being used as a verb, so it can only be modified by adverbs. "Regular" becomes "regularly" and "diligently" is actually an adverb already, so keep it the way it is. This also overlaps with **Parallelism** (Lesson 10).

2. A – NO CHANGE. "More accurately" is a phrase meant to modify the way that a sniper *shoots*, which is a verb. Since "shoots" is a verb, it requires an adverb form like "accurately," not an adjective form like "accurate" to modify it.

3. D – The key word is the adjective "easy."What did the author mean was "easy?" The intended meaning is that "it's easy *to make* a career change." *Making* or *doing* the career change is what's "easy." Since we're modifying an *action* in this sentence, our best choice is to use an adverb like "easily" to modify the verb "make."

4. A – NO CHANGE. "Quickly" is a modifier describing how you must run; "run" is a verb and requires an adverb form like "quickly" to modify it, not an adjective form like "quick." Choice D states that you "might" run quickly when in fact you "must" run quickly to win at the highly-competitive Olympics.

5. B - OK, so maybe great jazz music could be creatively described as "seamless," but it would probably be more logical if a "*blend*" was described as "seamless." Therefore, "seamless" shouldn't be modifying the noun "jazz" but rather the verb "melded," and must instead take the adverb form of "seamlessly," which only is available in Choice B.

If you were considering Choice D, use **Eliminating Details** (Prelesson B) take out the Parenthetical Clause between the commas (also see Lesson 9 on **Sentence Structure**) and the sentence will then read "Kei Tari was a Japanese comedian and musician who melded the two." The "two" what? It would be a clearer sentence if it said "melded the two *entertainment forms*," or something along those lines.

6. B – "Keen" is meant to modify the way the holiday is awaited. The adjective "awaited" is being used to modify the noun "holiday." Therefore, "keen" must be changed to an adverb form, since only an adverb can modify the adjective "awaited."

Choice C would mean that "Clean Your Computer Day" is awaiting something, which is ridiculous. Choice D is a **Wordier** way (see Lesson 13) to say the same thing as Choice B.

7. D – Ask yourself these two questions. Is "easier" an adjective or an adverb? (It's an adjective.) As it's used in this sentence, is "easier" modifying a noun? (No, it's modifying something else; specifically "easier" is modifying the way the professor speaks - a *verb* - which means we need an *adverb*...) Instead we use "more easily," the adverb form of "easier."

8. A - NO CHANGE. – The original version offers the proper pairing of "ending," which is acting as a verb, and "dramatically," an adverb correctly modifying that verb. Choice B tries to use an adjective instead of an adverb. Choices C and D are unnecessarily **Wordy** (see Lesson 13).

9. C – "Valiant" is a modifying word for how Sir Erec fights. "To fight" is a verb, so it must be modified by an adverb like "valiantly," as in Choice C. Unfortunately, Choice A uses an adjective form. Choice B correctly uses the adverb form "valiantly," but changes the word's location so that it now modifies the verb "required" instead of the verb "to fight." It's probably nonsense to say that Erec is "valiantly required," since - unlike fighting as a knight - "requirements" aren't something we typically associate with the quality of being "valiant." Choice D is **Wordy** (see Lesson 13).

10. A - NO CHANGE. "Haughty" is an adjective describing the noun "victory speech." It's correct in the original version. Choice C has a **Verb Tense** error (Lesson 2).

LESSON 4
Pronoun-Antecedent Clarity

This topic of this lesson is called "Pronoun-Antecedent Clarity," and it's the first of three major pronoun-based rules on the tests. Pronoun mastery will be responsible for quite a lot of points on your SAT or ACT Grammar score!

First, let's quickly review what we know about pronouns from **Prelesson A: Parts of Speech**.

Pronouns are the short, "anonymous" words like *it*, *he*, *them*, and *I*. These words act just like Nouns in many ways. However, they also must follow some important special rules.

Pronouns are useful words for shortening our sentences, avoiding repetition, and not having to say the same names, objects, and places over and over again. Indeed, that is their most valuable asset - pronouns save us time and repetition.

On the other hand, the *downside* of using pronouns is that they can be vague and confusing.

That's why I sometimes call pronouns "anonymous nouns" - they replace *specific* nouns with more general and vague words like "they" or "it."

For example: "My dog is running around. *She* is very excited." The specific noun "dog" is replaced by the generic pronoun "she."

Remember: There is a special term - the *antecedent* - for any noun that is replaced by a pronoun. In the example in the line above, we would refer to the noun "dog" as the *antecedent* of the pronoun "she."

WARNING: Pay special attention to the note in bold about the *antecedent*. Make sure you understand exactly what an "antecedent" is before continuing!

Now, once you understand:
A) What a pronoun is...
B) What an antecedent is, and...
C) Why using pronouns without clear antecedents is confusing...

Then this rule is easy, because Pronoun-Antecedent Clarity is nothing more than the requirement to have a *clear* and definite antecedent to match with each and every pronoun we encounter on the SAT & ACT grammar tests.

For example, if we were to write:

> Between cats and dogs, James likes *them* better.

Then we have a problem: the pronoun "them" does not have a clear antecedent. Are we referring to "cats" or to "dogs" as the animal that James prefers?

This is just a simple example of the Pronoun-Antecedent Clarity rule being broken. By adding details and nonessential parenthetical clauses (see Prelesson B on **Eliminating Details** and Chapter 9 on **Sentence Structure**) to distract your attention, the SAT & ACT tests can make this simple pronoun mistake much harder to find.

Be sure you are looking for these Pronoun Clarity issues in advance. You already *know* they will be on the test, so predict and anticipate them. It's much easier to notice Pronoun-Antecedent mistakes if you're already looking out for them at all times.

Let's take a look at an example of Pronoun-Antecedent Clarity from the Pretest:

> Cyclone Althea devastated portions of northern Australia in December 1971; the strong winds ripped roofs off houses, hail damaged vehicles and windows, <u>and it cost</u> the Australian federal government close to a billion dollars in modern-day adjusted values.
>
> (A) [NO CHANGE]
> (B) and they cost
> (C) and those cost
> (D) and the storm cost

Notice the pronoun "it" in the underlined portion, and other pronouns throughout the answer choices: "they" and "those." Choice D, on the other hand, replaces the pronoun with the specific noun "the storm." Could there be a reason?

There certainly is. The three pronoun choices all share the same problem: none of them have a clear and definite antecedent. Does "it" refer to the cyclone, or to the winds and hail? What about "they", or "those"? All three pronoun-based choices have the same issue: the antecedent to the pronoun is not clear enough.

Choice D is the correct answer - it sidesteps the problem entirely by not using any pronoun at all, and replaces instead with a specific noun, "the storm."

Pronoun-Antecedent Clarity Quick Reference

- A *pronoun* is an "anonymous noun" (like "it") that replaces a specific noun (like "table.")

- The *antecedent* is the specific noun (like "table") that is replaced by a pronoun (like "it.")

- Every pronoun must have a specific and clear antecedent.

- If the antecedent of a pronoun is ever unclear, this rule is being broken.

- Get these questions right by anticipating and looking for them in advance. Any time a pronoun is part of a grammar question, double-check that it actually has a clear antecedent.

Now let's try another Pronoun-Antecedent Clarity question from the Pretest:

Historical wolf hunts would include noblemen, conscripted peasant farmers, and trained wolfhounds, though <u>they were</u> often injured as the wolves attempted to defend themselves with teeth and claws.

(A) [NO CHANGE]
(B) it was
(C) the wolfhounds were
(D) these were

Explanation: Remember to anticipate Pronoun Clarity errors *any* time the sentence uses a pronoun, especially in an underlined portion. In this case, we see the pronoun "they" is underlined, along with replacement choices "it" and "these." As in our previous Pretest example, none of these pronouns are sufficiently clear. Do they refer to the entire hunting group: noblemen, farmers, and wolfhounds? Or is there a more specific antecedent who is being injured by the wolves?

Luckily, **Choice C** gives us a great option for eliminating any Pronoun Clarity issues by replacing the pronoun with a specific noun, "the wolfhounds."

It's not uncommon for the SAT and ACT Grammar tests to resolve Pronoun Clarity mistakes by simply removing the pronouns entirely and replacing with specific nouns. In this fashion, we can completely remove any possibility of confusion arising from pronoun usage.

Review & Encouragement

It's wise to always remain hyper-vigilant towards pronouns. Remember, Pronoun-Antecedent clarity is only the first of *three* major rules for pronouns.

You can never go wrong by noticing and evaluating the use of pronouns on a grammar test. Remain on your guard whenever pronouns are part of a question!

Pronoun-Antecedent Clarity
Practice Questions

1. The tree branch banged and rattled against the window all night, and in the morning, <u>it was</u> in pieces.

   (A) [NO CHANGE]
   (B) it is
   (C) it will be
   (D) the window was

2. Today in our class of thirty students, two policemen burst in the door and <u>arrested her in</u> the middle of the classroom.

   (A) [NO CHANGE]
   (B) arrested him in
   (C) arrested a female student in
   (D) arrested a female student on

3. The Russian ambassador spoke to the President of France and the delegate from <u>Spain, promising him</u> that their governments could work together in the future.

   (A) [NO CHANGE]
   (B) Spain promising
   (C) Spain, promising it
   (D) Spain, promising both

4. Strawberry jam from the chefs at my local French restaurant is my favorite treat; <u>they make it</u> fresh each day in their kitchen.

   (A) [NO CHANGE]
   (B) it makes it
   (C) they make them
   (D) the chefs make them

5. Cats, mice, and dogs don't always get along together - the dogs tend to chase the cats, and <u>they tend to</u> chase the mice.

   (A) [NO CHANGE]
   (B) they
   (C) it tends to
   (D) the cats tend to

6. You may want to take an extra science, math, or language arts class, <u>but it is</u> technically the only official requirement for graduation.

   (A) [NO CHANGE]
   (B) but math is
   (C) but they are
   (D) and they are

7. Today I saw two calico cats, a monarch butterfly, and three fluffy dogs on the way to work, but <u>they were</u> my favorite animals of the morning.

(A) [NO CHANGE]

(B) it was

(C) the eagle I saw was

(D) the turtles I saw were

8. The small group of soldiers could see the prince well-protected on one side of the battlefield and King Richard under vicious attack on the other, <u>so they rallied to him.</u>

(A) [NO CHANGE]

(B) so he rallied to them

(C) so they rallied to their king

(D) so the soldiers rallied to them.

9. My friends want to go to the party, but <u>they are not comfortable going to it</u> without getting their parents' permission.

(A) [NO CHANGE]

(B) these friends are not comfortable going to it

(C) my friends are not comfortable going to this party

(D) these friends of mine are not comfortable going to this party

10. In China and Korea, the chefs are known for their spicy food in certain regions and for more delicate fare in other parts <u>of it.</u>

(A) [NO CHANGE]

(B) of them.

(C) of the countries.

(D) of China and Korea.

11. The ocean can be easily distinguished from a lake by two things: the presence of kelp and <u>its distinctive smell</u>.

(A) [NO CHANGE]

(B) their smell

(C) smelling distinct

(D) a distinctive smell

12. The piano is known for its lovely and expressive sound; naturally, <u>a trained pianist will find it</u> especially beautiful.

(A) [NO CHANGE]

(B) these will find it

(C) a trained pianist will find this

(D) a trained pianist will find the sound

13. In a shocking turn of events, these illegal downloads are from protected government sources; <u>it cannot be accurately traced.</u>

    (A) [NO CHANGE]

    (B) they cannot be accurately traced.

    (C) tracing them is not possible.

    (D) as a result, the downloads cannot be traced.

Pronoun-Antecedent Clarity Answers

1. D
2. C
3. D
4. A
5. D
6. B
7. D
8. C
9. A
10. C
11. D
12. D
13. D

Pronoun-Antecedent Clarity Explanations

1. D - The pronoun in question is "it," which is singular. Unfortunately, there are two singular nouns in the sentence that could both be the antecedent: "branch" and "window." Either one of those singular nouns could be "in pieces" after a night of banging against each other, so the antecedent is not clear and the meaning of the sentence isn't either. Replace "it" with a specific noun: in this case, our only option is "the window."

2. C - The pronoun "her" doesn't have a clear antecedent. Our best option is Choice C, which replaces the unclear pronoun "her" with the specific noun "female student." Choice D is close, but commits a **Idioms & Prepositions** mistake (Lesson 16) with "on the middle" instead of "in the middle."

3. D - "Promising *him*" uses a pronoun (him) without a clear antecedent (it could be either "the President of France" or "the delegate from Spain," since we don't know their genders from the context of the sentence). Choice D just solves the problem by putting both of them together.

Choice B almost works, but would need a comma after "Spain" **(Punctuation Marks**, Lesson 8) to properly separate the "-ing" Parenthetical Clause (**Sentence Structure**, Lesson 9) like so: "Spain, promising him that…"

4. A - NO CHANGE. Despite taking a risk by using the pronouns "it" and "they," the original version still maintains perfect Pronoun-Antecedent Clarity: "it" must refer to "strawberry jam," the only singular noun, and "*they* make it" must refer to "chefs," since nothing and no one else in the sentence is capable of making jam. Luckily, the other choices all commit **Pronoun-Antecedent Agreement** errors (Lesson 5), which make it even easier to be sure of our choice.

5. D - The plural pronoun "they" doesn't have a clear antecedent, since it could refer to either "cats" or "dogs" who chase the mice. The easiest way to fix the problem is to replace the pronoun with a specific noun: in this case, "the cats", *specifically*, will chase the mice.

6. B - The singular pronoun "it" doesn't have a clear antecedent, so go with Choice B, the only option that replaces the unclear pronoun with a specific noun to avoid the clarity problem. Also, Choices C & D commit **Pronoun-Antecedent Agreement** mistakes (Lesson 5) by using the plural Pronoun "they" to refer to the singular Antecedent "an extra class."

7. D - In the original version, the plural pronoun "they" doesn't have a clear antecedent, so Choices C and D look good because they give specific nouns - either "the eagle" or "the turtles." To make your final choice, notice the plural noun "my favorite *animals*," which indicates we should match with a plural noun like "turtles." This question overlaps with the next lesson on **Pronoun-Antecedent Agreement** (Lesson 5).

8. C - The singular pronoun "him" could apply to either "the prince" or "King Richard," both masculine singular nouns. That's a Pronoun-Antecedent Clarity problem when matched with "him." Luckily, the meaning of the sentence clearly implies that the *king* was in danger and would need the small group of soldiers to rally to him for help. Choice C makes this clear.

9. A - NO CHANGE. Although the sentence risks a Pronoun-Antecedent Clarity disaster by using both "it" and "they," it is alright because the antecedents are clear. "It" is a singular pronoun that can only refer to the singular noun "party," and "they" is a plural pronoun that clearly refers to the plural noun "my friends."

Choices B, C, and D are redundant and a bit wordy with repetition of "my friends / these friends of mine" and/or "the party." When the choices have an equal level of clarity, the SAT & ACT prefer to use more concise answers (see Lesson 13 on **Redundancy & Wordiness**).

10. C - The original version of the underlined portion uses the unclear pronoun "it", which doesn't have a clear antecedent noun to refer back to. Choice B has a similar problem. Choice D's repetition of country names is **Redundant** (see Lesson 13) compared to Choice C because Choice C offers a shorter, less repetitive option that's equally clear.

11. D - The original version makes a subtle Pronoun-Antecedent Clarity mistake: does the pronoun "it" refer to the singular noun "ocean" or the singular noun "kelp"? Both of these nouns could have a "distinctive smell." Choice D removes the pronoun entirely, which is one way of solving a Pronoun Clarity mistake. Choice C commits a **Parallelism** error (Lesson 10).

12. D - The original sentence uses the singular pronoun "it" without a clear antecedent: both "piano" and "sound" are singular nouns that a trained pianist could find especially beautiful. Choice D does the best job of being clear - it's always worth the extra wordiness to be precise with your Pronouns or avoid them altogether, when your only other choices are options with unclear Pronouns like "this" or "it."

13. D - The plural pronoun "they" does not have a clear antecedent: is it the "illegal downloads" (plural) or the "government sources" (also plural) that need to be traced? Only Choice D explicitly states what needs to be traced.

LESSON 5
Pronoun-Antecedent Agreement (Singular-Plural)

This next topic - called Pronoun-Antecedent Agreement (Singular-Plural) - is closely related to the lessons on **Subject-Verb Agreement** (Lesson 1) and **Pronoun-Antecedent Clarity** (Lesson 4). Like those previous topics, Pronoun-Antecedent Agreement (Singular-Plural) deals with proper selection of *singular* and *plural* forms of nouns & pronouns.

Now that we're on our second pronoun-based lesson, let's get one thing out of the way:

Pronouns on the SAT & ACT Grammar sections are ALWAYS SUSPICIOUS. They are GUILTY until proven INNOCENT.

That's because there's just so darn much that can go wrong when pronouns are involved.(Now might be a good time to review pronouns in Prelesson A, **Parts of Speech**, if you have any questions about what "pronouns" or "antecedents" are).

The first and foremost rule of pronouns - as we just learned in Lesson 4 on **Pronoun-Antecedent Clarity** - is: *it must always be clear what antecedent noun a pronoun is referring to.* Because pronouns like *it* and *she* are "anonymous" by nature, there is plenty of room for confusion.

If you can't tell *exactly* what antecedent noun a pronoun is referring to, then it's already wrong because of Pronoun-Antecedent Clarity. Here's an example of such a situation to review:

"Mr. Johnson and Mr. Daniels both agree that he should go to the party after all."

"He" could refer to either Mr. Johnson or Mr. Daniels, so this sentence contains a pronoun clarity error!

But, that's just a review of our previous lesson on Pronoun-Antecedent *Clarity*. So it is to the next topic that we turn our attention: Pronoun-Antecedent *Agreement*.

The name of this grammar rule actually explains itself perfectly:

Pronouns must agree with the antecedent noun they replace in singular/plural!

Some pronouns are plural, like "they." Some pronouns are singular, like "it."

Many times you can use common sense. "He" can only refer to one man at a time, so *he* is a *singular* pronoun. "They" replaces several people, so *they* is a *plural* pronoun. "It" is a singular pronoun. "We" and "us" are plural because they involve two or more people at a time.

Let's look at an easy example of a Pronoun-Antecedent Agreement mistake:

"Daniel and Jeremy both went to the ice cream shop for treats, where *he* got one three-scoop cone and one ice-cream sundae."

Step 1: *Be suspicious of all pronouns.* I see the pronoun "*he*." This could cause trouble.

Step 2: *Identify the antecedent noun(s).* In this case, the logic of the sentence shows that two guys went to the ice cream shop, where they each got an ice cream treat. The singular pronoun "he" is referring back to the plural antecedent "Daniel and Jeremy."

Step 3: *Check singular/plural agreement.* "He" is a singular pronoun, but "Daniel and Jeremy" is a compound plural antecedent. Big mistake! We must change "he" to "they" to match a plural pronoun with a plural antecedent.

Be careful of certain singular nouns that may sound plural to you. This overlaps nicely with **Subject-Verb Agreement** (Lesson 1), and it never hurts to review that chapter.

Basically, to some students, some nouns like "company," "country," "school (of fish)," and certain other words *sound* plural because a company is made of many employees, a country has many people in it, and a school is a group of many fish.

However, these nouns are, in fact, singular – ONE company, ONE country, ONE school of fish. If the words were meant to be plural, they would take the plural form: companies, countries, schools of fish. Just be aware that the SAT & ACT will often try to exploit this trick on the grammar and English sections.

All Pronouns acting as subjects must agree with their verbs in Singular/Plural. This is exactly the same rule as **Subject-Verb Agreement** (Lesson 1). Since pronouns can be subjects, singular pronouns that act as subjects must connect to singular verbs, and plural pronouns must match with plural verbs.

"Tricky" Pronouns: Singular or Plural?

The SAT & ACT don't just test the easy & obvious pronouns, like "he" and "us." There are also trickier pronouns. Some of these are obviously singular or plural, but others are a little tougher to figure out. Here are some examples:

Easier: One (singular), those (plural), all (plural), many (plural), few (plural)

Harder: No one, neither, either, anyone, everyone, someone, every, each

The bottom list is slightly tougher, but here's something interesting: *all* of those "harder" pronouns are singular. Many of them have a clue built in: "no *one*," "any*one*," "every*one*," and "some*one*" all include "*one*" in them. That's a dead giveaway that they are *one* - singular!

"Every" and "each" also remind me of the word "one" (every one, each one).

"Neither" and "Either": Singular or Plural?

The only pronouns that I think are *really* tricky are **NEITHER** and **EITHER**.

"Neither" and "neither/nor" can be singular *or* plural depending on the situation. They will actually follow the *second* noun when determining their singular/plural nature.

For example, "Neither the cat nor the *dogs*" is plural. "Neither the dogs nor the *cat*" is singular.

Luckily, "either" follows the exact same rules as "neither."

Now let's look at Pronoun-Antecedent Agreement question from the Pretest:

> Despite the group's many musical successes, <u>they are struggling</u> to afford new instruments and gas money for the van.
>
> (A) [NO CHANGE]
> (B) they struggle
> (C) it is struggling
> (D) he and she are struggling

Step 1: Be suspicious of pronouns. I see the pronoun "they" hanging out in the underlined portion, so it might be causing trouble.

Step 2: Make sure you know exactly what antecedents the pronouns refer back to. I feel confident from the context that "they" is clearly meant to refer to "the group." No problem here. (Notice that this also takes care of Lesson 4, **Pronoun-Antecedent Clarity**.)

Step 3: Check singular/plural agreement. The pronoun "they" is plural, but it's being used to replace a singular antecedent noun, "the group." Instead of the plural form "they are," we need a singular form like "it is." **The correct answer is Choice C**.

Note that Choice D, "he or she," is also considered a singular pronoun, but "he or she" is not an appropriate replacement for the word "group."

Pronoun-Antecedent Agreement (Singular-Plural)
Quick Reference

- Pronoun-Antecedent Agreement is closely related to **Subject-Verb Agreement** (Lesson 1) because they are both about "number" (i.e. "singular-plural"). These two topics together make up a significant portion of the SAT & ACT English grammar tests.

- As we've already learned, pronouns' jobs are to replace specific antecedent nouns.

- Because of their multiple risk factors, you must treat pronouns on the SAT & ACT as *guilty* until proven *innocent*.

- If it is unclear exactly what antecedent a pronoun is replacing in the sentence, it's already wrong (Lesson 4 on **Pronoun-Antecedent Clarity**).

- Pronouns must match the antecedent noun they replace in singular/plural.

- Pronouns acting as subjects must also match their verbs in singular/plural.

- Many pronouns are obviously singular/plural, but some are trickier. Review them. The presence of "one" (anyone, no one, someone) is an indicator that the pronoun is singular.

- "Neither" and "either" are special pronouns - they follow the second noun's singular/plural number.

Here's another example from the Pretest:

> Neither the duck <u>nor the goose is able to</u> enjoy long periods of time without a nearby body of water.
>
> (A) [NO CHANGE]
> (B) nor the goose
> (C) or the goose is able to
> (D) nor the goose are able to

Remember what I said about the word "neither" being a tricky pronoun? When using "either" or "neither," the pronoun takes its singular or plural from the second noun in the list. (In this case, "the goose" is the second noun.)

So, if "neither" is a singular pronoun in this case because "goose" is singular, then we need a singular verb to match with it. (If this is confusing, review Lesson 1 on **Subject-Verb Agreement**).

Two of our choices use plural verbs: Choice D ("*are* able") and Choice B ("enjoy"). So, those are eliminated.

Only Choices A and C use the singular verb "*is* able." However, Choice C uses the wrong pair of conjunctions, "neither - *or*," when the pair must be "neither - *nor*."

Choice A is our only remaining option - it's singular and uses the proper conjunctions - so the right answer must be No Change.

Pronoun-Antecedent Agreement
Practice Questions

1. No one, including the professors, <u>were ready for</u> the probing questions asked by the members of the peer-reviewed scientific journal.

(A) [NO CHANGE]

(B) was ready for

(C) are ready for

(D) was ready for the answering of

2. The company is about to run out of funding for research, so <u>they are going</u> to turn to investors in hopes of securing a loan.

(A) [NO CHANGE]

(B) they will turn

(C) it is going

(D) they have gone

3. One style of teacher prefers to lecture, rather than interact with students; <u>they can often be found</u> at the front of the classroom.

(A) [NO CHANGE]

(B) find them

(C) it can often be found

(D) such an instructor can often be found

4. Someone can be both brilliant in one field and far below average in many others; <u>they are called "savants."</u>

(A) [NO CHANGE]

(B) they can be called "savants."

(C) the term for these is "savants."

(D) he or she can be called a "savant."

5. Everyone I know, including all my friends and <u>relatives, are going</u> to be celebrating the holidays with good cheer.

(A) [NO CHANGE]

(B) relatives, is going

(C) my relatives, are going

(D) relatives is going

6. As <u>it ran</u> from the poachers, the pack of wolves raced across the barren tundra.

(A) [NO CHANGE]

(B) they ran

(C) they run

(D) it will run

7. My young nephew reports that he knows some well-educated people who think <u>he or she deserves</u> a scholarship or grant.

(A) [NO CHANGE]
(B) it deserves
(C) one deserves
(D) they deserve

8. <u>Until it can be</u> exchanged for a more durable and inexpensive material, these alloys will continue to be used in bridge-building.

(A) [NO CHANGE]
(B) Until it is
(C) Until they can be
(D) Once they can be

9. Carlos predicted that anyone who attends the Bach and Mozart <u>performances are</u> open-minded about the idea of listening to classical music.

(A) [NO CHANGE]
(B) performances is
(C) performance are
(D) performances were

10. Only the gifted few with unique <u>talents are</u> likely to be remembered favorably by history in two hundred years.

(A) [NO CHANGE]
(B) talent is
(C) talents is
(D) talent was

11. <u>"Is," he asked</u> with curiosity, "both of your sisters attending the dance?"

(A) [NO CHANGE]
(B) "Are," he asked
(C) "Was," he asked
(D) "Will," he asked

12. Though the thought seems humorous now, we - both my friends and I - dreamed <u>of becoming a garbage-truck driver</u> when we were much younger.

(A) [NO CHANGE]
(B) of becoming garbage-truck drivers
(C) to become a garbage-truck driver
(D) to become garbage-truck drivers

13. Each swimmer should check that they have goggles, a swimsuit, and a towel before boarding the team's bus.

(A) [NO CHANGE]

(B) it has

(C) he or she has

(D) he or she have

14. Whoever our next mayor might be, <u>I believe that he or she</u> absolutely must protect our citizens from any further violence.

(A) [NO CHANGE]

(B) they

(C) I believe that it

(D) I believe that they

15. If nobody in the house is going to eat that pasta, <u>they ought to</u> refrigerate the leftovers so that the food stays fresh.

(A) [NO CHANGE]

(B) they should

(C) someone should

(D) he or she ought to

16. Alone on the prairie, one often begins to feel that <u>they have</u> a special connection to the desolate landscape.

(A) [NO CHANGE]

(B) it has

(C) one has

(D) we have

17. Many people, after touring the medieval fair, <u>become an apprentice</u> to blacksmiths or jewelry-makers.

(A) [NO CHANGE]

(B) be an apprentice

(C) become apprentices

(D) choose to be an apprentice

18. One of my classmates thinks that <u>their parents are</u> the most productive and generous members of society who ever lived.

(A) [NO CHANGE]

(B) his parents are

(C) their parents is

(D) one's parents are

19. What any particular antique violin <u>is worth is</u> determined by its age and maker.

    (A) [NO CHANGE]
    (B) are worth is
    (C) is worth are
    (D) are worth are

20. All of the watches in our collection, which is comprised of timepieces from distant <u>centuries, is highly valued</u> by connoisseurs of horology.

    (A) [NO CHANGE]
    (B) centuries, it is highly valued
    (C) centuries, are highly valued
    (D) centuries, being highly valued

21. Someone is at the door, but I am unaware of what purpose <u>they might be</u> visiting us for at this late hour.

    (A) [NO CHANGE]
    (B) they are
    (C) they could be
    (D) he or she might be

22. Each runner will have a lane on the track, which has recently been resurfaced, to <u>themselves</u> in order to minimize accidents.

    (A) [NO CHANGE]
    (B) oneself
    (C) him or her
    (D) himself or herself

Pronoun-Antecedent Agreement Answers

1. B
2. C
3. D
4. D
5. B
6. A
7. D
8. C
9. B
10. A
11. B
12. B
13. C
14. A
15. C
16. C
17. C
18. B
19. A
20. C
21. D
22. D

Pronoun-Antecedent Agreement
Explanations

1. B – The subject of this sentence is the pronoun "no one," which is singular (remember, it has "one" at the end). That means we need the singular verb "was," not the plural "were" (review Lesson 1 on **Subject-Verb Agreement**). Choice D is too wordy (**Redundancy & Wordiness, Lesson 13**).

2. C - "The company" is a singular antecedent noun, so it matches with a singular pronoun "*it*." Don't be tricked: a company is singular, even though many people may work there.

3. D – The *plural* pronoun "they" in the original sentence is incorrectly agreeing with the *singular* antecedent "style." The sentence is trying to say that "this *style* (of teacher) can often be found at the front of the classroom." Choice D is nice and clear and lets the reader know exactly who can be found at the front of the classroom, which also overlaps with **Pronoun-Antecedent Clarity** (Lesson 4).

4. D – This sentence incorrectly matches the singular noun "someone" with the plural pronoun "they." Instead, we should use "he or she" as a singular companion to "someone."

5. B – Remember, "every*one*" is singular – while it's true that there are many people included in the word "everyone," it still refers to just a single "everyone" So, use a singular verb like "is" instead of a plural verb like "are" (review Lesson 1 on **Subject-Verb Agreement**). Choice D has the correct Singular-Plural, but poor **Sentence Structure** (Lesson 9).

6. A – NO CHANGE. "The pack" is a singular antecedent noun (it's just a single pack, even though it's made up of many wolves). "They" is a plural pronoun, but it is referring to "the pack." Use the singular pronoun "it" instead.

7. D – "He or she deserves" is singular, but refers to the antecedent "some well-educated people," which is plural. Replace with the plural version of the pronoun and verb, "they deserve."

8. C – The plural antecedent noun "alloys" must be replaced by a plural pronoun, such as "they."Choice D uses the incorrect transition word "once" (**Conjunctions & Transitions**, Lesson 7) which gets the cause-and-effect of the sentence reversed.

9. B – "Anyone...*are* open-minded" uses a plural verb, but it's referring to "*anyone* who attends." As always, any*one* is singular, so it needs a singular verb like "is" (review Lesson 1 on **Subject-Verb Agreement**).

10. A – NO CHANGE. "Few" is a plural noun, because it represents to "more than one." Therefore, it's correct to use the plural verb form "are" (review Lesson 1 on **Subject-Verb Agreement**).

11. B – You can practice **Rearranging Word Order** (Prelesson C) to rephrase questions into statements and make any singular/plural mistakes more clear, like this: "*Both* of your sisters *is* attending the dance." Now it's obvious that "both," which refers to two people and is plural, is mismatched with the singular verb "is." Change "is" to the plural form "are" to fix the mistake (review Lesson 1 on **Subject-Verb Agreement**).

12. B - A classic 'career' mistake: "both my friends and I" is plural, so all those people *plural* can't dream of becoming the same, *singular* "garbage-truck driver." Change to "garbage-truck *drivers*" so they agree about being plural.

13. C - The plural pronoun "they" is being used to refer back to the singular antecedent noun "each swimmer." That's a classic Pronoun-Antecedent Agreement mistake, so let's change the plural pronoun "they" to the singular pronoun "he or she."

14. A – NO CHANGE. The singular pronoun "he or she" is properly being used to refer to the singular antecedent "our next mayor."

15. C – "Nobody" is a singular antecedent noun, so we can't use Choices A or B, which both use a plural pronoun "they." Choice C correctly matches "If *nobody*.... *someone* should..." Choice D tries "If nobody.... he or she should"; however "he or she" is not an appropriate pronoun to replace the antecedent "nobody," perhaps because "nobody" is no person at all, so cannot be either male or female.

16. C – "*They*" is a plural pronoun, but the sentence states that *one* (a singular antecedent) often begins to feel a connection to the landscape. Stay consistent and singular by using "*one*" a second time.

17. C - The classic career trick, as in Question 12: "many people" is plural, so all those people can't make the decision to become (singular) "*an* apprentice." Instead, those *plural* people would like to become *many* apprentices, *plural*. Therefore, change to the plural "apprentices."

18. B - "Their" is a plural possessive pronoun; it creates a Pronoun-Antecedent Agreement error with its antecedent "*one* of my classmates," which is singular. We can correct this mistake by changing the plural pronoun "their" to the singular pronoun "his."

19. A – NO CHANGE. This can be a tough one. "*What* any violin is worth" is a singular noun; we're talking about a singular "*what it's worth*," a single amount of value. Therefore, the plural verb "*are* worth" is disagreeing; change to the singular verb form "is" for better **Subject-Verb Agreement** (Lesson 1). Then, consider "*a violin*", which is also singular. Keep the singular verbs all around and go with "is" and "is."

20. C – Just make sure you realize that it's not the *collection* that is "highly valued," it's *all* the *watches* – which is plural. Change the verb to "*are* highly valued" to fix the singular/plural **Subject-Verb Agreement** (see Lesson 1). Choice B commits a **Sentence Structure** error (Lesson 9 by producing a Sentence Fragment.

21. D – The antecedent "some*one*" is singular, so we can't use the plural pronoun "they" or we'll cause a Pronoun-Antecedent disagreement. Change from the plural pronoun "they" to the singular pronoun "he or she."

22. D – "Themselves" is a plural pronoun, but the antecedent "each runner" is singular; that means it's a Pronoun-Antecedent Agreement error. Use the slightly-wordier, but grammatically correct singular form "himself or herself."

LESSON 6
Pronoun Case

"Pronoun Case" is the topic that covers the common question of whether we should say "my brother and *I* go to the park" or "My brother and *me* go to the park" - and many other situations as well.

There are two ways to deal with this common error on the SAT & ACT, and in real life as well:

Method #1: Test each noun *by itself* and trust your ear (about 90% effective) *or*
Method #2: Think about it the "grammar teacher" way (this is harder to learn, but more powerful – and allows you to achieve 100% accuracy and certainty)

I'll explain both ways, and you can pick the one you prefer. I myself use a blend of both – I trust my trained ear nine times out of ten, but when I'm uncertain, I take a "grammar teacher" approach to support my decision.

Approach #1: Try Each Noun By Itself & Trust Your Ear

This first style of solving Pronoun Case issues focuses on four steps:

1. Noticing the presence of pronouns in the sentence,
2. Trimming the sentence down to its basics,
3. Occasionally rearranging word order without changing sentence meaning, and
4. Trusting your "inner ear" to determine the right pronoun to use (he/him? They/them? etc.)

We will practice each of the four steps when we look at the questions from the Pretest, but for now let me lay them out for you:

Step 1: You should *always* be looking for pronouns on the SAT & ACT English grammar tests! This step overlaps with at least three other important topics: **Subject-Verb Agreement** (Lesson 1), **Pronoun Clarity** (Lesson 4) and **Pronoun Agreement** (Lesson 5). Every pronoun should be closely examined!

Step 2: Practice eliminating unnecessary detail (**Prelesson B**). As always, this is an important tool you can use on *every single SAT & ACT grammar question*, so you should always eliminate details, even if you are "pretty sure" you know what the grammar mistake is. You may be surprised once the details are removed and the core of the sentence stands exposed.

Step 3: When the SAT & ACT writers test Pronoun Case, they sometimes make the sentence appear more complicated than it really is by choosing a word order that is unnatural, compared to your everyday speech. In such cases, you can beat them at their own game by applying **Prelesson C** and *re*-rearranging the order of the sentence into a more familiar-sounding style of speech.

Step 4: "Trust your inner ear." Try changing the pronoun's case (more details on this in the next half of this chapter) in the reduced, re-ordered sentence. Then use the case that "sounds better" to you. You won't get it right every *single* time with this method, but you'll get it right a lot of the time.

Pronoun Case Quick Reference

- Always remain suspicious of pronouns!

- Pronoun Case on the SAT & ACT is often about choosing between "I" and "me" (or between "us" and "we.")

- Method 1: Eliminate unnecessary details and rearrange the sentence (apply Prelessons B and C); then, trust your inner ear. This will work about 90% of the time.

- Method 2: If you want to get this topic right 100% of the time, you'll need to study up on the difference between subjects and objects and the pronoun subject/object chart (coming up next in this chapter).

Now we're going to practice the first Pronoun Case method on a Pretest question:

<u>Charles and me love</u> to play dodgeball, and we have spent many an hour engaged in this exciting pastime.

    (A) [NO CHANGE]

    (B) Charles and I love

    (C) Charles and me loves

    (D) Charles and I loves

Step 1: Notice the pronouns: "me" and "we."

Step 2: Eliminate Details, with a twist.

First of all, we can reduce this sentence to *"Charles and me* love to play, and *we* have engaged."

Now the twist: Try both "Charles" and "me" by themselves. You will have to change the plural verb "love" to the singular form "loves," but that's fine - it's just a natural result of applying this pronoun test.

So, you'd try saying these two ways to yourself:

"Charles loves to play"/ *"Me* loves to play."

Doesn't that second version sound *awful*? Yes, because it's wrong, and your ear knows it!

Step 3: Rearrange the word order if necessary. (No need to do that here; the sentence structure is already in the most basic order.)

Step 4: Try saying the "problem pronoun" both ways. So you'd try:

"Me loves to play" / *"I love* to play."

First one sounds awful, second one sounds good – so trust your ear; we should use the "I" form of the pronoun, not the "me" form. That eliminates Choice A and Choice C.

We still have Choices B and D, but Choice D contains a **Subject-Verb Agreement** error (Lesson 1) between a plural subject and a singular verb: "Charles and I *loves*." (You should be getting good at this Subject-Verb Agreement stuff by now!)

That leaves **Choice B** as the correct answer, because it uses the correct Pronoun Case and avoids any singular-plural mistakes.

Simplifying and Reorganizing Sentences

Let me show you some quick simplifying and reorganizing tactics on this next Pretest sentence:

"Is it right that us workers must suffer due to incompetent management?"

Eliminating details gives:

"Is it right that us must suffer?"

Rearranging and simplifying again gives the core of the sentence:

"Must us suffer?"

This sounds awful. Try it the other way:

"Must *we* suffer?"

Now it sounds much improved, and it is in fact correct this way.

Approach #2: The Grammar Teacher Way

Now, if you want to catch **Pronoun Case** errors every single time, you need to understand this rule the "grammar teacher way." What you need to learn (or review) first is the concept of "Object" vs. "Subject."

Every complete sentence has a subject. The subject *does* the action - for example:

"**The dog** barks."

More complex sentences also have objects, for example:

"The dog barks *at* **the mailman**."

Objects are required for situations where someone **does something *to*** something else.

The dog barked "at" the mailman; barking was the thing done **to** the mailman, so he's the "object."

The "subject" is the dog, the main character, who happens to be **doing** the action like a subject should.

You usually don't have to think about this stuff, except when you're using pronouns like "it" instead of dog and "him" instead of mailman. Let's see what that would look like:

"It barks at him."

OK, on this SAT or ACT this sentence would be wrong already because of **Pronoun-Antecedent Clarity** issues (Lesson 4). However, let's set that issue aside for a moment and deal only with Pronoun Case. Here's where we pull out our handy mental chart of pronoun case...

Oh wait, you don't have one? OK, you can borrow mine for the moment! Make sure to get your own (i.e. memorize this chart if you're shaky on it):

Subject Pronoun	Object Pronoun
I	Me
He, She, It	Him, Her, It
We	Us
They	Them

This chart represents a written version of "trusting your ear" from the previous four-step approach to Pronoun Case. A lot of the time, your brain will just "know" this stuff through years of practice and experience with the English language.

Now, can you add up the pieces of the "grammar teacher" way to handle Pronoun Case questions?

1) We know how to tell the difference between a subject and an object.
2) We have a chart that tells us which pronoun to use depending on if it's a subject or object.

The dog was the *subject*, and has been replaced correctly with a *subject* pronoun from our chart: "It."

The mailman was the *object*, and has been replaced correctly with an *object* pronoun from our chart: "Him."

Therefore, the sentence "It barks at him" is correct in regards to pronoun case.

But, if we changed the sentence to "It barks at *he*," for example, we would have a Pronoun Case problem, because we replaced the mailman (who is an *object* in the sentence) with a *subject* pronoun ("he"). Notice how the chart also supports what I'm saying.

Let's try the "grammar teacher" method on the following Pretest question:

Is it right that <u>us workers must suffer due to</u> incompetent management?

(A) [NO CHANGE]
(B) we workers must suffer despite
(C) us workers must suffer despite
(D) we workers must suffer due to

OK – first of all, we're looking for pronouns, and one stands right out: "us."

Who does "us" refer to (what's the *antecedent* of the pronoun "us')? "The workers."

Is the pronoun "us" in the objective or subjective form? Check the chart: Objective.

Objective form means it's *not* the *subject*, the main actor of the sentence, but the *object* - having something done *to* it.

Now, think about the sentence as a whole. Does the sentence say anything is happening *to* the workers? No, it says the workers are *doing* something: they are "suffering."

If the workers are suffering, then they are the main characters of this sentence – they are the *subject*. Therefore, any pronoun standing for "workers" in this sentence must be in the *Subjective Case*.

Now, check the chart again for a reminder that "we" is the subjective form of "us."

At this point we should check our answer choices: Choices A and C use the incorrect objective form "us," so they must be wrong.

Choice B and D seem almost identical at first, but notice the conjunctions they use: "despite" vs. "due to." A direct cause-and-effect is logical here, so the conjunction "due to" is the correct choice over "despite." If this confuses you, study Lesson 7 on **Conjunctions**. The correct answer is **Choice D**.

Note: If this Subjective / Objective approach feels too technical for you, or you're short on time to prepare for your test, just stick with the previous method from earlier in this chapter: simplifying/rearranging the sentence and trying each pronoun by itself, then relying on your ear to help you. That will work for most questions, but it's even better to understand this topic from the technical angle as well.

Pronoun Case Practice Questions

1. As I have taught my little sister more and more about soccer, <u>she and me spend more time</u> kicking the ball around outside.

   (A) [NO CHANGE]

   (B) she and I have spent more time

   (C) she and I will spend more time

   (D) her and me have spent more time

2. On our travels through Germany, Raphael, Bill, and <u>me met both weary</u> travelers and excited explorers.

   (A) [NO CHANGE]

   (B) me met both wearily

   (C) I met both weary

   (D) I met both wearily

3. <u>Us students are</u> leading a solidarity march in order to protest the unfair treatment of migrant farm workers.

   (A) [NO CHANGE]

   (B) Ourselves are

   (C) Us students were

   (D) We students are

4. When I saw Kate jumping on the trampoline, I asked <u>my friends and she to be careful,</u> for the springs were old and worn-out.

   (A) [NO CHANGE]

   (B) them

   (C) she and my friends to be careful

   (D) my friends and her to be careful

5. <u>My puppy and I go</u> to the dog park as often as possible; I love to watch his rambunctious antics as he chases other friendly dogs and plays in the river.

   (A) [NO CHANGE]

   (B) I go

   (C) Me and my puppy go

   (D) My puppy and me go

6. Annabelle is an old acquaintance of our family; <u>my brother and her may</u> even get married someday.

   (A) [NO CHANGE]

   (B) she and he

   (C) her and my brother

   (D) she and my brother

7. When Debbie answers the phone, <u>she always responds "this is her."</u>

   (A) [NO CHANGE]
   (B) she always responds "this is she."
   (C) her always responds "this is she."
   (D) she always responding "this is she."

8. To a great artist such <u>as he, both</u> oil painting and charcoal sketching come quite naturally.

   (A) [NO CHANGE]
   (B) as his, both
   (C) as him, both
   (D) like him, both

9. He throws the ball accurately; she catches it consistently; together, <u>he and she make</u> a remarkably well-rounded team.

   (A) [NO CHANGE]
   (B) he and her make
   (C) he and she makes
   (D) he and her makes

10. The bear chased Xander and <u>me while Martha's climbing skills allowed her to perch</u> safely in a tree.

    (A) [NO CHANGE]
    (B) me to allow Martha's climbing skills to perch her
    (C) I allowing Martha's climbing skills to perch her
    (D) I while Martha's climbing skills allowed her to perch

11. Playing <u>the way us Wildcats do</u> is sure to guarantee victory in the tournament.

    (A) [NO CHANGE]
    (B) our way, us Wildcats
    (C) in our own way, we Wildcats
    (D) the way we Wildcats do

12. Concert audiences in the 1800s did not have access to recording technology and might only hear a song once in their entire life; <u>for they, an encore</u> was their only chance to hear a piece of music for a second time.

    (A) [NO CHANGE]
    (B) for these, an encore
    (C) for them, an encore
    (D) an encore, for these,

Pronoun Case Answers

1. B
2. C
3. D
4. D
5. A
6. D
7. B
8. C
9. A
10. A
11. D
12. C

Pronoun Case Explanations

1. B – Take out the details and split up the nouns using the "one at a time" test to identify the mistake in the original, like this: "*She* spends more time…" and "*Me* spend more time…" The first version sounds fine, the second sounds like a caveman. We need to use the pronoun "I" instead of "me," as in "*I* spend more time." Choice C commits a **Verb Tense error** (Lesson 2).

2. C – Use the "one at a time" test: "*Raphael* met…" / "*Bill* met…" / "*Me* met…" Whoa whoa – "*Me* met" doesn't sound so good. It should be the subjective pronoun case "I met," which should sound much more familiar. Choices B and D also make **Adjectives & Adverbs** mistakes (Lesson 3).

3. D – First, **Eliminate Details** (Prelesson B) to shorten the sentence. Then test Pronoun Case. It sounds awful to say "*Us* are leading a march," especially when you compare it to "*We* are leading a march," which sounds natural. We need a *subject* for this sentence, but the awful-sounding first version is incorrectly using the *objective*-case pronoun "*us*." The natural-sounding second version is correctly using the *subjective*-case pronoun "*we*."

4. D - Take out the details and use the "one at a time" test: "I asked *my friends* to be careful" vs. "I asked *she* to be careful." The second one sounds "off," doesn't it? Change the subjective pronoun "*she*" to the objective case "…asked *her* to be careful." Choice B uses the plural pronoun "them" without a clear antecedent (**Pronoun-Antecedent Clarity**, Lesson 4).

5. A – NO CHANGE. "*I* go to the park" would be correct, using the "one at a time" test. This test also confirms that you can't use "me": "*Me* goes to the park" definitely sounds like a caveman.

6. D – Use the "one at a time" test: "*My brother* may get married someday." "*Her* may get married someday." The second one sounds really bad, because it's trying to use an *objective*-form pronoun to do a *subjective*-form job. Change "*her*" to "*she*": "*She* may get married someday." Sounds better, right? Good.

7. B – A classic phone-etiquette question. Reduce the details to the bare minimum (**Eliminating Details**, Prelesson B) and rearrange the words (**Rearranging Word Order**, Prelesson C), and the mistake and proper solution will become more clear: we say "*She* is x," not "*Her* is x." For example, "*She* is happy," not "*Her* is happy." Therefore, by reversing the order, we get "Happy is *she*," not "Happy is *her*." And from there, we deduce it's better to say "*She* is this," or rearranged to "this is *she*," rather than "This is *her*."

8. C – Rearrange the sentence, like so: "Both painting and sketching come naturally to *he*." That sounds wrong because it's trying to use a *subjective* pronoun (*he*) as an *object*; try the sentence with the objective pronoun "*him*" instead of "*he*" and your ear will probably agree more with the new version.

9. A – NO CHANGE. "He" and "she" are already *subjective* form pronouns, which is great, because they are acting as *subjects* in this clause. Also, look out for "make" (plural verb) vs "makes" (singular verb). Review **Subject-Verb Agreement** (Lesson 1) if you miss this.

10. A - NO CHANGE. Use the "one at a time test" to notice the Pronoun Case error: "The bear chased *Xander*. "The bear chased *I*." Doesn't it sound much more normal to say "The bear chased *me*"? That's because "me" is an objective form - "me" is the *object* being chased by the bear, who is the *subject* of the sentence. Choice B is wrong because "The bear chased me... *to* allow" incorrectly implies that the bear made a calculated decision to allow Martha's escape.

11. D - Get rid of some of the details and the mistake is more clear, like this: "Playing the way *us* do..." We never say "Yes, *us do* like electronic music," do we? No, but "*we* do" sounds right. That's because "we" is the proper Pronoun Case: the subjective case, correctly playing the role of the sentence's subject.

Choice C gets the Pronoun Case right, but incorrectly mixes a plural pronoun and a singular verb ("We is"). If you miss this, review **Subject-Verb Agreement** (Lesson 1) and **Pronoun-Antecedent Agreement** (Lesson 5).

12. C – Rearrange the second half of the sentence (Prelesson C, **Rearranging Word Order**) in order to convince yourself that the sentence can be rewritten like this: "An encore was the only chance for *them* to hear a piece of music a second time." Then trust your ear.

LESSON 7
Conjunctions & Transitions

The central concept of this lesson, titled "Conjunctions & Transitions," is closely linked to *Conjunctions*, one of the eight **Parts of Speech** you can review in Prelesson A.

The difference between those "conjunctions" (the Part of Speech) and "Conjunctions & Transitions" (the SAT/ACT Grammar rule) is that this rule can apply either to the *smaller* level in the middle of a single sentence ("Conjunctions") or to the *bigger* level on a multiple-sentence or multiple-paragraph level ("Transitions").

Let's take a look back at what a conjunction is:

> A conjunction "joins" ideas A and B with a logical transition of some kind.
>
> Common examples of conjunctions are *and, however, but, or, because, although,* and many other "joining" or "transitioning" words.

"Conjunctions," the name for this important part of speech, comes from the word "conjoined," or simply "joined." A "junction" is a place where two things meet and connect – like two train lines, two sides of a bridge, or two different ideas. This might help you remember: *Conjunction*s are the words that *join* two ideas.

When two ideas are joined or connected, there are two possible situations: either the two ideas are closely related, which I call "*connectors*,", or they are in a disagreement of some kind, which I call "*divergers*."

Another way of saying this is that either the second idea *continues* or picks up where the first idea left off (a "connector"), or the second idea will *contradict* the first idea (a "diverger").

There are many different conjunctions, each with their own special "flavor" when it comes to connecting or diverging between two ideas – but in the big picture, all transitions will fall broadly into one of two categories: they either <u>connect</u> Idea B to Idea A, or they <u>diverge</u> from Idea A to Idea B!

Conjunctions & Transitions also have two possible "strength levels": *strong* and *weak*.

For example, the conjunction "because" is a *strong connector* that directly links Idea B to Idea A. It shows a paired "cause and effect" - one of the strongest possible connections. On the other hand, the conjunction "but" could be a *weak diverger* since it breaks a connection between two ideas without necessarily implying a total contradiction of the first idea.

Examples of Common Conjunctions

Here are a few examples of common conjunctions:

Strong Connecting Conjunctions:

Because, since, due to, as a result

Weaker Connecting Conjunctions:

And, for, in addition, furthermore

Strong Diverging Conjunctions:

However, despite, nevertheless, not, instead

Weaker Diverging Conjunctions:

But, although, still, regardless

On the SAT & ACT grammar sections, Conjunction errors are often tested in sentences with no obvious *grammatical* errors (for example, the Singular/Plural agreements are fine, the pronouns play by the rules, no bad Parallelism or Misplaced Modifiers, etc.) but the answer choices are focused on a selection of transitions or conjunctions - and in many cases, the sentence's meaning *on the whole* may make you shake your head in confusion and go "huh?"

In general, when the Conjunctions & Transitions are wrong, something about the *big* picture won't add up. The overall logic seems wrong - perhaps unclear - but maybe you can't quite put your finger on *why*. Look at your answer choices. Are the they playing with different conjunctions and transition words?

These are all signs that you need to look for two separate ideas ("Idea A" and "Idea B") and closely examine the conjunction or transition options to connect them. Make sure the logical pathway from Idea A to Idea B is expressed with maximum sense, logic, and clarity.

Let's look at an example from the Pretest:

> The soldier successfully pulled his ally from the <u>helicopter wreck, and since the</u> flames engulfed their craft, he was unable to repair the vehicle.
>
> (A) [NO CHANGE]
> (B) helicopter wreck, the
> (C) wreck of the helicopter, with the consequence that
> (D) helicopter wreck, but because

Check out the basic logic of this sentence as written: In the first half, the soldier *succeeds* at something (by saving his comrade). In the second half of the sentence, the soldier *fails* at something else (he is unable to repair his helicopter due to flames).

Are those ideas *connecting* or *diverging*? Well, if he succeeded first, but failed second, I would definitely have to say that these two ideas are *diverging*. If they were more connected, he would either *succeed* in both halves or *fail* in both halves.

Unfortunately, the conjunction "and" is used to *connect* two ideas, so it's illogical to use it in this context. For a simpler illogical example, imagine:

> "I usually can't stand gym class *and* sometimes I like it"

This is illogical for the same reason as the "burning helicopter" Pretest sentence. The conjunction "and" isn't good for connecting two *contrasting* ideas. Instead of the connecting word "*and*," it will make more sense to use a contradicting conjunction like "*but*" or "*yet*."

So, we know Choice A, "No Change," is wrong. Choice B makes a run-on sentence (see Lesson 9 on **Sentence Structure**); we need to change the conjunction, but that doesn't mean we can just skip using any conjunction at all! We need to replace the *connecting* conjunction with a *contradicting* one.

Choice C, "with the consequence that," provides another *connecting* conjunction that implies a direct cause-and-effect relationship between the two halves of the sentence. This is just as wrong as using "and," because it's still not logical to say that "rescuing his ally" causes the helicopter to be on fire.

Choice D uses "but," which is the type of *diverging* conjunction we were looking for. Now the soldier succeeds in the first half *but* fails in the second half - the sentence and its conjunctions make sense.

Double Conjunctions

OK – there's one other important way that the SAT & ACT hide conjunction errors. It's less common than what we just learned about, but still may make an appearance:

Important: Two ideas ("clauses") cannot be connected by more than one conjunction.

This doesn't mean an entire *sentence* is limited to just one conjunction (in fact, longer sentences can often have more than one conjunction in them). It just means that two ideas *within* the sentence must be connected by one conjunction and *only* one conjunction, whether they are agreeing with or diverging from each other.

Here's an example of a sentence that breaks this rule:

"Because I like fishing, *since* I'm very good at it."

Notice the double conjunction "Because... since..." That's not allowed when connecting two ideas.

The Boxcar Method

Now, I want to teach you an advanced method I use myself to handle tricky transition questions on the SAT & ACT. 99% of students never learn to do this, so they continually lose points to challenging Conjunctions & Transitions questions. Hope you're paying attention!

I call this method "the Boxcar method."To get the idea, first picture a line of boxcars - train cars - connected on *both sides* to other boxcars, forming an unbroken, connected chain of boxcars. There are little hooks on both ends of every boxcar, used to hook together with the previous and next boxcars in line so that the whole line of cars all connect.

Now, think of a Transition question as a set of three *"idea boxcars"* - each boxcar is one idea in a three-idea sequence, and each idea hooks together on both sides, just like a chain of boxcars. Our job is to *transition* from one idea to the next, so all three boxcars must hook together smoothly and firmly on both sides: Boxcar A into Boxcar B into Boxcar C. Notice that Boxcar B, in the middle, has the hardest job to do: it has to bridge between *two* connections, one on each side.

So, to appropriately use the Boxcar Method, you should identify and focus on what I call "Boxcar B" in the middle. Find this middle idea in the sequence of three ideas, and then split it into "first half" and "second half," which you should then summarize and *write down* on paper.

Now, use your summaries to eliminate any answer choices that do *not* link up the end of Boxcar A to the first half of Boxcar B. By *link up*, I mean "show a logical connection." (Remember, you're visualizing a line of connected "idea boxcars" from Boxcar A to Boxcar B to Boxcar C.)

Then, use your notes on the second half of Boxcar B to eliminate any options that don't link up the *back* end of Boxcar B to the start of Boxcar C.

Once you've patiently taken these methodical steps, it should become much easier to make your final answer selection for *any* Conjunctions and Transitions question.

This is much faster and less work than it sounds, but *only* if you practice the method carefully before the test. It was specially designed for SAT & ACT Transition & Conjunction questions, and is extremely effective, although it takes practice to work efficiently.

Conjunctions & Transition Quick Reference

- A "junction" is where two things join, like a railroad junction. A "conjunction" is a word that joins two ideas.

- "Conjunctions" connect two ideas *within* a sentence. "Transitions" connect larger ideas between sentences or paragraphs.

- Identify these questions by their answer choices: you are given various choices for conjunctions, connecting or transition words & phrases.

- There are two "flavors" of Conjunctions & Transitions: *connecting* and *diverging*.

- There are two "strengths" of Conjunctions & Transitions: *stronger* and *weaker*.

- Look at the "big picture" – the *grammar* may be fine, but does the *logic* make sense? Does Idea A properly flow into Idea B?

- Use the "Boxcar Method" to narrow down to a single conjunction with the correct "flavor" and "strength."

- Only use *one* single conjunction between *two* ideas/clauses.

Note: We've been looking at Conjunctions that transition between halves of a single sentence - but you should also be aware that the concept of Transitions and "boxcars" can be applied to multi-sentence situations. Many questions on both the SAT and the ACT will demand that you choose the optimal transition between two sentences, or even between two paragraphs.

The best way to approach these multi-sentence Transition questions is exactly the same as your standard Conjunctions questions: Analyze the first half and the second half with the "Boxcar Method," taking written notes as you go. Next, consider if a "Connector" or a "Diverger" would be more appropriate. Then eliminate your way down through the answers (don't forget to weigh "stronger" vs "weaker" transition options).

For now, we'll continue to focus on Conjunctions and single-sentence situations. Once you've mastered these situations and the "Boxcar Method," you can use Official SAT and ACT practice tests to identify and practice multi-sentence Transition questions.

Let's look at another example from the Pretest:

> Although deforestation is extremely detrimental to the planet's delicate ecology, <u>yet</u> many timber companies continue to harvest lumber for large corporate profits.
>
> (A) [NO CHANGE]
> (B) and
> (C) but
> (D) [DELETE the underlined portion]

The two ideas ("Boxcars") are: 1) Deforestation is harmful. 2) Many companies continue to harvest lumber.

Is this a direct cause-and-effect relationship, or is it contradicting? Definitely *contradicting*. The dangers of deforestation are *contrasted* with the continued timber harvesting. However, the sentence is already using the conjunctions "although" and "yet," both of which are diverging conjunctions - so that seems good....

Wait a second - the sentence is using *two* conjunctions?! No way – only *one* single conjunction is ever allowed to connect two ideas.

We can't mess with the conjunction "although," because it's not underlined. The second conjunction, "yet," *is* underlined, so we should take this opportunity to remove it. **Choice D** is the correct answer.

Conjunctions and Transitions
Practice Questions

1. The science institute was located in picturesque surroundings, <u>but the students are able</u> to relax among the lakes and fields after classes.

   (A) [NO CHANGE]

   (B) so the students are able

   (C) though the students are able

   (D) this allows the students

2. Dangerous Dan was a fictional detective and the star of many popular mystery <u>movies; however,</u> the actors that have played Dan are now worth millions of dollars.

   (A) [NO CHANGE]

   (B) Movies; despite that,

   (C) movies; in fact,

   (D) movies, and yet,

3. An "Iltizam" was a 17th century Egyptian farmland that earned the wealthy landowner a great deal of <u>profit; therefore, he left</u> only pennies to the peasants who actually cultivated the farm.

   (A) [NO CHANGE]

   (B) profit, to leave

   (C) profit, but left

   (D) profit, nor left

4. The Federal Trade Commission was established years ago to protect the American economy, <u>because since then it has</u> ended many unfair monopolies.

   (A) [NO CHANGE]

   (B) because in that time it has

   (C) and since then they have

   (D) and since that time it has

5. Ludwig van Beethoven may have been the greatest Viennese composer in <u>history, and he</u> almost missed his destiny when deafness threatened to end his musical career.

   (A) [NO CHANGE]

   (B) history, he

   (C) history, so he

   (D) history, but he

6. An excellent wrestler, David Tsinakuridze won the Olympic gold medal, <u>although his coach</u> was concerned about the athlete's recently-injured knee.

   (A) [NO CHANGE]

   (B) for his coach

   (C) for he and his coach

   (D) though he and his coach

7. You may know this simple device only as a "crowbar"; <u>furthermore,</u> in previous ages it was known as a "handspike."

(A) [NO CHANGE]

(B) indeed,

(C) however,

(D) in rebuttal,

8. Because mountain-climbing is an arduous and exhausting activity with serious risk of <u>injury, since</u> many mild-mannered people are unwilling to even attempt it.

(A) [NO CHANGE]

(B) injury,

(C) injury, so

(D) injury, and

9. Some motorcycles can appear to be quite intricate in their design, <u>but they all share</u> the same basic concept of unification between frame, wheels, and engine.

(A) [NO CHANGE]

(B) but it all shares

(C) and they all share

(D) furthermore, they all share

10. Charlie Daniels will be remembered as the songwriter of "Devil Went Down to Georgia," <u>therefore, although he wrote</u> many other tunes, none of them have remained popular.

(A) [NO CHANGE]

(B) therefore, writing

(C) but, although he wrote

(D) and since he wrote

11. <u>Although</u> these people run the risk of landing in unexpected places, aerial thrill-seekers, such as skydivers and hang-glider pilots, should carry a GPS locator and two-way radio.

(A) [NO CHANGE]

(B) Since

(C) Despite the fact that

(D) Indeed,

12. Charlie often enjoyed conversing with Veruca, whose controversial opinions always fascinated <u>him; however,</u> he was sometimes offended when she vehemently disagreed with his own views.

(A) [NO CHANGE]

(B) him; moreover,

(C) him, and

(D) him, being that

13. Songbirds often have to defend their nests from intruders that might prey on their <u>eggs, so sometimes</u> the birds will share nesting grounds with other woodland creatures such as squirrels or opossums.

(A) [NO CHANGE]

(B) eggs; in addition,

(C) eggs, while sometimes

(D) eggs; nevertheless, sometimes

Conjunctions and Transitions Answers

1. B
2. C
3. C
4. D
5. D
6. A
7. C
8. B
9. A
10. C
11. B
12. A
13. D

Conjunctions and Transitions Explanations

1. B – The original Diverging conjunction, "but," is a poor choice: these students are able to relax among the lakes and fields *because of* the pleasant surroundings, not *despite* them. We want a Connecting conjunction - and in this question, our only Connecting option is "so." Choice D doesn't have any conjunction, which makes it a comma splice error (two Independent Clauses connected without a conjunction) - see **Sentence Structure**, Lesson 9.

2. C – The first idea and second idea need a Connector, not a Diverger. It seems logical that the stars of a popular movie series would become millionaires. Choice C, "in fact," is our only Connecting conjunction, and it does a good job of further emphasizing the popularity of Dangerous Dan.

3. C – We need a Diverging conjunction: the landowner earned a great profit, but the working peasants received little compensation. That eliminates the Connectors in Choices A and B. We can't use the word "nor" for this transition - usually we use that word as part of a comparison or a "neither-nor" word pair. Choice C, "but," is a simple and effective Diverging conjunction that logically transitions from the first idea to the second idea.

4. D – For this sentence, we'll want a Connector: the first half (protection of the economy) matches nicely with the second half (ending unfair monopolies). However, we don't want such a strong cause-and-effect Connector as "because." Look closely and you'll see that the commission was established "years ago," which would be *before* it ended any monopolies. "And" is a better choice of word, indicating a connection without implying a direct cause-and-effect.

Did you notice how Choice C is almost right, but makes a **Pronoun-Antecedent Agreement** error (Lesson 5) by using the plural pronoun "they" to refer back to a singular noun, "commission?"

5. D – We can logically assume that deafness would not help a composer become the greatest in history, so a Diverger like "but" would be a better conjunction than connectors like "and" or "so." Beethoven became a great composer *despite* his deafness, not *in addition* to it.

6. A - NO CHANGE. Notice how the first and second parts of this sentence are diverging from each other? If the athlete's knee was recently injured, we wouldn't expect him to win the gold medal. That's why a diverging conjunction like "although" will nicely represent the idea that this wrestler won *despite* his injuries.

Choice D contains a singular-plural **Subject-Verb Agreement** error (Lesson 1) because "he and his coach" is a compound (plural) subject and cannot be paired with the singular verb form "was concerned."

7. C – This sentence contains a divergence between its first and second halves: the first half mentions something you might *already* know, but the second half provides some *new* information that you probably did not know. Also, the first half implies that a crowbar has only one name, while the second half informs us that in fact there is at least one *other* name for the same device.

On that basis, we can get rid of the Continuing conjunction "furthermore," a word which implies the continuation of a similar set of ideas. "Indeed" has a similar problem – it agrees with and continues any ideas that came before. "In rebuttal" indicates conflict, so it might seem right, but a "rebuttal" is an attempt to completely discredit or prove wrong what came before. It's *too* strong of a contradicting word for this context.

We're left with the Diverging conjunction "however," which fits into the sentence by gently informing us that there might be unexpected or new information that we are about to learn.

8. B - It's inappropriate to use a second conjunction here, since we already have the conjunction "because" at the beginning of the sentence.Only one conjunction allowed to connect between any two ideas!

9. A – NO CHANGE. The main point of the sentence is that even though some motorcycles look quite complicated, they are actually very simple in their basic idea. That means we want a Diverging conjunction like "but." Notice that Choice B includes a singular-plural **Pronoun-Antecedent Agreement** error (Lesson 5) with "motorcycles... *it* shares"

10. C – The main idea behind this sentence is that Daniels wrote one great song, but none of his other work has stayed popular. We need some sort of Diverging word like "but" instead of a Continuing word like "therefore."

11. B – Ask yourself "do the two halves of this sentence *agree* or *disagree*?" They agree, because if you might land in an "unexpected location," it would be logical to carry some sort of emergency gear.

The diverging conjunction "although" would indicate a disagreement between the two halves of the sentence. Fix it by using a conjunction that indicates agreement between cause and effect, like "because" or "since."

12. A – NO CHANGE. The two halves of this sentence feature a contradiction or divergence: Charlie likes to talk with Veruca most of the time, *but* sometimes she offends him when she goes too far.

We can't change to a continuing conjunction like "and" or "moreover" (which essentially means "in addition"); these conjunctions would be properly used when continuing logically with new ideas that are *similar* to ones that were previously expressed.

13. D – This sentence is a bit subtle in its meaning, but the main idea is that songbirds are at risk of having their eggs stolen by other animals. The more animals nearby, the more risk to the birds, so it's *surprising* (notice a divergence!) to learn in the second half of the sentence that the birds will still live among squirrels and other critters.

The word "so" indicates a strong cause/effect connection, but what we really need is some sort of *diverging* conjunction like "but" - or even better, "*nevertheless*," which means "despite what you might have expected."

LESSON 8
Punctuation Marks

There are 7 punctuation marks tested on the SAT & ACT tests:

Periods .

Commas ,

Semicolons ;

Colons :

Parentheses ()

Dash Marks -

Apostrophes '

You should not expect to see any questions on the SAT or ACT about question marks (?), exclamation points (!), or quotation marks (" ").

The majority of the tested punctuation marks - six out of seven of them - are used in connection with clauses and **Sentence Structure** (the topic of the next lesson). The *apostrophe* is the only punctuation mark tested on the SAT or ACT that does *not* relate to Sentence Structure.

Let's go over the basics of each of these seven punctuation marks.

The Period

The period is our most familiar punctuation mark. Periods are used to end complete sentences.

Period Usage:
My dog is barking. My cat is watching birds.

That's it - pretty simple. Also see the next lesson on **Sentence Structure** for more information about Independent Clauses.

The Comma

The comma is the hardest punctuation mark for most students to master. Commas are not for *pauses* or *breaths* as many students erroneously believe. Actually, Commas are used to separate *clauses* (again, see the next chapter on **Sentence Structure** for related information). Commas are also used to separate *lists* of three or more items.

> **Comma Usages:**
> My dog is barking, and my cat is watching him.
> My dog, who is still a puppy, is barking.
> My dog is barking, jumping, and running.

The Semicolon

Semicolons are very easy punctuation marks to master. The semicolon is used to separate two complete sentences. On the SAT & ACT, semicolons work exactly like periods do. Don't worry right now about advanced nuances you may have heard before, such as "semicolons connect two similar ideas." Instead, just act like semicolons are periods, and you will always understand their usage on the SAT and ACT.

> **Semicolon Usage:**
> My dog is barking; my cat is watching birds.

The Colon

Using colons is easy, but almost everyone misunderstands them. The most common misunderstanding is the idea that "colons are for lists." If this is what you think, you need to change your definition - NOW.

Here's how colons actually work. There are exactly two criteria.

The first criteria is crucial, but also easy and quick to identify, so check it first:

> **Colon Criteria #1:** A colon *must* be preceded by a complete sentence.

The second criteria is what colons actually *do*:

> **Colon Criteria #2:** "Colons introduce one or more examples, or a definition."

Never, ever worry about the second colon criteria until after you've checked the first one. Colons must *always* be preceded by a complete sentence. Knowing this one rule makes colon usage 100x easier.

> **Colon Usages:**
>
> My house is filled with a variety of animals: dogs, cats, and birds.
>
> I have a favorite animal: hedgehogs.
>
> The musician played the lute: a classic instrument similar to an ancient guitar.

Parentheses

Parentheses are used to show optional, extra, or nonessential information that adds extra detail to a sentence. You must be able to read the sentence *without* the parenthetical info and still have the sentence work without it. Parentheses always come in pairs: an open parentheses and a close parentheses.

> **Parentheses Usages:**
>
> My dog (a puppy) is barking.
>
> I have two animals (a cat and a dog) who live at my house.

Notice that these examples can be read without the parenthetical info and still stand on their own as complete sentences.

Dash Marks

Dash Marks can imitate either of two other punctuation marks: Parentheses *or* Colons. This is determined by context.

When used as colons, dash marks follow exactly the same rules as colons. Easy!

However, dash marks are more often used like parentheses, with a few special notes:

First of all, when in the middle of a sentence, dash marks tend to come in pairs, just like parentheses do. However, when used to add extra information at the *beginning* or *end* of a sentence, a single dash mark is allowed to exist by itself. This would never allowed with parentheses, which always have to be in an open-close pair.

Also, a bit of bonus info - though not essential for SAT/ACT testing - is that parentheses contain extra information that is *less* important than the main sentence, while dash marks are meant to contain info that is *extra*-important. Dashes call *extra* attention, while parentheses *decrease* the amount of attention.

> **Dash Mark Usages:**
>
> My dog - still a puppy - is barking.
>
> I have two animals - a cat and a dog - who live at my house.
>
> I have a favorite animal - hedgehogs.

Apostrophes

These punctuation marks are a special case - apostrophes are the only marks on this list that do *not* have anything to do with **Sentence Structure** (see the next lesson for more info).

Apostrophes mainly serve two purposes: to show *possessive case* for nouns and pronouns (for example, *Tim's jacket* or *the birds' cages*), and to form *contractions* (shortened versions of a pair of words).

Some students get mixed up when using the "plural possessive" form of a noun, which typically places an apostrophe *after* the plural "s" at the end of a noun. For example, we might have four birds in our house, living in four separate cages. In that case, to show that the birds "owned" their cages, we'd put the apostrophe *after* the "s", like so: "the birds' four cages."

> **Apostrophe Usages:**
>
> That is Tim's jacket.
>
> There are piles of seeds in the birds' cages.
>
> I can't come to the door right now.
>
> It's time for dinner.

Note a special word in the last example above: its / it's / its. One of these words doesn't actually exist!

> **Rules of its / it's / its':**
>
> it's = Contraction of "it is"
>
> Ex: It's hot outside today.
>
> its = Singular pronoun, possessive case
>
> Ex: The cat was licking its tail.
>
> its' = *This word does not exist in English!*

Now let's try a simple practice question from the Pretest.

> There are several activities that I like to practice <u>every day; motorcycling,</u>
> <u>running, and songwriting.</u>
>
> (A) [NO CHANGE]
> (B) every day: motorcycling,
> (C) every day, motorcycling,
> (D) every day. Motorcycling,

Since we are given a set of choices including semicolons, colons, and a periods, the first question to ask is "can the first part of the sentence stand on its own?" (See Lesson 9 on **Sentence Structure** for more on this topic.)

The answer is "yes" - the first half is a complete Independent Clause with its own subject and verb. It could easily stand alone as its own sentence: "There are several activities that I try to practice every day."

The next question is, "What about the second half of the sentence? Can it stand on its own as a complete, independent clause?"

The answer is *no* - the second half is *not* a complete sentence: "motorcycling, running, and songwriting."

We can now eliminate Choice D, which uses a period - that would require two complete sentences, one on either side of the period. For the same reason, we can also eliminate Choice A, "No Change," because it uses a semicolon. Semicolons act exactly like periods and require a complete sentence on both sides.

Can we use a comma? Unfortunately not, because there is no conjunction or connecting word linking the first and second halves of the sentence. That means Choice C is eliminated.

Does a colon work? It might. We have a complete sentence *before* the colon (criteria #1). And, the colon is followed by one or more examples (criteria #2). Perfect! This is the right moment to use a colon, so **Choice B is the correct answer.**

Punctuation Marks Quick Reference

- There are seven punctuation marks to master for the SAT & ACT: periods, commas, semicolons, colons, parentheses, dash marks, and apostrophes.

- Periods and semicolons come in between two complete sentences (also called "Independent Clauses").

- Colons have two criteria: a complete sentence *before* the colon, and one or more examples or a definition *after* the colon.

- Dash marks can act like parentheses *or* colons, depending on context.

- Commas are challenging and require a mastery of clauses and **Sentence Structure** (see the next lesson for more information).

- Apostrophes are different than the other punctuation marks, because they don't usually affect Sentence Structure. Instead, they are used for *possessive case* and *contractions*.

- Be well aware of the formal and technical differences between its / it's / its'.

Let's try another practice question.

> There are many kinds of dogs, but mine - a golden <u>retriever, is my favorite,</u>
> <u>he</u> is very loyal and friendly.
>
> (A) [NO CHANGE]
> (B) retriever - is my favorite; he
> (C) retriever - is my favorite, he
> (D) retriever) is my favorite; he

One of the best ways to get this Punctuation question started is to look for complete sentences (or "Independent Clauses" - see the next chapter on **Sentence Structure** for more information).

We find an Independent Clause at the end of the sentence: "He is very loyal and friendly." This suggests that a period or semicolon must come just before this portion of the sentence, since those are the two types of punctuation marks that can separate Independent Clauses.

We don't have any answer choices with periods, but we do have Choices B and D, which both use semicolons appropriately. So, let's eliminate Choices A and C, which improperly use commas to separate two Independent Clauses.

Now we can analyze the difference between Choices B and D. Choice D uses a close parentheses ")" where Choice B uses a dash mark "-". We can eliminate Choice D, because there is no open parentheses in the sentence to pair with the close parentheses.

That leaves us with the correct answer, Choice B, which uses a pair of dash marks to isolate a Parenthetical Clause ("a golden retriever") and also uses a semicolon to separate two Independent Clauses from each other.

We'll continue to learn more about the challenges of commas and other punctuation marks in the next chapter, because punctuation is closely tied with the upcoming lesson on clauses and **Sentence Structure**.

Punctuation Marks
Practice Questions

1. David was surprised to learn that frogs were primarily <u>carnivorous, he had assumed</u> that they mostly ate plants and vegetables.

   (A) [NO CHANGE]
   (B) carnivorous, he had assumed,
   (C) carnivorous (he had assumed
   (D) carnivorous; he had assumed

2. A synthesizer - an entirely electronic musical <u>instrument: can</u> usually be categorized into either an "East Coast" or a "West Coast" design philosophy.

   (A) [NO CHANGE]
   (B) instrument, can
   (C) instrument - can
   (D) instrument; can

3. There are a wide variety of modern dance forms and styles to <u>enjoy. That's</u> one reason my hometown has many different dance studios.

   (A) [NO CHANGE]
   (B) enjoy that's
   (C) enjoy, that's
   (D) enjoy (that's

4. A professional long-distance <u>runners</u> life revolves around his or her workout schedule, sleep routine, and dietary needs.

   (A) [NO CHANGE]
   (B) runner
   (C) runner's
   (D) runners'

5. Though the words "vintage" and "classic" are often applied interchangeably, there is a subtle <u>difference: "vintage"</u> has a primary reference to age, while "classic" can add an additional connotation of elegance.

   (A) [NO CHANGE]
   (B) difference, "vintage"
   (C) difference ("vintage"
   (D) difference, so "vintage"

6. Musicians should carefully craft a strategy for their online <u>streaming - the ability</u> for their music to be heard instantly via the internet through a computer or mobile device) to achieve maximum popularity.

   (A) [NO CHANGE]
   (B) streaming (the ability
   (C) streaming. The ability
   (D) streaming; the ability

7. Alvin is struggling in math class <u>this year; and there are</u> many topics in Precalculus that he finds both challenging and frustrating.

   (A) [NO CHANGE]

   (B) this year (there are

   (C) this year, there are

   (D) this year; there are

8. Surfing (riding the waves on a wooden or plastic board) gained <u>much of its' popularity</u> in the 1950s and 60s in Hawaii, California, and Australia.

   (A) [NO CHANGE]

   (B) much of its popularity

   (C) much of it's popularity

   (D) much of their popularity

9. The art exhibit's brochure read like a "who's who" of famous Italian <u>artists; Michelangelo,</u> Raphael, Leonardo da Vinci...

   (A) [NO CHANGE]

   (B) artists, Michelangelo

   (C) artists: Michelangelo

   (D) artists (Michelangelo

10. Anyone who has had <u>siblings - younger</u> or older, brother or sister) will know that they are, at various times, a source of both great joy and great frustration.

   (A) [NO CHANGE]

   (B) a sibling. Younger

   (C) a sibling, younger

   (D) a sibling (younger

11. When working at the kennel, Samantha was often astonished at the sheer variety of <u>the dogs' collars</u>, including spiked ones, simple ones, and colorful ones.

   (A) [NO CHANGE]

   (B) the dogs' collar

   (C) the dog's collars

   (D) the dogs collars

12. Brian Eno is the foremost composer of <u>ambient music (a genre</u> based in slow, evolving soundscapes that can be either ignored in the background or attended to carefully, as the listener may determine for himself or herself.

   (A) [NO CHANGE]

   (B) ambient music; a genre

   (C) ambient music - a genre

   (D) ambient music. A genre

Punctuation Marks Answers

1. D
2. C
3. A
4. C
5. A
6. B
7. D
8. B
9. C
10. D
11. A
12. C

Punctuation Marks Explanations

1. D - Choice C is no good, because it uses an open parentheses with no close parentheses. Choices A and B won't work, because this sentence is made of two Independent Clauses (see next chapter on **Sentence Structure**), and we can only use a comma to connect two Independent Clauses if we also add an appropriate conjunction or subordinating word (see Lesson 7, **Conjunctions & Transitions**). That leaves us with Choice D, which is perfect: a semicolon acts just like a period, and is effective for dividing two "complete sentences" or Independent Clauses, as we have in this situation.

2. C - This is the perfect time to use a dash mark in the same way we use parentheses. The dash mark in Choice C will partner with the first dash mark in the sentence to create a "Parenthetical Clause" (see next chapter on **Sentence Structure**). This separates the sentence into two main chunks: the Independent Clause ("A synthesizer… can usually be categorized…") and a Parenthetical Clause in the middle ("an entirely electronic musical instrument") that is opened and closed by a pair of dash marks.

3. A - NO CHANGE. This practice question is best left as a pair of complete, independent sentences, given our options. We can't use Choice D, because it uses an open parentheses with no close parentheses. Choice C is out, because you can't connect two Independent Clauses with only a comma (see also next chapter on **Sentence Structure**). Choice B uses no punctuation mark at all, creating a Run-On Sentence.

4. C - This question tests our understanding of apostrophes, possessives, and singular-plural. We can tell we have a singular "runner" because of the clues "a… runner" and "his or her," which both are singular. That eliminates Choices A and D, which are plural. Choice A also doesn't included a possessive form, and neither does Choice B. That leaves only Choice C, which is perfect, because it is both singular and possessive: this sentence describes a single runner's life. In other words, the apostrophe helps show that our singular runner "possesses" his or her own life.

5. A - NO CHANGE. Elimination helps here. Choice C uses an open parentheses without a close parentheses. Choice B improperly uses a comma to connect two Independent Clauses without a conjunction or subordinating word. Choice D uses a "double conjunction" ("Though... so...") which is not allowed (review Lesson 7, **Conjunctions & Transitions**). That leaves us with Choice A, which uses a colon. Evaluate according to the two colon criteria: Is it preceded by a complete sentence? (Yes). Does it introduce one or more examples or a definition? (Yes!)

6. B - This question is easy. Notice the close parentheses already given in the sentence after "mobile device." That close parentheses doesn't currently have a matching open parentheses to pair with, so it's our job to provide one by selecting Choice B.

7. D - Choice B is out instantly: it uses an open parentheses with no close parentheses. Choice A won't work because you can only use a semicolon between two complete sentences, but the second half begins with "and" - a subordinating conjunction that prevents the second half from standing on its own (see next chapter on **Sentence Structure**). Choice C is out because you can't use a comma to connect two Independent Clauses without a conjunction. Choice D is perfect because it uses a semicolon to separate two complete Independent Clauses.

8. B - This question tests usage of the word "its" combined with apostrophes. Remember that *its'* is not a real word, so we can eliminate Choice A immediately. Choice D is wrong because it commits a **Pronoun-Antecedent Agreement** mistake (Lesson 5) by using the plural pronoun "their" to refer to the singular antecedent "surfing." Choice C incorrectly uses the contraction *it's*, meaning "it is," when a possessive singular pronoun is what we actually need. That leaves us with only Choice B, *its*, which is the correct singular possessive pronoun form.

9. C - This sentence is a textbook example of the ideal time for colon usage. Check the two colon criteria. First, there is a complete sentence before the colon. Second, the colon introduces one or more examples or a definition. Choice D uses an open parentheses without a close parentheses, and Choice A uses a semicolon, but the second half of the sentence is not an Independent Clause (see Lesson 9 on **Sentence Structure**).

10. D - This question is easy, if we just notice the lonely close parentheses after "sister." That requires us to supply an open parentheses in our answer - only Choice D will work.

11. A - NO CHANGE.This question tests the use of apostrophes to show singular and plural possessive nouns. We are talking about multiple *dogs* with multiple *collars*, so we definitely want to stick with our plural options. That eliminates Choice C, which is a singular "dog." Also, Choice B refers to only a singular "collar," so that's out as well. Choice D lacks any possessive apostrophe. Only Choice A correctly uses both plural form and applies the possessive apostrophe to the end (*dogs'*).

12. C - This question makes use of a dash mark acting like a colon. Let's narrow things down first with some elimination. Choice B uses a semicolon, but lacks an Independent Clause in the second half of the sentence (see next chapter on **Sentence Structure**). Choice D is wrong for a similar reason - after the period is an incomplete sentence, and we also know that semicolons and periods follow the same rules as each other. Choice A uses an open parentheses without a close parentheses, which isn't allowed. That leaves Choice C. Imagine that the dash mark is a colon and evaluate according to the two colon criteria - you will see that the rules apply perfectly.

LESSON 9
Sentence Structure

Sentence Structure is a grammar topic that is intimately tied with **Punctuation Marks** (Lesson 8), because one of the main uses of punctuation marks is to support the "structure" of a sentence (and you'll learn more about what *exactly* this means in just a moment).

I have often noticed that high school students struggle to master Sentence Structure, but it's worth a lot of points on the SAT & ACT, so we should strive to understand the rules of good Sentence Structure.

What is Sentence Structure?

What do I mean by "Sentence Structure"? Specifically, I refer to the way a sentence is built out of smaller phrases or "clauses" and how those clauses fit together to form a grammatically-acceptable sentence.

So, before we master Sentence Structure we will need to go over the *three types of clauses*. I will make it as painless and quick as possible!

A "clause" is defined as "a unit of grammatical organization just below the sentence in rank." That basically means any group of words working together in a single "phrase." There are three types of clauses:

1. **Independent Clause:** A complete idea that can stand on its own. It contains a Subject and a Main Verb, but *not* a subordinating word or conjunction (words like *and, because, so, or, but*, etc.)

2. **Dependent Clause:** A "Dependent Clause" is essentially an "Independent Clause" *with* a subordinating word (e.g. *and, because, so, or*, etc.) attached to it. This creates an idea that cannot stand on its own, and must be attached to an Independent Clause to survive.

3. **Parenthetical Clause:** A "Parenthetical Clause" does not need its own Subject-Verb pair (a topic explored in Lesson 1). Instead, it contains *supporting details* - the kind we could enclose in parentheses (thus the name "Parenthetical" clauses). Parenthetical Clauses can always be completely removed from sentences without harming the underlying basic meaning or structure.

Examples of the Three Types of Clauses

Here is a set of examples showing all three types of clauses:

> 1. The dog barked.

Above is an Independent Clause with "dog" as the subject and "barked" as the main verb.

> 2. The dog, *a golden retriever*, barked.

We've added a *Parenthetical Clause* inside of the Independent Clause, marking the separation with commas.

> 3. The dog barked, *but his owner did nothing*.

We've taken the Parenthetical Clause back out and instead linked a *Dependent Clause* to the Independent Clause.

> 4. The dog barked, but his owner, *my neighbor*, did nothing.

We've added a *Parenthetical Clause* inside of the Dependent Clause.

> 5. The dog, *a golden retriever*, barked, but his owner, *my neighbor*, did nothing.

All together now: the first half of the above sentence is an Independent Clause ("The dog barked") with a *Parenthetical Clause* inside it; the second half of the sentence is a Dependent Clause ("but his owner did nothing") with its own *Parenthetical Clause* inside it, too.

Next up, some more details and finer points about the three types of clauses...

Independent Clauses

Every Independent Clause has a *subject*. The subject will always be a Noun, Pronoun, or Gerund (a verb that's been made into a noun, like *running* in the sentence "*Running* is fun.") Since verbs are "doing" or "being" words, the subject is the primary "*do*-er" of action or the "*be*-er" that is being described.

Every Independent Clause also has a *main verb*, the action that the subject is doing ("The dog *runs*," "The boys *go* to school"), or a "being" verb (as in "The cat *is* happy," "Our old house *was* painted red," or "The children *are* playing").

Finally, every Independent Clause expresses a complete idea that can stand on its own. "The cat is happy" can stand on its own. (On the other hand, the clause *"because* the cat is happy" *cannot* stand alone - the subordinating word *"because"* makes it a Dependent Clause.)

That's it! All you need for a complete Independent Clause is a subject and a main verb that add up to one complete idea.

Dependent Clauses

Independent Clauses may provide the most essential structure to our sentences, but *Dependent* Clauses are also useful. These clauses usually have a subject and verb pair, but can't quite stand on their own because they also contain a *subordinating word*.

Subordinating words include many conjunctions (such as *and, but, because, or,* and *not*). Some of these conjunctions are part of the "FANBOYS" family (for, and, nor, but, or, yet, so). These are sometimes called "coordinating conjunctions."

An example of a Dependent Clause that cannot stand on its own is *"because* I am happy." Notice the subordinating word *"because."*

Without an Independent Clause to attach to (such as "I am smiling"), this Dependent Clause CANNOT stand alone!

We could create a combined sentence with an Independent and Dependent Clause such as "I am smiling, *because* I am happy."

Parenthetical Clauses

Parenthetical Clauses are frequently used to add additional details or explanation. They're definitely important - they're just not as important as Independent or Dependent Clauses.

For example, we've already seen the Parenthetical Clause "a golden retriever" used to modify a "dog," as in the example "The dog, *a golden retriever*, barked." You can see how the Parenthetical Clause is adding interesting, but non-essential detail, to the Independent Clause. You might also observe that you could us parentheses - (a golden retriever) - instead of commas.

Parenthetical Clauses are frequently introduced by an "-ing" word, as in "The dog, *barking* loudly, jumped at the fence." Other common introductions to a Parenthetical Clause are certain subordinating words like *who, where,* or *which* - these are called "Relative Pronouns" - as in "The dog, *who* barked loudly, jumped at the fence."

Parenthetical Clauses can be completely removed from a sentence without affecting the essential meaning or structure of the sentence.

Identifying Different Types of Clauses

Part of your job is to get good at telling which types of the three clauses you're dealing with. One way to make that easier is to use **Eliminating Details** (Prelesson B) to trim down the extra details in the sentence.

Example 1:

Let's try analyzing the following sentence:

"The brown bear jumped from tree to tree."

What are the subject and main verb?

Subject: The bear (If you said "brown" bear, notice that "brown" is just an adjective that gives more details and is not as crucial as the subject noun, "bear.")

Main Verb: Jumped (the action word that the subject is *doing*)

We can ignore the prepositional phrase "from tree to tree," which simply adds detail about the location of the bear. Prepositional phrases can always be ignored when analyzing clauses (you can review Prelesson A on **Parts of Speech** for more info about prepositions.)

Can this idea ("The bear jumped") stand on its own? Sure, it's a complete thought. This is an Independent Clause and it stands on its own just fine.

Example 2:

What about this example?

"But the roller coaster is fun."

What are the subject and main verb?

Subject: The roller coaster

Main Verb: Is

Can this idea stand on its own? No! This clause says "*but* the roller coaster is fun."

"But" what, exactly?

This thought seems to be contradicting some other idea, but it can't stand alone. This clause needs to connect to something to be complete! The word *but* is an example of a subordinating word (it's a FANBOYS coordinating conjunction), which turns this phrase into a Dependent Clause.

We could fix it by connecting it to a complete idea:

> "The merry-go-round is boring, *but the roller coaster is fun.*"

OK, so that example was a little simplistic. The way the SAT & ACT make clause analysis more difficult is by adding a heap of extra unessential details into the sentence in the form of adjectives, adverbs, prepositional phrases, and Parenthetical Clauses.

These unessential details often arrive with a bunch of commas surrounding them, and act like camouflage for grammatical problems hidden below the surface. For example, once you remove the details, you may find only a collection of Dependent Clauses with no strong, heroic Independent Clause to support them all. You may even find a "Sentence Fragment," or incomplete Independent Clause.

In other words, eliminating extra details is a trick you will use throughout the SAT & ACT Grammar sections on nearly every single question. If you're not already a pro at eliminating details, re-read Prelesson B on **Eliminating Details**!

Example 3:

Let's take a look at another example and analyze the clauses:

> "The duck, who is eating pancakes, likes breakfast, and he also enjoys pickles."

First we should look for an Independent Clause. Where is the subject noun of this sentence? (If you said "duck," you are correct.)

Now let's find the main verb. It's a little tricky - the main verb is *likes*, not "eating." The complete Independent Clause is "The duck likes breakfast."

This Independent Clause is interrupted by a Parenthetical Clause: "who is eating pancakes." Notice that this Parenthetical Clause is introduced by the relative pronoun *who*.

There is also a Dependent Clause at the end of the sentence: "and he also enjoys pickles." Observe that this Dependent Clause is essentially an Independent Clause (including the subject "he" and main verb "enjoys") paired with the subordinating FANBOYS conjunction "*and*".

Example 4:

Here's an example where you should **Eliminate Details** to make the main clauses more obvious:

"The brown bear, which is known for eating various foods left behind by picnickers, who visit national parks on the weekends."

What are the unessential descriptive details in this sentence? Remove them first:

1) "which is known for eating various foods" is a big Parenthetical Clause that just describes the bear. (Note that this clause is introduced by the Relative Pronoun "which.")

2) "left behind by picnickers" is a prepositional phrase that simply describes the location of the foods.

3) "who visit national parks on the weekends" is a Parenthetical Clause that describes the picnickers (notice that the clause is introduced by the Relative Pronoun "who.")

Take descriptive phrases 1, 2, and 3 out, and suddenly the camouflage of the sentence is gone: we're left holding a sentence with nothing left in it besides "The brown bear."

Where's the main verb? What *"is"* the bear, or what does it *do*? Absolutely NOTHING! The main verb is missing in action; we're left holding only a subject with no main verb. This is called a "Sentence Fragment," and this incomplete sentence is a huge Sentence Structure no-no.

Using Punctuation Marks for Better Sentence Structure

It's important to understand that **Punctuation Marks** (see the previous lesson) and **Sentence Structure** work hand-in-hand to produce good grammatical results.

Remember and apply the following rules:

1. *Periods* end complete sentences.

2. *Semicolons* are very similar to periods and go between two Independent Clauses.

3. *Colons* must be preceded by an Independent Clause and followed by one or more examples or a definition.

4. *Commas* are used to separate clauses. For example, a comma could separate an Independent Clause from a Dependent Clause, or separate a Parenthetical Clause from an Independent or Dependent Clause. There is one important exception: commas cannot be used between two Independent Clauses, or you will have a "Comma Splice" error (see below).

Comma Splices

A "Comma Splice" error will occur if you try to connect two Independent Clauses with only a comma. For example:

> "James threw his fork, he was not happy with his meal."

This sentence contains two Independent Clauses (the first half and the second half). But, we cannot simply use a comma to connect these two Independent Clauses, because that creates a Comma Splice error.

The three main options for fixing this mistake include:

1) Use a period between the two Independent Clauses:

> "James threw his fork. He was not happy with his meal."

2) Use a semicolon between two Independent Clauses:

> "James threw his fork; he was not happy with his meal."

3) Use a comma + subordinating conjunction to change one of the Independent Clauses into a Dependent Clause:

> "James threw his fork, *because* he was not happy with his meal."

Sentence Structure Quick Reference

- Every sentence needs at least one Independent Clause. Without an Independent Clause, we have a Sentence Fragment error.

- An Independent Clause requires two things: a subject and a main verb. It should also express a complete idea that can stand alone.

- Independent Clauses can end with a period, a semicolon, a comma + Dependent Clause, or a colon used properly according to the rules of colon usage (review the previous chapter on **Punctuation Marks**).

- Dependent Clauses have a subject and verb but *not* a complete thought; they use a *subordinating conjunction* (like *but*, *because*, or *yet*) and must attach to an Independent Clause via a comma.

- Parenthetical Clauses contain supporting details that could be enclosed in parentheses. You can always ignore these clauses without changing the sentence's essential meaning or structure. These are frequently separated from other clauses by commas, parentheses, or dash marks.

- Two Independent Clauses cannot be connected with only a comma or you will have a Comma Splice error. You could use a period or a semicolon. If you choose to use a comma, you must change one of the two Independent Clauses into a Dependent Clause by adding a subordinating conjunction like "because" or "so."

- **Eliminating Details** (Prelesson B) - especially adjectives, adverbs, prepositional phrases, and Parenthetical Clauses - is a good way to simplify a sentence and expose hidden errors in its Sentence Structure.

Let's take a look at a question from the Pretest:

The "desert rally," an endurance race by dune buggies across hostile terrain, <u>that only the fiercest competitors qualify for.</u>

   (A) [NO CHANGE]

   (B) which only the fiercest competitors can qualify for.

   (C) and only the fiercest competitors qualify for it.

   (D) is a contest that only the fiercest competitors qualify for.

Take a look at the original sentence. We're going to practice **Prelesson B: Eliminating Details**. Find and remove all the unessential details to make the underlying Sentence Structure more clear.

First, "an endurance race by dune buggies across hostile terrain" is a nonessential Parenthetical Clause adding details about the "desert rally." We can remove it without affecting the underlying sentence.

Second, "that only the fiercest competitors qualify for" is a descriptive phrase that adds additional details about the "desert rally." It also can be removed.

Take out phrases 1 and 2 and you're left with only "The desert rally," which is the subject of this clause. But where's the main verb? It's nowhere to be found, which means this is a Sentence Fragment error!

Repeat this analysis with Choices B and C and you'll notice the same problem.

Choice D adds the main verb *is*. Phew – now the desert rally "*is*" something! The new & improved sentence has a subject, a main verb, and expresses a complete thought. That's good. Now we have a complete Independent Clause, and **Choice D is the right answer.**

Let's check out another example from the Pretest:

> The intrepid explorers of the wilderness discovered a new <u>river, they also</u>
> <u>found</u> a pair of mountains they named "Dipyramid."
>
> (A) [NO CHANGE]
> (B) river, found
> (C) river; they also find
> (D) river and found

In the original version, notice the comma hanging out in the middle - *without* a subordinating word, such as a FANBOYS conjunction, to create a Dependent Clause? Uh-oh, that's often a bad sign for Sentence Structure problems.

First off, are there any Independent Clauses ? Here's where simplification can come in handy. We can use **Eliminating Details** (Prelesson B) to reduce this sentence to the following:

"The explorers discovered a river, they also found mountains."

Yes - unfortunately, we do have two complete Independent Clauses joined only by a weak comma. It's a Comma Splice error.

Choice C might seem like a logical pick, with the semicolon between two Independent Clauses, but it creates a **Verb Tense** error by changing the past-tense "found" to a present-tense "find." This creates a mismatch between the tenses of the first and second half of the sentence. If you rush through this question, it's easy to overlook this error. Don't rush!

What other option do we have, besides a semicolon? Well, the two clauses in the sentence connect logically – they both describe things that the explorers discovered. A simple, connecting FANBOYS conjunction such as *"and"* would work nicely:

"The explorers discovered a river and found mountains."

That's why **Choice D is perfect** for this situation, and the Comma Splice error is fixed. Choice B almost works (because the second half of the sentence loses its subject, "they," and so isn't an Independent Clause any longer), but it would need a coordinating conjunction after the comma.

Here's another Pretest question:

> Authors selected for the philosophy journal must be respected in <u>their field, and</u> should hold advanced degrees and have a great deal of practical experience.
>
> (A) [NO CHANGE]
> (B) his or her field, and
> (C) their field, they
> (D) their field, such authors

Let's **Eliminate Details** (Prelesson B) and simplify the sentence to analyze the clauses more easily:

> "Authors must be respected, and should hold degrees."

Right now we have an Independent Clause and a Dependent Clause connected by a comma and conjunction ("and'), a textbook example of good Sentence Structure. Let's look at our other choices, just to be sure.

Choice B maintains good Sentence Structure, but unfortunately adds a **Pronoun-Antecedent Agreement** (Lesson 5) error: the singular pronoun "his or her" doesn't match with the plural antecedent "authors."

Choices D creates a Comma Splice error: there is an independent Subject-Verb pair on *both* sides of the comma ("Authors must" and "authors should hold"). This creates two Independent Clauses connected by only a comma with no conjunction - exactly the type of error we must avoid.

Choice C has the same problem, because it simply replaces the noun "such authors" with the pronoun "they," which doesn't fix the underlying problem of a Comma Splice created by an improperly-punctuated pair of Independent Clauses.

Only **Choice A** prevents a Comma Splice by using a comma paired with the subordinating FANBOYS conjunction *"and."*

Let's do one more example from the Pretest:

> The pine tree, known for its majestic appearance and sweet scent, and its needles can be used to brew tea.
>
> (A) [NO CHANGE]
>
> (B) The pine tree, known for its majestic appearance and sweet scent, has needles that can be used to brew tea.
>
> (C) Known for its majestic appearance and sweet scent, the pine tree's needles can be used to brew tea.
>
> (D) The pine tree, its needles can be used to brew tea, is known for its majestic appearance and sweet scent.

Let's analyze for clauses and Sentence Structure. Starting with the original sentence, eliminate any camouflaging unessential details. First, the Parenthetical Clause "known for its majestic appearance and sweet scent" can be removed without affecting the underlying sentence.

Now the sentence is just "The pine tree and its needles can be used to brew tea."

This sentence contains a logical error that's camouflaged by its structure: you would not use a *pine tree* and its needles to brew tea - you would only use the *needles*. Can you imagine the ridiculousness of trying to brew tea with an entire *tree*? This is an example of how Sentence Structure can be used to hide critical underlying mistakes in the meaning of the sentence.

Choice C is wrong not because of Sentence Structure, but because of a combined **Pronoun-Antecedent Agreement** (Lesson 5) and **Misplaced Modifier** error (Lesson 11) that incorrectly uses the singular pronoun "its" to refer to the plural antecedent "needles" and also makes it seem like the *needles* are "known for their majestic appearance," when really the *tree* would be more likely be known for its majestic appearance.

Choice D is wrong because of a Comma Splice error. Break the sentence into three sections: the first ("The pine tree") provides a subject, which is paired with a main verb at the end of the sentence ("is known") - so, that's one Independent Clause already. Unfortunately, the middle section provides a second Independent Clause with the Subject-Verb pair "needles can be used." The two Independent Clauses are mashed together with only commas to connect them. No periods, no semicolons, no subordinating words... not an acceptable way to join two Independent Clauses.

Choice B is correct. Removing all details, including the central Parenthetical Clause "known for its majestic appearance and sweet scent" as well as the descriptive phrase "that can be used to brew tea," leaves behind a single Independent Clause: "The pine tree has needles." Our meaning is also clear and accurate. Finally, we've achieved good Sentence Structure!

Sentence Structure Practice Questions

1. Coffee, a beverage that many entrepreneurs depend on, <u>it is not only stimulating and delicious, but also comforting.</u>

   (A) [NO CHANGE]

   (B) stimulating, delicious, and comforting.

   (C) is not only stimulating and delicious, but also comforting.

   (D) because it is not only stimulating and delicious, but also comforting.

2. The people of Qalif frequently follow their family <u>trade, they work</u> mainly in fishing, oil, and education.

   (A) [NO CHANGE]

   (B) trade;

   (C) trade working

   (D) trade, working

3. <u>A worldwide authority on horticulture, Gerald Holmes, after training at the finest academies in France.</u>

   (A) [NO CHANGE]

   (B) A worldwide authority on horticulture, Gerald Holmes trained at the finest academies in France.

   (C) A worldwide authority on horticulture; Gerald Holmes trained at the finest academies in France.

   (D) Gerald Holmes, who trained at the finest academies in France, becoming a worldwide authority on horticulture.

4. The Trenton Thunder is a Minor League <u>baseball team, it is</u> from Trenton, New Jersey.

   (A) [NO CHANGE]

   (B) baseball team, they are

   (C) baseball team

   (D) baseball team; they are

5. In 1686, at the age of only eight, Heinrich Gustav was appointed captain in the German <u>army, he was</u> a prince and was therefore required to serve in the armed forces.

   (A) [NO CHANGE

   (B) army;

   (C) army; he was

   (D) army, who was

6. I one met a Harvard math professor, considered preeminent in his <u>field; and</u> at the forefront of economic analysis.

(A) [NO CHANGE]

(B) field, and was

(C) field, who was

(D) field, he was

7. Carnegie-Mellon <u>University, which has one of the finest computer science programs in the nation, and</u> its students are recruited by top companies every year.

(A) [NO CHANGE]

(B) University: which has one of the finest computer science programs in the nation, and

(C) University, because it has one of the finest computer science programs in the nation,

(D) University has one of the finest computer science programs in the nation, and

8. St. Michael's Church, in Longstation, England, is an example of what is called a "redundant" <u>church, it is</u> no longer used for regular church services.

(A) [NO CHANGE]

(B) church: it is

(C) church; they are

(D) church, the church is

9. Eddie Mottau is an American <u>guitarist who has played</u> on albums written by innovators such as John Lennon and Yoko Ono.

(A) [NO CHANGE]

(B) guitarist, he played

(C) guitarist, he has played

(D) guitarist, played

10. Llyn Conwy is a picturesque lake in north Wales, <u>many tourists and families visit it</u> each year.

(A) [NO CHANGE]

(B) many tourists and families visiting it

(C) which many tourists and families visit

(D) where many tourists and families visit it

11. Departing the port of Boston in 1913, the <u>battleship cruised the U.S. coast, protected</u> merchant fleets.

(A) [NO CHANGE]

(B) battleship, cruised the U.S. coast, protected

(C) battleship cruised the U.S. coast and protecting

(D) battleship cruised the U.S. coast and protected

12. The warm summer sun that radiated onto earth, and the birds sang while dragonflies hovered all around us.

 (A) [NO CHANGE]

 (B) The warm summer sun radiated onto earth, and

 (C) The warm summer sun radiated onto earth; and

 (D) The summer sun, it radiated warmth onto the earth, and

13. The modern-day tennis player, who has access to rackets enhanced by technological innovations, and who is able to set new world records more easily than players of the past.

 (A) [NO CHANGE]

 (B) and can

 (C) is able to

 (D) they can

14. Mt. Austin, which offers a beautiful view from the summit, is in Australia, and is a popular tourist attraction.

 (A) [NO CHANGE]

 (B) Australia is

 (C) Australia, is

 (D) Australia, which is

15. CAT scans are a medical procedure used to peer inside the human brain without surgery; they are commonly used to diagnose concussions.

 (A) [NO CHANGE]

 (B) surgery; commonly

 (C) surgery, they are commonly

 (D) surgery and it is commonly

16. Amidst the majestic hills of South Dakota, where iron ore was once mined, that young sparrows once frolicked.

 (A) [NO CHANGE]

 (B) Amidst the majestic hills of South Dakota; iron ore was once mined and young sparrows once frolicked.

 (C) Where iron ore was once mined amidst the majestic hills of South Dakota: now young sparrows frolic.

 (D) Young sparrows once frolicked, and iron ore was once mined, amidst the majestic hills of South Dakota.

17. In an era of smartphones and text-messaging, one may find it difficult to find a moment of silence; at times our technology can seem like a burden.

 (A) [NO CHANGE]

 (B) silence, it

 (C) silence, our technology

 (D) silence, at times our technology

18. Though often misunderstood, SAT question-writers actually have the best of <u>intentions, want to help you clarify your written and spoken communication.</u>

(A) [NO CHANGE]

(B) intentions; wanting to help with you clarifying your written and spoken communication.

(C) intentions, they want to help you clarify your communication, both written and spoken.

(D) intentions, and want to help you clarify your communication, both written and spoken.

19. Any great opera depends upon a well-written libretto, the text that will be <u>sung, requires, in most cases, the</u> services of a second author who is not the composer of the music.

(A) [NO CHANGE]

(B) sung; requiring, in most cases, the

(C) sung, which, in most cases, requiring

(D) sung, requiring, in most cases, the

20. <u>Automated book-summary technology, programmers believe, may soon be available, so</u> some investors are buying stocks in related new companies.

(A) [NO CHANGE]

(B) Automated book-summary technology may soon be available,

(C) Programmers, believing that automated book-summary technology may soon be available, and

(D) Programmers, who believe that automated book-summary technology may soon be available, so

Sentence Structure Answers

1. C
2. D
3. B
4. C
5. C
6. C
7. D
8. B
9. A
10. C
11. D
12. B
13. C
14. A
15. A
16. D
17. A
18. D
19. D
20. A

Sentence Structure Explanations

1. C – Eliminate the Parenthetical Clause ("a beverage that many entrepreneurs depend on"). Now you're left with a dangling subject, "Coffee," at the beginning of the sentence - it doesn't have a main verb to partner with. The end of the sentence is a complete Independent Clause: "It is not only stimulating, but also comforting." So, as it stands, the sentence is a Sentence Fragment error connected to an Independent Clause - not a good thing.

Choice C is the best answer, because it removes the subject pronoun "*it*" from the Independent Clause at the end of the sentence. Now the subject "Coffee" can pair with the main verb "is" for a single Independent Clause ("Coffee... is not only stimulating, but also comforting") with a Parenthetical Clause in the middle ("a beverage that many entrepreneurs depend on").

2. D – As it stands, this sentence is a Comma Splice error, because it connects two Independent Clauses ("people follow" and "they work") with only a comma. Choice B uses a semicolon, but now the second half of the sentence is *not* an Independent Clause (review the previous lesson on **Punctuation Marks**). Choice C turns the end of the sentence into a Parenthetical Clause ("working mainly in fishing, oil, and education"), but doesn't use a comma to separate it from the Independent Clause. Choice D correctly uses a comma to separate an Independent Clause from a Parenthetical Clause.

3. B - In the original sentence, after removing the introductory Parenthetical Clause ("A worldwide authority on horticulture" and the Prepositional Phrase at the end ("after training at the finest academies in France"), we are left with only a Sentence Fragment - the dangling subject "Gerald Holmes."

Pair this subject with a main verb, like "trained," to get a complete Independent Clause - but don't pick Choice C, which incorrectly uses a semicolon without having an Independent Clause before it (review the previous lesson on **Punctuation Marks**).

4. C – The sentence begins as a Comma Splice error with two Independent Clauses connected by only a comma. Choice B has the same problem, but it's even worse because it contains a **Pronoun-Antecedent Agreement** error (Lesson 5) by trying to replace the singular noun "team" with a plural pronoun "they." Choice D contains the same pronoun mistake, although at least it does correctly use a semicolon to separate two Independent Clauses (review the previous lesson on **Punctuation Marks**).

Choice C is the correct answer, which reduces the final section of the sentence from its own Independent Clause complete with subject and verb ("It is from Trenton, New Jersey") into a simple prepositional phrase ("from Trenton, New Jersey") that can no longer stand on its own.

5. C - The sentence as written has two Independent Clauses glued together with only a comma to connect them – the classic Comma Splice error. Choice B uses a semicolon, but now the second half of the sentence has been altered to *not* be an Independent Clause (also review the previous lesson on **Punctuation Marks**). Choice C correctly uses a semicolon to separate two Independent Clauses. Choice D contains a **Misplaced Modifier** error (Lesson 11) because the Parenthetical Clause at the end ("who as a prince...") is incorrectly modifying "the German army."

6. C - The current situation is misusing a semicolon, a **Punctuation Mark** (Lesson 8) which can only be placed between two Independent Clauses. The second half of this sentence is not Independent ("*and* at the forefront of economic analysis" cannot stand on its own) Choice D *would* work, except that the semicolon has now been changed to a comma, which creates a Comma Splice error between two Independent Clauses.

Choice C is the best option, because it turns the second half of the sentence into a Parenthetical Clause ("who was at the forefront of economic analysis.") Notice the use of a Relative Pronoun ("who") to introduce this Parenthetical Clause with a useful subordinating word.

7. D - Practice **Eliminating Details** (Prelesson B) and remove the middle section of the sentence ("which has one of the finest computer science programs in the nation"). Notice that this is a Parenthetical Clause introduced by the relative pronoun "which". Also ignore the final section, which is a Dependent Clause ("and its students are recruited by top companies every year.")

Now you're left with a Sentence Fragment in the form of a dangling subject ("Carnegie-Mellon University") that doesn't have a main verb to pair with. Choice D fixes the problem by adding a main verb *has*, creating an Independent Clause: "Carnegie Mellon University *has* one of the finest computer science programs in the nation..." Notice that Choice B fails the first criterion of colon usage - it is not preceded by an Independent Clause (review Lesson 8 on **Punctuation Marks**).

8. B –The original sentence is a Comma Splice. Analyze the clauses - remove the Parenthetical Clause ("in Longstation, England") to see the first Independent Clause ("St. Michael's Church is an example…") Unfortunately, this is followed by another Independent Clause ("it is no longer used…") connected only by a comma - no subordinating word, no conjunction - which creates a Comma Splice error.

Choice D commits the same error, merely swapping the pronoun "it" for the noun "the church." Both of these nouns/pronouns can act as subjects, so nothing has been improved. Choice C commits a **Pronoun-Antecedent Agreement** error (Lesson 5) by using the plural pronoun "they" to replace the singular antecedent "church."

Choice B correctly uses a colon according to the rules of this **Punctuation Mark** (review the previous lesson). There is an Independent Clause before the colon, and it introduces a definition of a "redundant church."

9. A – NO CHANGE. As it stands, the sentence is correct. There is an Independent Clause ("Eddie Mottau is an American guitarist") followed by a description introduced by the Relative Pronoun "who" ("*who* has played on albums…"). Choices B and C create Comma Splice errors by adding a new subject, "he," which creates a second Independent Clause ("he played" or "he has played"). Choice D contains a free-floating Sentence Fragment at the end ("played on albums…") - it's neither Independent, Dependent, nor Parenthetical.

10. C – The original sentence contains a basic Comma Splice error between two Independent Clauses. Choice C correctly turns the second half of the sentence into a Parenthetical Clause by using the subordinating word "which" to introduce the clause. Now there's an Independent Clause followed by a Parenthetical Clause, separated by a comma.

Choice B has several problems: the second half of the sentence isn't an Independent Clause because it lacks a main verb ("visiting" is acting as a descriptive word, not a main verb), but it's also not Dependent, yet it's not a Parenthetical Clause either. It's sort of a **Verb Tense & Form** error (Lesson 2). Choice D would probably work if we removed the pronoun "it," but this pronoun seems to make the second half more independent than it should be, and also contains a clumsy use of the Relative Pronoun *where* ("where tourists and families visit it").

11. D – This sentence contains a list of two things the battlecruiser did: it "cruised" and "protected." When making a list of two things, we should use the conjunction "*and*" without using any commas. The proper form of a two-item list is "X *and* Y," not "X, Y." By this principle, both Choices A and B are wrong, while Choice D is correct. Choice C contains a **Parallelism** error (Lesson 10) by mingling the forms "cruis*ed*" and "protect*ing*."

12. B – The original sentence is incorrect because the first half is a Sentence Fragment ("The warm summer sun that radiated onto earth") which is missing a main verb. You can ignore the phrase "that radiated onto earth," by the way. This fragment is connected to a Dependent Clause - so there's no Independent Clause anywhere. Choice B correctly removes the subordinating word "that," allowing the subject ("sun") to connect to a main verb ("radiated").

Choice C incorrectly uses a semicolon without an Independent Clause on both sides (review the previous lesson on **Punctuation Marks**). Choice D uses commas to place an Independent Clause inside another Independent Clause, which isn't allowed.

13. C – With the details taken out (Prelesson B, **Eliminating Details**), the original Sentence Fragment is obvious. Remove the Parenthetical Clause ("who has access to rackets enhanced by technological innovations"). Then notice the end of the sentence is a Dependent Clause ("and who is able to set new world records more easily than players of the past.") Now all you're left with is the dangling subject "The modern-day tennis player," which is a Sentence Fragment.

Choice C removes the subordinating relative pronoun "who," so now the subject ("tennis player") can link directly to the main verb ("*is*"): "The modern-day tennis player *is* able..."

14. A – NO CHANGE. Best to **eliminate some details** (Prelesson B) and analyze the clauses, looking in particular for an Independent Clause. Remove the Parenthetical Clause ("which has a beautiful view from the summit" - notice that it is introduced by the Relative Pronoun "which"). Now you can see the Independent Clause: "Mt. Austin *is* in Australia." The subject is "Mt. Austin" paired with the main verb "*is*". That leaves the final Dependent Clause ("and is a popular tourist attraction") correctly introduced by a comma and subordinating FANBOYS conjunction ("and"). The sentence is correct the way it is.

For the incorrect Choice D, notice that this mischaracterizes *Australia* as "a popular tourist *attraction*," which is clearly more applicable to "Mt. Austin." A large region like Australia would be better described as a popular tourist *destination*, not an "attraction." This is a **Vocab Word Choice** error (Lesson 12).

15. A – NO CHANGE. Nothing wrong with the original, which correctly uses a semicolon between two Independent Clauses (review the previous lesson on **Punctuation Marks**). Choice C is a Comma Splice, because it has two Independent Clauses connected by only a comma. In fact, a Comma Splice will always result if you replace a correctly-used semicolon with a comma. Notice that Choice D commits a **Pronoun-Antecedent Agreement** error (Lesson 5) by using the singular pronoun "it" to replace the plural antecedent "CAT scans."

16. D - The original "sentence" is actually composed of three fragments (a prepositional phrase and two Parenthetical Clauses), none of which have the subject/main verb pair that we so desperately need for an Independent Clause. Choice D, although it may sound a little clumsy, correctly produces an Independent Clause ("Young sparrows once frolicked") with a Dependent Clause ("and iron ore was once mined") followed by a prepositional phrase ("amidst the majestic hills of South Dakota.") Choice B incorrectly uses a semicolon, and Choice C incorrectly uses a colon (review the previous lesson on **Punctuation Marks**).

17. A - NO CHANGE. This sentence breaks into three sections: A prepositional phrase ("in an era of smartphones and text messaging"), an Independent Clause ("one may find it difficult to find a moment of silence") and another Independent Clause ("at times our technology can seem like a burden.") The two Independent Clauses are correctly separated by a semicolon, so everything is fine the way it is.

All other choices, B through D, create Comma Splices errors because they replace the semicolon with a comma while maintaining the Independent Clause after the comma (review the previous lesson on **Punctuation Marks**). You may also need to review *prepositions* in Prelesson A, **Parts of Speech**, if you're unclear on the idea of a "prepositional phrase."

18. D - In the original, the final clause ("want to help you clarify your communication") is a fragment - neither Independent, Dependent, nor Parenthetical. Choice B lacks an Independent Clause to follow the semicolon. Choice C is a Comma Splice. Choice D fixes the problems by using an Independent Clause in the first half of the sentence ("SAT writers have the best of intentions"), paired with a subordinated Dependent Clause in the second half ("*and* want to help you clarify your communication).

19. D - This is a beast of Sentence Structure analysis. Let's look at the various sections. First, there's an Independent Clause with subject and verb: "Any great opera depends upon a well-written libretto." Then there's a Parenthetical Clause ("the text that will be sung") separated by commas.

The next part gets confusing. Realize that "in most cases" is a Parenthetical Clause, which we can ignore. Also ignore the descriptive phrase "who is not the composer of the music." Now you're left with the second half of the sentence - "requires the services of a second author." This isn't Independent, nor Parenthetical, but it's also not a proper Dependent, because it's not connected to the main sentence by a conjunction or subordinating word - it's just a mess!

This is why Choice D is ideal. It changes the verb "requires" to the descriptive *-ing* form "requiring" and transforms this final section into a Parenthetical Clause. Now the end of this sentence is a Parenthetical Clause with a prepositional phrase ("in most cases") inside it! Crazy!

20. A - NO CHANGE. Despite how awkward the original version may sound, it's actually correct. Remove the Parenthetical Clause ("programmers believe") and you're left with an Independent Clause ("Automated book-summary technology may soon be available") followed by a Dependent Clause ("so some investors are buying stocks in related new companies"), which is connected by a subordinating conjunction ("so").

LESSON 10
Parallelism & Comparisons

When's the last time you thought about the word "parallel" outside of math class? Maybe never, so this could be a first for you!

In math class, "parallel" lines could be described as lines *that are going exactly the same direction as one another*. They'll never bump in to each other, because they're in perfect alignment.

Believe it or not, grammar has "parallel" situations, just like math – and the concept is similar.

In math you must have *at least two lines* for them to be parallel (a single line, by itself, isn't really parallel to anything, is it?). However, you don't have to stop with two lines; you can have as many different parallel lines as you want, as long as they're all going in exactly the same direction.

The same holds true in grammar. "Parallelism" issues come up in sentences involving *lists or comparisons of two or more things*.

There are three main situations when Parallelism will happen:

1) In a simple list (like a grocery list).

2) Between two or more longer phrases.

3) Within a comparison.

Parallelism Type #1 is the simplest style, so let's look at it first...

Parallelism Type #1: "Grocery Lists"

One extremely common example of Parallelism would be a list, such as the following:

Example of a good parallel list:

"I went to the store for *eggs*, *milk*, and *cheese*."

The list doesn't have to *actually* be a grocery list, but it's one of the easiest examples to remember (a non-grocery list example could be "I like running, jumping, and swimming").

We have three items in this grocery list, all of which are *nouns* (reviewing your **Parts of Speech** from Prelesson A is very helpful when studying Parallelism). That's good; the list follows proper parallel structure because all three items in the list are the same Parts of Speech. In our math analogy, three nouns would be like three lines that all go the same direction – they are parallel and don't bump into each other, which is good.

Where we'd have a Parallelism *problem* would be if we mixed and matched nouns and some other parts of speech in our list, like so:

Parallelism Mistake Version:

> "I went to the store for eggs, milk, and *to buy cheese*."

Now one of our grocery list items has changed direction, grammatically speaking – the noun "cheese" has changed into "to *buy* cheese," a phrase which includes a verb. *This breaks the pattern and commits a Parallelism error.* **All items in a list of two or more things must be the same Parts of Speech in the same forms.**

When it comes to making a list or comparison of two or more items, nouns match only with other nouns. Verbs match only with other verbs of the same form. Words ending in "-ing" match only with other "-ing" words (running, jumping, swimming.) None of these categories can be mixed and matched within the same list or comparison, or it will cause a Parallelism error.

Here are some BAD examples of grocery lists that break parallel form:

> "I went to the store for eggs, milk, and buying cheese."
>
> "I went to the store for eggs, to buy milk, and bought cheese."
>
> "I went to the store for buying eggs, to get milk, and cheese."
>
> "I went to the store and bought eggs, was getting milk, and cheese."

Here are some GOOD examples of grocery lists that follow parallel form:

> "I went to the store for eggs, milk, and cheese." (Three nouns)
>
> "I went to the store to buy eggs, to find milk, and to sample cheese." (All three items follow the same pattern: "to [verb] [noun]"

Let's look at an example from the Pretest:

> The bass guitar differs from standard guitars in that the bass <u>has fewer strings, a longer neck, and the ability to produce lower notes.</u>
>
> (A) [NO CHANGE]
> (B) has fewer strings, a longer neck, and can produce lower notes.
> (C) having fewer strings, a longer neck, and can produce notes more low.
> (D) with lower strings, a longer neck, and lower notes.

First, take a look at Choice B and notice the Parallelism mistake: The bass has a list with three items in it: "fewer strings" (a noun), "a longer neck" (a noun), and *"can produce* lower notes" ("can produce" is a *verb*!)

We need the third item in this list to be another *noun* so that the whole list is nice and parallel.

Here's another way to look at this error - break the list in Choice B down into three traits of the bass guitar and test one at a time to expose the mistake:

1) The bass has fewer strings. (check!)
2) The bass has a longer neck. (check!)
3) The bass has *can produce* lower notes. (uh... what?!?)

Choices B and C both contain the same Parallelism mistake. Choice D fixes the Parallelism problem, but removes the main verb "has." Now the subject "the bass" no longer has a main verb attached to it, creating a Sentence Fragment (review Lesson 9 on **Sentence Structure** for more details).

Choice A is correct; compared to Choice B, it changes the third item in the list, "can produce lower notes," to "the *ability* to produce lower notes." "*Ability*" is a noun, so now the list is made up of three nouns: "strings, neck, and ability," and the law of Parallelism is satisfied.

Parallelism Type #2: Parallelism in Longer Phrases

This is the "big brother" of Type 1 Parallelism ("grocery lists"), and requires a little more care and attention. Most people can easily recognize grocery-style lists of three simple items, but it's harder to notice a "list" that is made up of larger phrases, rather than individual words. Often, these sentences will only have two items in the list.

Here's an example of a Parallelism mistake of this type:

"Would you prefer *to be eaten by an alligator* or *getting digested by a shark*?"

The "list" in this sentence is only two items long: One, "to be eaten by an alligator," or two, "getting digested by a shark."

The first step is to recognize the list of two items and identify the risk of a Parallelism mistake. The second step is to investigate the parallel structure: are "to be eaten" and "getting digested" the same Parts of Speech in the same form as each other? The answer is *no*: although both items are both based on verbs, the forms of the verbs are different ("to be x-ed" vs "x-ing").

If you want to fix the Parallelism of this sentence, you have two options:

Option A) "to be eaten" and "to be digested"

Option B) "getting eaten" and "getting digested"

But we can't mix and match "to be" and "getting" because they're verbs in different forms.

This kind of Parallelism error can definitely be tricky to notice. **The biggest giveaway** for this kind of mistake is to look for conjunctions such as "and," "or," and "not only.. but also." When listing or comparing things, the items you're listing or comparing should be the same Parts of Speech in the same forms.

It's easier to see what I mean with some examples. The *words in italics* are the things that must be parallel to each other, while **the words in bold** are the giveaway connecting/comparing words:

Wrong: *"Going to the rodeo* is **more fun than** *to go biking.*" ("Going" and "to go" are different verb forms)

Right: *"Going to the rodeo* is **more fun than** *going biking.*"

Wrong: "My brother likes **not only** *his life in the dorm,* **but also** *to jump on his bunk bed.*" ("his life" is a noun, but "to jump" is a verb.)

Right: "My brother likes **not only** *living in his dorm,* **but also** *jumping on his bunk bed.*"

Here's another example from the Pretest:

Beethoven's music is known for being logical, yet emotive; challenging, yet occasionally simple; and unique, yet <u>derived from previous styles.</u>

(A) [NO CHANGE]

(B) previous styles influenced it.

(C) was derived from previous styles.

(D) it was derived from previous styles.

Here we have a complex list of three things that Beethoven's music is known for, with the first two items following the pattern "adjective, yet other contrasting adjective."

It's the last item in the list that we're particularly interested in, because it's underlined. Does it break the pattern?

Well, let's look at our options. Choice D breaks the Parallelism pattern with "it was derived" (pronoun "*it*" + verb "*was derived*"). These new Parts of Speech are suddenly introduced into the list, conflicting with the Parallelism pattern of "adjective, yet other contrasting adjective" that was already established by the first two items of the list.

Similar Parallelism problems crop up in Choice B (which contains an unwelcome verb, "influenced," that doesn't fit into the established pattern) and Choice C (which also contains a verb, "derived").

The best choice is to maintain the Parallelism pattern that's already established - use **Choice A**, which keeps the last part of the sentence as a short modifying phrase, "derived from previous styles."

A modifying phrase (like "occasionally simple," or "derived from previous styles") can act the same way as a single adjective (like "emotive.") This makes sense if you think about it, because modifying phrases are like extended versions of single adjectives – both share the function of adding description or detail to a target noun.

Be aware that "modifying phrase" is simply another name for "Parenthetical Clauses," which you can review in-depth with Lesson 9 on **Sentence Structure**!

Side Note: Using Semicolons in Lists

If you're wondering about our unusual usage of semicolons in the previous example, did you know that semicolons can be used to punctuate lists?

Usually we use commas to punctuate items in a list:

> "I need eggs, milk, and chicken."

However, for complex lists we can use semicolons as separators, as when you make a list of cities:

> "I've visited Austin, TX; Buffalo, NY; and Los Angeles, CA."

See how we can use semicolons to punctuate complex lists - especially if the items in the list already have commas *within* them? That's the same technique we use in the "Beethoven" Pretest example above.

Parallelism Type #3 - Parallelism in Comparisons

When any sort of *comparison* is made between two or more items, those items must be logically comparable *and* follow the rule of Parallelism.

It's easy to demonstrate. Here are some items that CAN be properly compared:

Cats vs. Dogs (they are both animals)

Apples vs. Oranges (they are both fruit)

Firemen vs. Policemen (they are both professions/types of people)

Speed of a car vs. Speed of a motorcycle (they are both velocities)

Now, here are some items that could NOT be properly compared:

Cat *hair* vs. *Dogs* (we can't compare "hair" to an animal like a "dog"; it's not a logical comparison to make; change it to cat *hair* vs. dog *hair*)

Apples vs. Orange *Trees* (one is the fruit, the other is the tree it grows on)

Firemen's *salaries* vs. Policemen (one is money, the other is a person/profession)

A car vs. *speed of* a motorcycle (one is a vehicle, the other is a velocity)

The Parts of Speech must still match in your comparisons, as with all Parallelism situations. Here is an example of what happens when this rule is broken within a comparison:

BAD Comparison / Parallelism: I like *to run* more than *jumping*.

The example above is wrong because it uses different verb forms and breaks Parallelism. You could fix it either by pairing "running" and "jumping," or by pairing "to run" with "to jump." Just no mixing-and-matching of forms.

One tricky Comparison variation. Does the following sentence sound wrong to you?

"The length of this train is more impressive than any bus I've ever seen."

This may sound acceptable, **but it is wrong.** Take a look at exactly what's being compared:

"*Length* of this train" vs. "any *bus*." It's illogical to compare a *length* to a *vehicle*. Fix the sentence by changing to "the *length of* any bus."

As you train yourself to notice this error, watch out for any kind of "comparing" word; this can range from "more" to "bigger," "wiser," "louder," etc.

In fact, **the single biggest giveaway** that this Parallelism / Comparison error might be under your nose is the word "*than*" - a word that always indicates a comparison.

Parallelism & Comparisons Quick Reference:

- In math, "parallel" lines are when two or more lines are all going the exact same direction as each other - not bumping into one another.

- In grammar, words in a comparison or list of two or more items are all "going the exact same direction" if they have the same Parts of Speech in the same forms as each other.

- **Simply stated, the rule of Parallelism is:** "In any list or comparison, all items must be the same parts of speech in the same forms."

- Comparisons must always be between items that are logically comparable to each other. In addition, all Comparisons must follow the rule of Parallelism.

- Train yourself to watch out for lists and comparisons and double-check that they are consistent all the way through.

- The most common giveaway for a comparison is the word "than." Words that end in "-er" (like "more" or "taller") are another way to notice comparisons.

- The harder Parallelism questions may present two longer phrases linked by a conjunction. Both phrases should be formed as similarly as possible to one another, using the same Parts of Speech in the same forms.

Let's look at a Parallelism / Comparison example from the Pretest:

> The use of robots on farms is growing rapidly, since it is often <u>more cost-effective than</u> human farm workers.
>
> (A) [NO CHANGE]
> (B) more cost-effective than the use of
> (C) more effective than using
> (D) less costly than

Notice the words "*more* cost-effective *than*," which indicate a comparison.

What two things are being compared to each other? "The *use* of robots" vs. "human farm *workers*." This is no good; *use* is not parallel to *human worker*.

The two ways to fix this would be to compare "*use of* robots" to "*use of* human workers," or compare the nouns "robots" to "workers," but regardless of which you choose, it's incorrect to mix-and-match. **Choice B** is the only option that properly compares "the *use* of robots" to "the *use* of human farm workers," maintaining the law of Parallelism.

Choice C and D continue the original Parallelism / Comparison mistake by comparing "use" to "using" in Choice C (different **Verb Forms**, see Lesson 2) or comparing "use" to "human workers" as in the original mistake.

Here's a final Pretest question:

> I think that most Japanese manufacturers' cars get better mileage and are more reliable than <u>American automakers</u>.
>
> (A) [NO CHANGE]
> (B) making cars in America
> (C) American automakers' cars
> (D) what they make in America

Notice now how this sentence is trying to compare the *cars* from Japan to the *auto makers* from America? You know by now that this breaks the rules of Parallelism & Comparison, so go with **Choice C**, which correctly compares *cars* made by Japanese manufacturers to *cars* made by American automakers.

Go forth and conquer in your Comparisons & Parallelism! It will earn you a ton of extra points on your grammar sections. This is a really simple topic that you just have to train yourself to become aware of - I promise you'll see it often on the SAT & ACT tests, once you start actively looking for it!

Parallelism & Comparison
Practice Questions

1. A rural airstrip presents a pilot with two primary difficulties: <u>to land on dirt, and avoiding</u> dangerous crosswinds.

   (A) [NO CHANGE]
   (B) landing on dirt and avoiding
   (C) landing on dirt and the avoidance of
   (D) the landing of the plane on dirt, and avoiding

2. I prefer my Japanese history class to <u>sitting and listening to American history</u>.

   (A) [NO CHANGE]
   (B) American history
   (C) my American history class
   (D) sitting in American history class

3. Getting an article published can be quite tedious; once written, it must still be <u>edited and reviewed</u> before it is distributed.

   (A) [NO CHANGE]
   (B) edited and pass review
   (C) reviewed and will be edited
   (D) reviewed and they will edit it

4. Though wax candles pose a risk of fire hazard, due to their open flames, they generate a light that is more relaxing than <u>electric candles</u>.

   (A) [NO CHANGE]
   (B) electric ones
   (C) an electric candle
   (D) that of electric candles

5. <u>To put berries in your breakfast cereal is one healthy idea;</u> putting bananas in your oatmeal is another.

   (A) [NO CHANGE]
   (B) To put berries in your breakfast cereal is one healthy idea;
   (C) Putting berries in one's breakfast cereal is one healthy idea;
   (D) Putting berries in your breakfast cereal is one healthy idea;

6. Unlike <u>the</u> flu, people who suffer from the common cold may only have to deal with a headache and a congested nose for twenty-four hours.

(A) [NO CHANGE]

(B) having the

(C) people with the

(D) when you have the

7. The website's stated mission was "<u>to preserve the internet, and we will record</u> illegal online censorship."

(A) [NO CHANGE]

(B) the preserving of the internet and to record

(C) to preserve the internet and to record

(D) to preserve the internet and keeping records of

8. My friend makes electronic <u>music by sampling classic tunes and combining them</u> into a remix.

(A) [NO CHANGE]

(B) music by sampling classic tunes and combines them

(C) music, samples classic tunes, combines them

(D) music with samples of classic tunes and combining them

9. This <u>omelet calls for more ingredients than any other recipe's instructions.</u>

(A) [NO CHANGE]

(B) omelet's recipe calls for more ingredients than any other recipe.

(C) omelet, calling for more ingredients than any other recipe's instructions.

(D) omelet calls for more ingredients than the instructions of any other recipe.

10. <u>To keep her life private and protecting</u> her family, the pop star wore masks and costumes during her live shows.

(A) [NO CHANGE]

(B) To keep her life private, protect

(C) Keeping her life private and to protect

(D) To keep her life private and protect

11. The hands and feet of chimpanzees are far more versatile and dexterous than <u>humans</u>.

(A) [NO CHANGE]

(B) humans are

(C) that of humans

(D) those of humans

12. This calculator's <u>processing power is greater than that of</u> the computers that NASA used in the 1960s to land a man on the moon.

    (A) [NO CHANGE]

    (B) processes more great than

    (C) processing power is greater than

    (D) processing power is greater than those of

13. Kishore Kumar was a multitalented man who was mainly known as a singer, actor, and <u>wrote screenplays</u>.

    (A) [NO CHANGE]

    (B) screenwriter

    (C) for his screenplays

    (D) he wrote screenplays

14. Having read many of both authors' novels, I prefer those of Ernest Hemingway to <u>Victor Hugo</u>.

    (A) [NO CHANGE]

    (B) those of Victor Hugo

    (C) Victor Hugo's writing

    (D) what Victor Hugo wrote

15. Teeth-grinding, fidgeting, and <u>excessive energy</u> are a few negative side effects of overconsumption of energy drinks.

    (A) [NO CHANGE]

    (B) to have excess energy

    (C) to be overly-energetic

    (D) more than enough energy

16. Hibernation, the act of resting and conserving energy when food is scarce, is <u>a behavior more common to bears than</u> most other mammals.

    (A) [NO CHANGE]

    (B) more like bears than

    (C) more common to bears than to

    (D) more common to bears than to the behavior of

17. There are many famous architects who began as furniture designers, interior decorators, or <u>worked in construction</u>.

    (A) [NO CHANGE]

    (B) in construction.

    (C) construction workers.

    (D) who worked in construction.

18. Human infants, unlike <u>the young of</u> other species, are born without yet knowing the basic instincts that are necessary for their survival.

(A) [NO CHANGE]

(B) with

(C) that of

(D) [DELETE the underlined portion]

19. The length of this completed essay, almost eighteen pages long, is far more impressive than <u>that</u> poorly-researched rough draft.

(A) [NO CHANGE]

(B) a

(C) this

(D) the length of that

20. For our feature on your achievements, would you like to be interviewed online, in the newspaper, or <u>captured on video</u>?

(A) [NO CHANGE]

(B) on video

(C) a video interview

(D) interviewed on video

21. Strict vegans monitor more than just their eating habits; they refuse to use any animal products for clothing or <u>to decorate</u>.

(A) [NO CHANGE]

(B) decoration

(C) decorate with them

(D) use them for decoration

22. More citizens of New York City (with its affordable subway network) utilize public transportation than <u>those of any</u> other city.

(A) [NO CHANGE]

(B) any

(C) that of any

(D) the public transportation of any

23. One minor tragedy of life is that you must choose to follow only a single path rather than <u>going down</u> all possible roads.

(A) [NO CHANGE]

(B) down

(C) go down

(D) following down

24. If you are planning a solo wilderness adventure, some important necessities are <u>a compass, a map, a supply of water, and to tell people where you are going.</u>

   (A) [NO CHANGE]
   (B) a compass, a map, water, and to tell people where you are going.
   (C) having: a compass, a map, a supply of water, and telling people where you are going.
   (D) to tell people where you are going and to bring a compass, a map, and a supply of water.

25. The newest models of seismographs, which are scientific devices designed to measure the movements of tectonic plates, are now more sophisticated than <u>previous eras.</u>

   (A) [NO CHANGE]
   (B) it used to be
   (C) eras once were
   (D) the seismographs of previous eras

26. Ear-piercing has many social functions; it not only is a sign of rebellion, but also is an indicator of fashion sense or <u>demonstrates belonging.</u>

   (A) [NO CHANGE]
   (B) belonging
   (C) demonstrated belonging
   (D) to demonstrate belonging

27. The nighthawk is a bird that eats primarily insects, <u>much like the diet of many other birds around the world.</u>

   (A) [NO CHANGE]
   (B) as do many other birds around the world
   (C) much like the diet of many other birds around the world
   (D) much like what many other birds around the world eat

Parallelism & Comparison Answers

1. B
2. C
3. A
4. D
5. D
6. C
7. C
8. A
9. B
10. D
11. D
12. A
13. B
14. B
15. A
16. C
17. C
18. A
19. D
20. B
21. B
22. A
23. C
24. D
25. D
26. B
27. B

Parallelism & Comparison Explanations

1. B - We have a list of two piloting-related difficulties in this question – and any list of two or more items is a chance for a Parallelism error. Both items in the list should be verbs that take the same form: either "to land" and "to avoid," or "landing" and "avoiding," but we can't mix and match. Choice B repairs the Parallelism error in the original with a concise and elegant solution that pairs two "-ing" form verbs.

2. C – Choice C is the most logical and well-matched comparison ("class" to "class"), so it's the easy winner here. Notice the nice parallel structure: "[Country X history class]" to "[Country Y history class]". Choice B incorrectly compares a *class* to *history*, and Choices A and D make a Parallelism error by comparing a *noun* ("class") to a *verb* ("*sitting*").

3. A - NO CHANGE. The two-item list in this sentence is already parallel the way it is: "edited" and "reviewed" are both past-tense verbs. All other options mismatch the verb tenses of these two items and so break the law of Parallelism.

4. D – As written, there is an improper comparison between a *light* and a *candle*. We must compare one *light* to another *light*, or one type of *candle* to another type of *candle*, but we can't mix and match "*light* of a candle" vs. "electric *candle*." It's picky, but those are the rules of Parallelism and Comparisons. Choices A, B, and C all incorrectly compare *light* to *candles*. Choice D properly compares the *light* of one type of candle to *that [light]* of another type of candle.

5. D - In Choices A and B, there is a Parallelism error: "to put" and "putting" are verbs in different forms. Choice D properly matches the first idea, "putting berries," with its *-ing* partner, "putting bananas." Choice C correctly follows Parallelism rules, but it creates a **Pronoun-Antecedent Agreement** mismatch (Lesson 5) between "*one's* breakfast cereal" and "*your* oatmeal."

6. C – As written, the sentence illogically compares the *flu*, a virus, to *people*. Instead, compare *people* to *people*, like so: "Unlike *people* with the flu, *people* who suffer from the common cold…"

7. C – As written, the sentence contains a Parallelism error (the different verb forms of "to preserve" vs. "will record"). Choice C corrects the Parallelism mistake by properly using the matching verb forms "to preserve" and "to record."

8. A – NO CHANGE. There is no error in this sentence. "Sampling" and "combining" are both *-ing* verbs that share the same form and don't cause Parallelism problems. Choice C is also parallel ("makes… samples… combines"), but notice that the third item of the list doesn't contain a conjunction (like "and") to properly end the list.

9. B - We can't compare an "omelet" (a food) to "instructions" (not a food). Only Choice B properly compares *recipes* to other *recipes*. The other choices all mistakenly mix-and-match comparisons between *foods* and *recipes*.

10. D – There's a Parallelism error in the original sentence when the verb form switches from "to keep" to "protecting." Choice D solves the Parallelism error with the matching verb form pair "keep" and "protect" (the "*to*" before "keep" is understood to be shared by both "keep" and "protect," so you don't have to repeat the "to" in "*to* protect.")

11. D – The original sentence contains a Comparison error: we can't compare the *hands and feet* of chimpanzees to *humans*. Changing "humans" to "the hands and feet of humans" would be acceptable and ensure that we are comparing similar things to each other. In this case we can save a few words by replacing "the hands and feet" with the pronoun "*those*." Choice C commits a **Pronoun-Antecedent Agreement** error (Lesson 5) by using the singular pronoun "that" to replace the plural antecedent "hands and feet."

12. A – NO CHANGE. The original sentence correctly compares "processing power of calculators" to "that [processing power] of computers." It's less consistent to compare "*processing power*" to "*computers*." Choice D commits a **Pronoun-Antecedent Agreement** error (Lesson 5) by using the plural pronoun "those" to replace the singular antecedent "processing power."

13. B – We have a basic three-item list here ("singer, actor, and wrote screenplays") so according to Parallelism rules, everything in that list must use the same **Parts of Speech** (Prelesson A) in the same forms. *Singer* and *actor* are nouns, while *wrote screenplays* uses a verb; fix the error by replacing "wrote screenplays" with its noun form, "screenwriter."

14. B – You can't compare "those [*books*] of Ernest Hemingway" to a *person* like "Victor Hugo." It doesn't make sense to compare books to people; you can only compare books to books, or people to people. Choice B correctly uses both a logical comparison and a parallel structure to compare "those [novels] of Ernest Hemingway" to "those [novels] of Victor Hugo."

15. A – NO CHANGE. In some cases, an -*ing* word can act like a noun instead of a verb (this is known as a "gerund.") Such is the case in this list: "teeth-grinding" and "fidgeting" are both acting as nouns. That's why the current sentence is our best option: "excessive *energy*" is also a noun, so Parallelism is already maintained.

16. C – Ask yourself "what is being compared here?" We should compare bears to other animals. Choice A has a Parallelism error because of an absent *preposition* (**Parts of Speech**, Prelesson A) in the second item of the list- we're missing the "*to*" in "*to* bears than *to* other mammals." Choice B compares *hibernation* (an action) to *bears* (an animal): "*hibernation*…is more like *bears* than other animals." Choice D makes an improper comparison between *bears* and *behavior*. Only Choice C correctly follows Parallelism and makes a logical comparison.

17. C – We have a list of three professions at the end of this sentence. The first two are nouns, but the third contains a verb ("*worked in*") and breaks the rule of Parallelism that all items in a list must be the same **Parts of Speech** (Prelesson A) in the same forms. Replace with a noun like "construction workers" for a perfect parallel match among the three items in the list.

18. A – NO CHANGE. This sentence is correct as it is. "Infants" are compared to "the young" of other species. Both are nouns, so Parallelism is satisfied, and the comparison of young humans to young animals is also logical. Choice C commits a **Pronoun-Antecedent Agreement** error (Lesson 5) by replacing the plural antecedent "infants" with the singular pronoun "*that* of." Choice D would compare "infants" to "other species" - an Illogical Comparison, because infants are an age group, not a separate species.

19. D – What is being compared here? It may seem like an "essay" and a "rough draft" are compared at first glance, but take a closer look. The sentence is really comparing the *length* of an essay to a *rough draft*. We need to compare "*length*" to "*length*" or "*draft*" to "*draft*"; otherwise the comparison is illogical. Choice D correctly compares "the *length* of this essay" to "the *length of* that rough draft."

20. B – We have a list at the end of the sentence that includes three different interview media: online, newspaper, and video. The problem is that the first two items in the list follow the same **Parts of Speech** (Prelesson A) pattern of [*preposition*] [noun]: "*on*-line" and "*in* the newspaper," while the third item throws in a verb ("*captured*") that breaks Parallelism. Choice B simply removes the verb "captured" to properly continue the list's original pattern of [preposition] [noun] with the choice "*on* video."

21. B – When using an "X or Y" list, the two items must maintain parallel form. This sentence mixes "clothing," a noun, with "to decorate," a verb. Fix the list by replacing the verb "to decorate" with its noun form "decoration."

22. A – NO CHANGE. It's easy to misunderstand the comparison: it could seem like this sentence is comparing "New York City" to other *cities*, but this sentence is actually comparing "*citizens*" of New York City to "[those] *citizens* of any other *city*." The sentence is correctly obeying Parallelism and making a logical comparison already. Choice C commits a **Pronoun-Antecedent Agreement** error (Lesson 5) by replacing the plural antecedent "citizens" with the singular pronoun "that of."

23. C – This is a list with two options ("to follow" and "going"). However, first item in the list uses the verb form "*to follow*"while the second item uses a different verb form "*going*" (**Verb Tense and Form**, Lesson 2). Of course, this breaks the rule of Parallelism, which states that all items in a list must be the same **Parts of Speech** (Prelesson A) in the same forms. Choice C correctly matches the infinitive verb form *to go* with the infinitive verb form *to follow* (the "*to*" before "*follow*" can be shared with the verb "*go*").

24. D - This list of "important necessities" forgot how important it is to use the same forms throughout a list! The first three items ("a compass, a map, a supply of water…") are all nouns – no problems here. However, Parallelism gets messed up near the end when the list shifts from nouns to a verb: "*to tell* people…"

Choice D fixes Parallelism by splitting the big list into two smaller parts: first, a two-item list with "to tell" and "to bring." Then there is a "sub-list" of three items contained under "to bring" - these three items are all nouns ("a *compass*, a *map*, and a *supply*"). This question is a very interesting situation with *two* cases of Parallelism and a list-within-a-list!

25. D – You can't logically compare *"eras"* (a time period) to *"seismographs"* (scientific instruments). Choice D fixes the error by comparing *seismographs* to *seismographs*. Choice C contains a **Pronoun-Antecedent Agreement** error (Lesson 5) by replacing the plural antecedent "seismographs" with the singular pronoun "it."

26. B – Parallelism requires that all items in a list must be the same **Parts of Speech** (Prelesson A) in the same form. In this case there is a list of two items: "an indicator of *fashion sense* [a noun] or *demonstrates* [a verb] belonging." In this case, simply remove the verb "*demonstrates*" and you are left with a list of two nouns: "*fashion sense* or *belonging*." (Remember that *-ing* words can often act like nouns - these words are called "gerunds.")

27. B – There is a sneaky Illogical Comparison in the original: "the nighthawk" is compared to "the diets" of other birds. Only Choice B correctly compares "the nighthawk" to "other birds," and it also maintains perfect Parallelism while doing so.

LESSON 11
Misplaced Modifiers

Misplaced Modifier errors are one of my favorite mistakes in the SAT & ACT Grammar sections. In a test that is almost entirely boring and humorless, this type of mistake can bring a little bit of comedy to your experience. You just have to know how to appreciate it...

What is a "Modifier"?

A "modifier" or "modifying phrase" is essentially another name for a "Parenthetical Clause" (review Lesson 9 on **Sentence Structure** for more details.) These phrases are never essential to the main sentence; they simply add extra details about other elements of the sentence.

Here's an example of a "modifying phrase" (or Parenthetical Clause).

"who worked as a fireman for many years"

This phrase cannot stand on its own, but it adds detail and description to *something* – in this case, it would provide background information about a person mentioned elsewhere within the sentence. Notice that these commonly start with Relative Pronouns, like "who" or "where."

These modifying details need to be attached to *something* or *someone* – they can't just stand on their own. Modifiers will never be independent; they are always attached to something else from the main sentence.

Continuing with the fireman example, the modifying phrase might be attached to a sentence in the following way:

"Jeremy, *who worked as a fireman for many years*, was able to rescue the cat from the tall tree."

Notice that the modifying phrase (or Parenthetical Clause) is not essential to the main sentence. Take it out, and you'll be left with "Jeremy was able to rescue the cat from the tall tree," which is still perfectly able to stand on its own.

Now, in the case above, the modifying phrase has *not* been "misplaced." That's because "Jeremy," the person who is being *modified* or described in more detail, is right next to the modifying phrase "who worked as a fireman for many years."

It's really, really important that a modifier is right next to the person or thing it is modifying, so that we know who the description is meant to "attach" to.

If this rule is broken, creating what we call a "Misplaced Modifier" error, then prepare for some hilarious misinterpretations. Check out the ridiculous results of moving the modifying phrase to a different location in the sentence, far away from "Jeremy":

> "Jeremy was able to rescue the cat, who worked as a fireman for many years, from the tall tree."

Heh heh. Silly sentence – cats can't work as firemen! By placing the modifying phrase next to "cat" instead of next to "Jeremy," the modifier has been "misplaced," and the meaning of the sentence is now completely altered - not for the better!

The big trick to catching these errors every time they show up is to *expect* them. Any modifying phrase should be considered "suspicious." Treat these descriptive phrases as "guilty" until proven innocent. Make sure the descriptive phrase is attaching to the correct noun.

Once you've found such a mistake, the next step is to look for answer choices that fix the modifier by putting it next to the person or thing it was actually meant to describe. Use your common sense and make sure that the modifying phrase matches up with (and is placed right next to) something or someone that it's actually meant to describe.

Let's look at a Pretest question that might have sent you to this chapter:

<u>While it panted and strained at its leash, the dog's owner attempted to restrain the puppy</u> when it saw a squirrel at the dog park.

(A) [NO CHANGE]

(B) The dog's owner attempted to restrain the puppy while it panted and strained at its leash

(C) While it panted and strained at its leash, the puppy's owner attempted to restrain it

(D) The dog's owner, while it panted and strained at its leash, attempted to restrain the puppy

First, notice the modifying phrase at the start of the sentence: "While it panted and strained at its leash..."

This modifying phrase gives extra details about *something*, but *what*? The phrase can't stand on its own - until we read further, it's unclear *what* or *who* this modifying phrase attaches to.

The way modifiers work is to attach to whatever person or thing they are closest to. In this example, the nearest person or thing would be "the dog's *owner*." (Note the common trick of using a possessive like "the dog's *owner*" - many readers will only see "the *dog*" and not catch the fact that "dog's *owner*" actually refers to a person, not to an animal).

Isn't it ridiculous to imagine a dog's *owner* panting and straining at a leash? I certainly hope so... otherwise, your life is a lot weirder than mine is. Yes, the original sentence contains a Misplaced Modifier error!

Now that we've identified the mistake, start eliminating answer choices that repeat the same flaw. Choice C makes the same Misplaced Modifier mistake by continuing to use the possessive form to refer to a *person* instead of the *puppy*.

Choice D continues the Misplaced Modifier error, even though it shifts the modifying phrase into the middle of the sentence. "The *owner*" is still the closest noun for the modifying phrase to attach to.

Choice B is the correct solution: the phrase "while it panted and strained at its leash" is now nestled up right next to "puppy," the thing it describes. The Misplaced Modifier is fixed and the meaning of the sentence is clear. Excellent!

Misplaced Modifiers Quick Reference

- Practice looking for Parenthetical Clauses, which are also called "modifying phrases": nonessential phrases that add extra detail or description. They cannot stand on their own.

- Modifying phrases / Parenthetical Clauses are often set apart from the rest of the sentence by commas, and frequently begin with Relative Pronouns like "who" or "where," or with "-ing" words. Review **Sentence Structure** (Lesson 9) and **Punctuation Marks** (Lesson 8) for more tips on Parenthetical Clauses and commas.

- The beginning or end of a sentence is usually the most common place to find a Misplaced Modifier error; however, Misplaced Modifiers can also be hidden in the middle of the sentence.

- Use common sense and logic to decide if a modifying phrase is describing the "wrong" person or thing: Can cats be firemen? Do dog owners walk on leashes?

- Learn to appreciate the unintentional humor of Misplaced Modifiers so that you enjoy looking for them and finding them.

- Fix these errors by moving modifying phrases so that they are right next to the person or thing they are actually meant to describe.

Now let's look at the second Pretest example of a Misplaced Modifier error:

Bursting with color, the pale hospital patient appreciated her friend's gift of flowers.

(A) [NO CHANGE]

(B) Bursting with color, the pale hospital patient's friend's gift of flowers was appreciated.

(C) The pale hospital patient, bursting with color, appreciated her friend's gift of flowers.

(D) The pale hospital patient appreciated her friend's gift of flowers, which was bursting with color.

Notice that the sentence starts off with a modifying phrase again: "Bursting with color." What, exactly, is supposed to be "bursting with color?" Would a "*pale* hospital patient" be "bursting with color," or would a "gift of flowers" probably be more colorful?

In context, the "color" definitely should refer to the "gift of flowers." That means the modifying phrase "bursting with color" is in the wrong place! So, Choice A is out, as is Choice C (which has a similar structure).

Choice B actually fixes the Misplaced Modifier error (it's hard to tell with all the possessives, but "bursting with color" actually *does* apply to the "flowers" in this sentence). However, compared to the correct answer, it is very poorly-written; we would hope for a better option than the multiple-possessive form "the hospital patient's friend's gift of flowers was appreciated," which is clumsy, confusing, wordy, and passive. See Lesson 13 on **Redundancy & Wordiness** for more info.

Choice D is correct: It fixes the Misplaced Modifier mistake by placing the modifying phrase "which was bursting with color" next to the thing it is meant to describe: the "gift of flowers." The meaning is clear, direct, and logical. Excellent!

Misplaced Modifier Practice Questions

1. <u>Because they eat mosquitoes, many home owners have</u> considered building bird houses in their backyards.

   (A) [NO CHANGE]

   (B) Because birds eat mosquitoes, many home owners have

   (C) Home owners, because they eat mosquitoes, have

   (D) Because mosquitoes are eaten by birds, many home owners have

3. <u>As the crowd's favorite athlete, Janet Lynn's figure-skating earned</u> cheers and applause that surely swayed the judge's opinion.

   (A) [NO CHANGE]

   (B) As the crowd's favorite athlete, Janet Lynn figure-skating earned

   (C) As the crowd's favorite athlete, the figure skating of Janet Lynn earned

   (D) Janet Lynn's figure-skating, as the crowd's favorite athlete, earned

2. <u>Buffeted by strong, gusty winds, the skyscraper's tenants felt the building</u> leaning to and fro.

   (A) [NO CHANGE]

   (B) The skyscraper's tenants, buffeted by strong, gusty winds, felt the building

   (C) As the building was buffeted by strong, gusty winds, the skyscraper's tenants could feel it

   (D) When buffeted by strong, gusty winds, the skyscraper's tenants felt the building

4. <u>Green workers, known for their focus on the environmental impact of large projects, are in high demand.</u>

   (A) [NO CHANGE]

   (B) Known for their focus on the environmental impact of large projects, demand is high for so-called "green" workers.

   (C) Known for focusing on the environmental impacts of large projects, there is a high demand for so-called "green" workers.

   (D) Green workers, known for their focus on large projects and its environmental impact, are in high demand.

5. Chilly in the winter, a space heater would make this basement more comfortable.

    (A) [NO CHANGE]

    (B) Chilly in the winter, space-heating would make this basement more comfortable.

    (C) A space heater would make this basement, chilly in the winter, more comfortable.

    (D) A space heater, chilly in the winter, would make this basement more comfortable.

6. Formed while its members were in college, the four-piece band toured all over Europe.

    (A) [NO CHANGE]

    (B) Formed while its members were in college, Europe was toured all over by the four-piece band.

    (C) The four-piece band toured all over Europe, formed while its members were in college.

    (D) All over Europe, formed while its members were in college, the four-piece band toured.

7. Using GPS technology, getting lost was easily dealt with by the savvy traveler.

    (A) [NO CHANGE]

    (B) Using GPS technology, the savvy traveler's getting lost was easily dealt with.

    (C) The savvy traveler using GPS technology, easily dealt with getting lost.

    (D) Using GPS technology, the savvy traveler easily dealt with getting lost.

8. Standing in Northumberland County, invading armies were never able to breach the thick stone walls of Warkworth Castle.

    (A) [NO CHANGE]

    (B) Invading armies were never able to breach the thick stone walls of Warkworth Castle, which stands in Northumberland County.

    (C) Invading armies, never breached the thick stone walls of Warkworth Castle, standing in Northumberland County.

    (D) Invading armies, standing in Northumberland County, were never able to breach the thick stone walls of Warkworth Castle.

9. Founded in 1968, attendees of the Clarion Workshop are taught to improve their science-fiction writing.

    (A) [NO CHANGE]

    (B) Founded in 1968, improving their science-fiction writing is the goal of attendees of the Clarion Workshop.

    (C) The Clarion Workshop is attended by those, founded in 1968, who are taught to improve their science-fiction writing.

    (D) Attendees of the Clarion Workshop, which was founded in 1968, are taught to improve their science-fiction writing.

10. As the race car reached speeds of over 200 miles per hour, its engine noise became nearly deafening to the spectators.

    (A) [NO CHANGE]

    (B) As it reached speeds of over 200 miles per hour, the race car's engine noise became

    (C) Reaching speeds of over 200 miles per hour, the race car's engine noise became

    (D) The race car's engine noise, reaching speeds of over 200 miles per hour, became

11. An author of passionately nationalistic novels, Carl Gustaf Verner's writing depicts Swedish life and traditions.

    (A) [NO CHANGE]

    (B) Authoring passionately nationalistic novels, Carl Gustaf Verner's writing depicts Swedish life and traditions.

    (C) Carl Gustaf Verner, an author of passionately nationalistic novels, depicts Swedish life and traditions in his writing.

    (D) Authoring passionately nationalistic novels, Swedish life and traditions were depicted by Carl Gustaf Verner's writing.

12. Studying intensively, the Department of Public Administration was where Felix received an excellent education.

    (A) [NO CHANGE]

    (B) The Department of Public Administration, studying intensively, was where Felix received an excellent education.

    (C) Studying intensively, at the Department of Public Administration was where Felix received an excellent education.

    (D) Studying intensively, Felix received an excellent education at the Department of Public Administration.

13. Agreeing after hours of debate, the decision of the jury was to let the citizen go without legal charges.

   (A) [NO CHANGE]
   (B) The jury's decision, agreeing after hours of debate, was to let the citizen go without legal charges.
   (C) The citizen, agreeing after hours of debate, was let go without legal charges by the jury.
   (D) The jury, agreeing after hours of debate, decided to let the citizen go without legal charges.

14. Finding contemporary classical music "arrogant," Lutz Glandien's music embraces rock influences and older styles alike.

   (A) [NO CHANGE]
   (B) Lutz Glandien's music is influenced by both rock and older styles.
   (C) Lutz Glandien embraces rock influences and older styles alike in his music.
   (D) rock influences and older styles alike are embraced by Lutz Glandien's music.

15. There is nothing more annoying than trying to work while a fly buzzes behind your ear.

   (A) [NO CHANGE]
   (B) There is nothing more annoying than a fly buzzing behind your ear, trying to work.
   (C) There is nothing more annoying than a fly buzzing behind your ear while trying to work.
   (D) A fly buzzing behind your ear: there is nothing more annoying while trying to work.

16. The abilities of squirrels, running across power lines and racing up even the tallest trees, have always amazed me.

   (A) [NO CHANGE]
   (B) Running across power lines and racing up even the tallest trees, the abilities of squirrels have always amazed me.
   (C) Squirrels have always amazed me with their ability to run across power lines and race up even the tallest trees.
   (D) Running across power lines and racing up even the tallest trees, squirrels' abilities have always amazed me.

17. Born in 1810, Robert Schumann's life is a fascinating tale of a composer driven to madness by schizophrenia.

(A) [NO CHANGE]

(B) Born in 1810, the life of Robert Schumann is a fascinating tale

(C) Born in 1810, the tale of Robert Schumann's life is

(D) Born in 1810, Robert Schumann lived a life that makes for a fascinating tale

18. The mythical painting was said to draw magical power from both its age and its master's skills, dead for over 900 years.

(A) [NO CHANGE]

(B) age and, dead for over 900 years, the skills of its master.

(C) age and the skills of its master, who had been dead for over 900 years.

(D) master's skills, dead for over 900 years, and its age.

19. The road racer was given a citation racing too close to other bicyclists in the race.

(A) [NO CHANGE]

(B) The road racer was given a citation for racing too close to other bicyclists in the race.

(C) A citation, racing too close to other bicyclists in the race, was given to the road racer.

(D) Racing too close to other bicyclists in the race, a citation was given to the road racer.

20. Experimenting in a new kind of land partnership, the farmers turned the land into a cooperative cropland after purchasing it in 1804.

(A) [NO CHANGE]

(B) After purchasing the land in 1804, the farmers turned it into a cooperative cropland experimenting in a new kind of land partnership.

(C) The farmers turned the land, experimenting in a new kind of land partnership, into a cooperative cropland after purchasing it in 1804.

(D) Experimenting in a new kind of land partnership, the land purchased in 1804 was turned into a cooperative cropland by the farmers.

21. <u>Though she is known as a murderer, the newspaper reports that the suspect may actually have had good intentions.</u>

(A) [NO CHANGE]

(B) The newspaper reports that, although she is known as a murderer, the suspect may actually have had good intentions.

(C) The newspaper, though she is known as a murderer, reports that the suspect may actually have had good intentions.

(D) Though she is known as a murderer, good intentions may actually have been had by the suspect, the newspaper reports.

Misplaced Modifiers Answers

1. B
2. C
3. B
4. A
5. C
6. A
7. D
8. B
9. D
10. A
11. C
12. D
13. D
14. C
15. A
16. C
17. D
18. C
19. B
20. A
21. B

Misplaced Modifiers Explanations

1. B – In the original version, the modifier "because they eat mosquitoes" will attach to the closest noun - in this case, "home owners." Of course, most people ("home owners") don't eat mosquitoes. The same Misplaced Modifier problem causes Choice C to be incorrect.

Choice B correctly fixes the Misplaced Modifier by making it clear that *birds* eat mosquitoes, so homeowners are building more birdhouses to attract birds for pest control. Choice D isn't as good - it fixes the Misplaced Modifier, but uses a passive, wordier version - "because mosquitoes are eaten by birds" - compared to Choice B (see **Redundancy & Wordiness**, Lesson 13).

2. C – What should be buffeted by strong winds - the people inside the skyscraper, or the building itself? Definitely the *building*, not the *people*! It's a Misplaced Modifier to describe the people as "buffeted by the winds" instead of the building.

This question uses the possessive case ("skyscraper's tenants") to camouflage the Misplaced Modifier error: "the skyscraper's tenants" may seem (to the untrained eye) like it focuses attention on the skyscraper, but it actually focuses on the *tenants* - the people who live inside the skyscraper. Choice C clearly states that the *building* is struck by wind, and the people inside are able to feel the building leaning as a result.

3. B - There's a Misplaced Modifier mistake in the original version and in Choices C and D: "Janet Lynn's *figure-skating*" can't be modified by "the crowd's favorite athlete." Notice the use of a possessive to seem like we're talking about a *person*, but actually it's an *activity*, "figure-skating," that's being mistakenly being modified and called an "athlete."

4. A – NO CHANGE. The modifying phrase ("known for their focus on the environmental impact of large projects") is already correctly attached to a person or a group of people ("green workers") who can be logically "known for focusing" on something. Choice B incorrectly attaches this modifying phrase to "demand." Choice C creates a large and confusing separation between the modifying phrase and its distant target, "green workers."

Choice D looks tempting, but it commits a crucial **Pronoun-Antecedent Agreement** error (Lesson 5) in the middle when it replaces the plural antecedent "large projects" with the singular possessive pronoun "its."

5. C – Only Choice C correctly modifies the *basement* as being "chilly in the winter." The other choices all create a Misplaced Modifier by describing the *heater* as "chilly in the winter."

6. A – NO CHANGE. There's nothing wrong with the original. It's clear that the band formed while its members were in college, and then toured all over Europe. Choices B, C, and D use several versions of a Misplaced Modifier error to describe *Europe* as being "formed while its members were in college," instead of the band.

7. D – There is a Misplaced Modifier in the original sentence, because the modifier "using advanced GPS technology" should be next to the person who used it ("the savvy traveler"). "Getting lost" is not something that is able to use a GPS device.

Choice B commits the same error because of the possessive form, "the savvy traveler's getting lost." This construction still mistakenly implies that "getting lost" is "using advanced GPS technology." Using a possessive noun like this is a common distraction used when attempting to conceal a Misplaced Modifier error. Choice C contains a Sentence Fragment error (review Lesson 9 on **Sentence Structur**e for more help.)

8. B – The modifying phrase "standing in Northumberland County" is clearly supposed to give details about Warkworth Castle, not about the "invading armies," who obviously don't just stand in one place the way that a castle does! Choice B correctly places the modifying phrase ("standing in Northumberland County") next to its intended target, "Warkworth Castle." Choice C also commits a **Sentence Structure** error (Lesson 9) with a Sentence Fragment arising from poor use of a comma (also see Lesson 8 on **Punctuation Marks**.)

9. D – The modifying phrase "founded in 1968" could describe something like a *workshop*, but it definitely can't describe "attendees," who are *people*! We would never describe people as being "founded," which is a word used to describe the establishment of organizations, companies, scholarships, etc. Choice D properly puts the modifying phrase ("founded in 1968") next to the "workshop" that was founded in 1968.

10. A - NO CHANGE. The original version is correct, while the other choices all contain Misplaced Modifier errors. It's the "race car" that would "reach speeds of over 200 miles per hour," not the "engine noise."

11. C – The original sentence, as well as Choice B, are trying to conceal a Misplaced Modifier error by using a distracting possessive. The phrase "an author of passionately nationalistic novels" is supposed to be modifying "Carl Gustaf Verner," but the Misplaced Modifier incorrectly states that his *writing* is an "author." Choice C correctly describes Verner as an author. Choice D incorrectly attaches the modifier "authoring passionately nationalistic novels" to "Swedish life and traditions" and also veers into passive, wordy territory (see **Redundancy & Wordiness**, Lesson 13).

12. D - "Studying intensively" is the modifying phrase in this sentence; it should modify a *person* who is studying (like "Felix"), not a *department*. All other choices contain a Misplaced Modifier error that describe the "Department of Public Education" as "studying intensively."

13. D - A decision can't "agree after hours of debate" - it's the jury - the *people* - who would be debating and agreeing, not their *decision* ("decisions" can't "debate"). Choice C commits a logical error, because it's illogical that the citizen would debate for hours before letting himself go free. Choice D properly places the modifying phrase "agreeing after hours of debate" next to the "jury," which is clearest and makes the most sense out of all our options.

14. C - Here's another attempt to use a possessive form to conceal a Misplaced Modifier error. "Lutz Glandien's music" wouldn't "find contemporary music arrogant"; that is a judgment that only a *person* - not *music* - could make. Choice B makes the same mistake as Choice A. Choice D also contains a similar Misplaced Modifier mistake to the first two choices, although in this case it's the "rock music" that "finds contemporary music arrogant."

15. A – NO CHANGE. The original version of the sentence is clear and correct. Some of the other options are worth laughing at - imagine an annoyed person, with a fly holding a clipboard and wearing glasses and work clothes buzzing behind that person's ear. After all, Choices B and C state that the fly is trying to work! Choice D incorrectly uses a colon, a punctuation mark which must be preceded by a complete sentence. Review both **Punctuation Marks** (Lesson 8) and **Sentence Structure** (Lesson 9) for more information.

16. C – The modifying phrase "running across power lines and racing up even the tallest trees" should apply to *squirrels*, not to "the abilities of squirrels" (*abilities* can't climb trees!) Choices A, B, and D use a variety of Misplaced Modifier errors to incorrectly attach "running… and racing…" to the *abilities* of the squirrels, rather than the squirrels themselves.

17. D – This is a favorite Misplaced Modifier trick of mine: at first it's hard to see that anything is wrong here, but think about it – can a "life" be born in 1810, or would it be more appropriate to say that a *person* (like "Robert Schumann") was born in 1810? It's definitely the second: it's not "lives" that are born, but *people* who are born. Choice C makes a similar mistake with "the tale" being born in 1810. Only Choice D correctly attaches the modifier ("born in 1810") to the *person* who was born ("Robert Schumann").

18. C – There's a Misplaced Modifier suggesting that "the skills of its master" have been "dead for over 900 years." A *person* can be dead, but we don't say their *skills* have died. Choice B commits the same error - still saying the *skills* were dead for 900 years. Choice C puts the modifying phrase ("dead for over 900 years") right next to the "master" that it modifies, and adds the Relative Pronoun "who" for additional clarity to further avoid any potential misunderstandings.

19. B – As written, there's a Misplaced Modifier error, making it seem that the *citation* was "racing too close to other bicyclists," when actually the meaning should be that the *racer* was racing too close. All three choices, other than Choice B, are incorrectly modifying the *citation* as "racing too close," instead of modifying the *racer*.

20. A – NO CHANGE. The sentence is correct as it is. It describes the "farmers" as "experimenting in a new kind of partnership," which makes perfect sense. Choices B, C, and D all contain Misplaced Modifier mistakes that imply the land itself is choosing to experiment in a new kind of partnership.

21. B – As written, there is a major Misplaced Modifier error. "Though *she* is known as a murderer" is a modifying phrase that is currently attached to "the newspaper," when this phrase really should be describing "the suspect." In other words, it seems like the *newspaper* is a murderer, which is obviously not the intended meaning. Choice C commits the same mistake as the original. In Choice D, the modifying phrase is incorrectly being applied to "good intentions," rather than "the suspect." The phrasing, "good intentions may have been had by the suspect," also exhibits a passive, wordy structure (see Lesson 13 on **Redundancy & Wordiness**). Choice B correctly solves the Misplaced Modifier error, while remaining clear, concise, and direct.

LESSON 12
Vocab Word Choice

Congratulations! You've made it through the majority of the "hardcore grammar rules" contained in this book. This is perhaps the first lesson that's not really about *grammar* in the literal sense. This new topic - **Vocab Word Choice** - revolves around *vocabulary:* choices of similar words with different tones or connotations.

Usually these questions look relatively short and sweet.- you're just given four choices of individual words. **For example, from the Pretest:**

> The small house built in the field used the <u>average</u> building materials that were available in the region: wood, stone, brick, and glass.
>
> (A) [NO CHANGE]
> (B) arbitrary
> (C) stereotypical
> (D) characteristic

Notice that all four words have something in common: they are a loosely-clustered group of similar words that can overlap in meaning in certain contexts and usages. However, they all have subtle differences in meaning and tone that can make a crucial difference when deciding which word to use for the job.

Priorities of Vocab Word Choice Questions

The **first priority** in any Vocab Word Choice question should be to eliminate any words that don't have an *accurate meaning* that is fitting for the situation.

In the question above, we can safely eliminate Choice B, "arbitrary," which means "based on a random whim, rather than any reason or system." The sentence tells us that the building materials are selected specifically from what is available in the region, so "based on a random whim" isn't a good definition.

The **second priority** in a Vocab Word Choice question is to eliminate any words that don't fit the *context.*

On this ground, we can most likely eliminate Choice A, "average," which fits best in a mathematical context when dealing with sets of data, or in a more informal context when comparing an individual to a larger group. This sentence does not present a particularly mathematical or data-based context, so it's unlikely that "average" will be the best word choice for the job.

The **third priority** in a Vocab Word Choice question is to narrow your remaining choices down by *tone*: the "positive," "negative," or "neutral" connotations, and the "formal" or "informal" connotations of each remaining word choice.

Of our remaining choices, Choice C, "stereotypical," has a negative connotation. This word implies "an *oversimplified* idea of a particular type of person or thing." Our sentence is neutral and informational in tone, and there's no negative connotation of being overly simple.

The best word for the job is **Choice D**, "characteristic." It's nothing fancy, but it's perfect for the job - a neutral, relatively formal word meaning "typical of a person, place, or thing."

There's **one more priority** to think about on a Vocab Word Choice question, which blends into the next lesson on **Wordiness and Redundancy**. (These two topics are sometimes blended together.)

For an example, what if Choice C had been "not unusual," instead of the given option, "stereotypical"? If that were the case, "not unusual" might pass the third priority's test - it's quite neutral, without any negative connotations. However, the double negative of "not unusual" would be unnecessarily *wordy* compared to the simpler option, "characteristic."

In a Vocab Word Choice question in which two choices both fit the *meaning*, *context*, and *tone*, then look for the most concise answer choice. It will usually be the correct one.

Levels & Difficulties of Vocab Words

These vocabulary questions aren't generally focused on high-level "difficult" vocabulary. They are mostly focused on the *nuances* of similar common words.

The majority of the vocab words will sound familiar to you - although you may find yourself worrying about the *exact* usage of each word, when you're faced with this type of question.

Remember, this topic isn't so much about the "difficulty" of the vocab words as it is about their exact meanings, appropriate contexts, connotation, tone, and brevity (which means "being short, exact, and concise.")

At the same time, you should be prepared to occasionally see more advanced vocabulary words. Sometimes I think the test authors like to provide three "easy and familiar" words alongside a single "challenging / advanced" vocab word - just to cause stress and chaos if you aren't sure whether the "advanced" vocab word would be a better choice than one of the three words that you're more familiar with.

Vocab Word Choice Quick Reference

- Recognize these questions by their simplicity and appearance. You're given four similar - but not identical - vocabulary words, and you're supposed to select the best option for the current context.

- First, focus on accurate *meaning*. Eliminate any words with unsuitable definitions.

- Next, eliminate any words that don't fit the *context* of the sentence, based on the topic.

- Now focus on appropriate *tone*. Does the situation call for a word with positive, negative, or neutral connotations? Is the setting more formal and academic, or more informal and conversational?

- The final check should be for *wordines*s. All things being equal, the shorter answer is better. This overlaps with Lesson 13 on **Wordiness and Redundancy**.

- To improve in this topic, read more books and articles each day to start learning the specific contexts, connotations, and meanings of new words. Deliberately spend time developing your vocabulary by looking up definitions and opening your mind to the subtle differences in similar word choices. This will also help immensely with your Reading scores on the SAT & ACT tests.

Following are a few details from my personal research into the SAT & ACT and their use of Vocab Word Choice questions. One point became immediately clear: vocabulary is *much* more important on the SAT Grammar test than it is on the ACT Grammar test.

ACT Vocab Word Choice

On the ACT Grammar section, this topic appears consistently, but in low frequencies. On average, it is seen approximately just once per test (once per 75 questions) This means that vocabulary questions are just over 1% of the whole ACT Grammar test, a very low percentage.

Here are a few word-choice selections from actual ACT Vocab Word Choice questions:

- illuminate, emanate, emulate, eliminate

- arouse, stimulate, awaken, disturb

- voluminous, immeasurable, mountainous, large

- heaps, a high number, hundreds, plenty

SAT Vocab Word Choice

On the SAT Grammar section, Vocab Word Choice questions are much more common. On average, it is seen approximately three times in a single test (three times per 44 questions). That makes this topic about 7% of the whole SAT Grammar test - nearly *six times* higher in importance than on the ACT.

Here a some selections of vocabulary words from actual SAT Vocab Word Choice questions:

- outdo, defeat, outperform, outweigh
- satiated, fulfilled, complacent, sufficient
- share advice, give some wisdom, proclaim our opinions, opine
- reducing, reductions, deducting, deducts
- devour, dispatch, overindulge on, dispose of
- austere, egregious, unmitigated, stark
- sinister, surly, abysmal, icky
- tight, firm, stiff, taut
- decreed, commissioned, forced, licensed
- confided, promulgated, imparted, unveiled
- preserve, carry on, maintain, sustain
- life-altering, galvanizing, intriguing, weird
- site, cite, sight
- emphatic, paramount, eminent, important
- swear, subscribe, vow, promise
- persecuted, prosecuted
- pinnacle, triumph, culmination, apex

- taking on, undertaken in, overtaking, taking off from
- blockade, scolding, interference, condemnation, drag, reproof, deterrent, rebuke
- weirdnesses, deviations, oddities, abnormalities
- keep pace, maintain the tempo, get in line, move along
- bolstering, amping up, arousing, revving up
- elderly, old, mature, geriatric
- elaborated, developed, evolved, progressed
- annihilating, eliminating, ousting, closing the door on
- potent, sturdy, influential, commanding
- scrupulous, super-rigorous, spot-on, intense
- deformation, alteration, transformation, modification

Let's look at the other Pretest question that might have sent you to this chapter:

I prefer modern boat designs, and although my cousins enjoyed the interior styling of the old steamship, I considered the decor fairly primordial.

(A) [NO CHANGE]
(B) elderly
(C) old-fashioned
(D) ancient

First, notice any words that don't have an accurate *meaning* for the situation. Interestingly, all of these words could *possibly* fit, since they all have a connection to "oldness." However, Choice A, "primordial," has the dictionary meaning of "existing at the beginning of time." It's unlikely that this is the ideal definition, since steamships did not exist at the beginning of time!

Next, move on to *context*. "Elderly" is a word most often seen in the context of *people*. Although it is possible to use "elderly" to describe machinery or other objects, it's an unusual context, and chances are that we've got a more straightforward option available.

Finally, let's move on to *connotation*. Although Choice D, "ancient," could possibly be used in this context, it has a connotation of "the very distant past." Compared to our other option - "old-fashioned" - it seems that "ancient" would imply a *much older* age, while "old-fashioned" is more moderate option.

We could still *try* Choice D if we were uncertain, which would give us the phrase "fairly ancient." It should sound a bit ridiculous to you, because "ancient" implies *extremely* old, but the word "fairly" is providing a more moderate tone that clashes with the more extreme connotation of "ancient."

That's why Choice C is the correct solution: "Old-fashioned" has a straightforward accuracy that fits the meaning, context and connotation of the "fairly old-fashioned" style of decoration aboard an old steamship, without going to extremes.

Review and Encouragement

Don't forget: the number-one way to improve your results on Vocab Word Choice questions is to *read more*. Develop a curiosity for the meanings of words, their exact definitions, precise usages and related synonyms. This will not only raise your SAT & ACT Grammar scores, it will also make you a faster, better reader.

Not least of all, this will also make you a better writer and speaker, and you'll find it easier to express your own ideas with powerful, clear, persuasive, and precise language!

Vocab Word Choice
Practice Questions

1. Still undecided, the financial committee <u>deliberated</u> who they would send to speak to the president of the company about the decreased profits this year.

   (A) [NO CHANGE]
   (B) authorized
   (C) nominated
   (D) delegated

2. Upon attempting to enter the military base, the reporter was <u>tested</u> by the guard, who called out a simple request for identification.

   (A) [NO CHANGE]
   (B) dared
   (C) challenged
   (D) taxed

3. My grandparents fell deeply in love with each other from the moment they met; my grandpa, in particular, always described feeling <u>attentive to</u> my grandma from the first time he saw her.

   (A) [NO CHANGE]
   (B) enamored with
   (C) armored with
   (D) concerned with

4. As a political science major writing a thesis paper on the behavior of crowds on voting day, I <u>followed</u> the elections with excitement and interest.

   (A) [NO CHANGE]
   (B) stalked
   (C) imitated
   (D) came after

5. Despite the best efforts of a federal team of business experts and politicians, the economic <u>miniaturization</u> continued to affect the lives of millions of citizens.

   (A) [NO CHANGE]
   (B) procession
   (C) lessening
   (D) recession

6. When in the grips of a major seizure, a patient's body and limbs may <u>trample</u> uncontrollably.

   (A) [NO CHANGE]
   (B) tremble
   (C) wobble
   (D) vibrate

7. When traveling through an area with many pickpockets, regardless of police presence and other security measures, you must stay attentive - no one can <u>warranty</u> the safety of your belongings better than yourself.

   (A) [NO CHANGE]
   (B) underwrite
   (C) swear
   (D) guarantee

8. Only the most <u>isolated</u> classical pianists will earn renown in the modern era, for the popularity of classical music has been waning as the audiences for rock and rap music have grown.

   (A) [NO CHANGE]
   (B) freakish
   (C) exceptional
   (D) abnormal

9. Although the world traveler had seen many impressive sights, she could not decide whether the stone ruins of Machu Picchu were more <u>confounding then</u> the colossal Great Pyramid at Giza.

   (A) [NO CHANGE]
   (B) confounding than
   (C) astonishing then
   (D) astonishing than

10. To <u>demolish</u> the volume of human trafficking across the border, the government implemented new security measures, but this did not complete eliminate the problem.

(A) [NO CHANGE]
(B) knock down
(C) diminish
(D) raze

11. The warring tribes competed for land and resources throughout history, but neither tribe was ever able to completely <u>conquer</u> the small island.

(A) [NO CHANGE]
(B) defeat
(C) trounce
(D) overcome

12. When restoring a vintage car or motorcycle, it is wise to proceed carefully and slowly to avoid breaking the original parts that can no longer be <u>superseded</u>.

(A) [NO CHANGE]
(B) replaced
(C) returned
(D) swapped

13. Generally stopping short of outright blackmail or violence, the mobster was famous for publicly making <u>veiled</u> threats towards witnesses who planned to testify against him.

(A) [NO CHANGE]
(B) secretive
(C) concealed
(D) hidden

14. When babysitting an infant, a sitter must be <u>frugal with</u> the needs of the child, especially the need for food, security, and sleep.

(A) [NO CHANGE]
(B) shrewd about
(C) attentive to
(D) thrifty with

15. The bank robbers are still at large, but the police are carefully tracking <u>there</u> whereabouts.

(A) [NO CHANGE]
(B) they're
(C) their
(D) its

16. Groups of elite actors working on a film
    together must control their <u>egos</u> to prevent
    fights from breaking out among prima donnas.

    (A) [NO CHANGE]
    (B) characters
    (C) self-images
    (D) roles

17. Ever since I accidentally offended my boss in
    the staff meeting yesterday, he has been
    treating me in a <u>freezing</u> manner and ignoring
    all of my attempts to apologize.

    (A) [NO CHANGE]
    (B) frigid
    (C) subzero
    (D) rigid

Vocab Word Choice Answers

1. A
2. C
3. B
4. A
5. D
6. B
7. D
8. C
9. D
10. C
11. A
12. B
13. A
14. C
15. C
16. A
17. B

Vocab Word Choice Explanations

1. A - NO CHANGE. The sentence explains that the committee is "still undecided," which matches best with "deliberated," a word that indicates that a decision is still being considered, without a final choice having been made. Choices B, C, and D ("authorized," "nominated," and "delegated") imply a level of certainty that would fit better in a context where the decision of who to send had already been made.

2. C - A "challenge" can be a request for identification called out by a guard or gatehouse to an unknown person who is approaching. This word would perfectly fit the meaning and context. A "test" is closer in meaning to a "quiz" or an "exam" - not something that could easily and simply be shouted at a distance. Neither "dared" nor "taxed" are good fits for the required meaning - and certainly not better than "challenged."

3. B - The primary context clue is "fell deeply in love with," which perfectly matches the precise definition of the word "enamored." Choice A ("attentive to") and Choice D ("concerned with") don't have any connection to "falling deeply in love." Choice C, "armored with," is a similar-sounding word that has a completely different meaning - of course, "armor" relates to equipment worn for protection, not to "love." Remember to look closely at your word choices - small differences in spellings can mean major differences in meanings!

4. A - NO CHANGE. To "follow" the news is a common phrase meaning "to keep track of what is happening." The other choices are not so good: "stalking" implies following *stealthily;* the narrator isn't "imitating" or copying the news, and "came after" could either mean "started a fight" or "came (sequentially) after (in time)," neither of which is appropriate for the intended meaning.

5. D - This question is easy if we understand that "recession" is a word meaning "a temporary economic decline", an appropriate term to describe large-scale economic events (supported by the clue words "federal," "business experts and politicians," "economic," and "millions of citizens"). Choice A, "miniaturization," is typically related to the physical size of an object; Choice B, a "procession," is a ceremonial parade; and Choice C, a "lessening," has nothing in particular to do with economics, and so is not nearly as relevant to the context as our first choice, "recession."

6. B - Choice A isn't right, because the meaning of "trample" is to "tread on and crush," and someone having a seizure is shaking uncontrollably throughout their entire body - unlikely to be standing upright, much less "treading" (or "walking upon") anything. Choice D, "vibrate," is closer to describing the body's motions during a seizure, but is a bit too strong - "vibrate" has the connotation of extremely rapid shaking, often mechanical in nature. Choice B, "tremble," is ideal - it has a similar meaning to "vibrate," but a bit more moderate in speed, and "tremble" is a word often applied to organic life, like the leaves of trees or human beings. Choice C, "wobble," is not intense or accurate enough for a seizure - it usually implies a loss of upright balance on a larger scale - the whole body, instead of individual limbs - and typically this word also relates to a slower rate of motion.

7. D - Choice A doesn't work, because a "warranty" is a written guarantee provided by the manufacturer of an item. Choice B, "underwrite," is a financial term for someone who guarantees that a loan will be repaid. Choice C, "swear," implies that someone is taking a solemn oath or promise, but Choice D, "guarantee" works best because one of its primary meanings is to "give a certainty of outcome" - in this case, only *you* can protect your belongings and provide the certainty that they will not be stolen by pickpockets.

8. C - Choice A, "isolated," means to be far away or having little contact with others. This contradicts two clue words in the sentence: "renown" (having great fame) and "popularity." Choices B and D, "freakish" and "abnormal," do correctly indicate that there is something extraordinary or unique about the pianist in question; however, they have strongly negative connotations, which again clash with the positive-tone clue words "renown" and "popularity." Choice C, "exceptional," fits perfectly for a famous and popular pianist: a positive-tone word that has a primary meaning of "unusually good or outstanding."

9. D - The first observation to make is the difference between the words "*then*" and "*than.*" Although there is only a one letter difference between them, it's crucial: "then" relates to time periods or to cause-and-effect (e.g. "if this, *then* that.") On the other hand, "*than*" is a comparison word, as in "greater than" or "lesser than." Since we're making a *comparison* between the ruins of Machu Picchu and the Great Pyramid of Giza, we definitely want to eliminate the "then" choices and keep the "than" choices.

Now let's turn our attention to the choice between "astonishing" and "confounding." In some ways these words are similar - both can indicate a sense of surprise - but "astonishing" implies "extremely impressive or amazing," which fits perfectly with the clue words "impressive sights." "Confounding" is typically understood as "confusing or defeating." Although both words imply a sense of surprise, we should avoid the negative tone of "confounding" and stick with "astonishing" for a positive tone that closely matches with the clue words "impressive sights."

10. C - The clues here are "new security measures" that "did not *completely* eliminate the problem." To "raze" or "demolish" imply "to completely destroy," which eliminates Choices A and D. Choice B, "knock down," has a physical connotation of actually pushing someone or something to the ground. Choice C, "diminish," is best - a simple, neutral word meaning "to make less."

11. A - NO CHANGE. Of course, we use the word "conquer" to describe the act of taking control of a specific place (like an "island") by force, which is appropriate for "warring tribes" who are "competing for land and resources." Choices B, C, and D all fail for the same reason - they each change the focus of the action to defeating or overcoming *the island itself*, rather than taking control of the island by defeating the other *tribes* on the island.

12. B - The clues are that we must avoid breaking "original parts," which can no longer be... what? Probably not Choice A, "supersede," which means to take the place of something old with something new and improved. That would defeat the meaning of "original" parts. Choice C also won't work, because logically we can't *return* broken parts for an old, out-of-date car. (Plus, we'd still need new replacement parts anyway, or the car wouldn't work.) In Choice D, a "swap" is an "exchange of one thing for another," but nothing in particular is mentioned to "swap" the parts with. Choice B, "replaced," is best for the context - the old parts of a vintage car are irreplaceable, so we must be careful not to break them.

13. A - NO CHANGE. To make a "veiled threat" is a commonly-used phrase meaning "to make a *subtle* threat" - to hint at inflicting pain or damage without coming right out and saying so. The fact that "veiled threat" is a common phrase with an appropriate meaning makes it a good choice already - and Choices B, C, and D all look worse - especially when we consider the clue word "publicly," which defeats the meanings of "secretive," "concealed," and "hidden." (It is self-contradictory to give a "hidden" threat "publicly.") On the other hand, it's still possible to make a "veiled" threat in public - that would just mean you're hinting at a risk of danger, without coming out and making an obvious, direct threat.

14. C - The clue words are "babysitting" and "needs of the child," which weaken Choice A ("frugal") and D ("thrifty"). These two vocab words are associated with connotations of money and personal finances. If we had no better option, then Choice B, "shrewd," would be a decent choice for its meaning of "sharp powers of judgement." The one issue is that "shrewd" tends to have a certain edge to it - not quite *negative* (although it's useful to know that "shrewd" historically had a more negative connotation), but definitely implying a sort of *sharpness* or *keenness*, often used in negotiations or tense situations. Again, it would probably work if we didn't have a better option for the context; however, we do have Choice C, "attentive to," and that's perfect for how a babysitter should behave towards the needs of a child, so it's the safest choice.

15. C - A common word choice mistake combined with **Pronoun-Antecedent Agreement** (Lesson 5). We can't use the word "there," meaning "at that location," because the underlined word is referring back to the antecedent noun "robbers," which means we need to use the **Part of Speech** (Prelesson A) known as a "pronoun." Choice D won't work: "its" refers to a *singular* antecedent, but "robbers" is a *plural* antecedent (again, review Lesson 5 if this is confusing to you). Choice B isn't the simple possessive pronoun that we need - it's a contraction meaning "they are." That leaves us with Choice C, the correct plural possessive pronoun to refer back to the robbers and their whereabouts.

16. A - NO CHANGE. "Elite actors" and "fights breaking out among prima donnas" point us towards a conflict of *egos*, meaning a person's *sense of importance* - something that could cause those clashes between competing actors. None of the other options capture the implication of clashes between the actors based on their senses of self-importance. Choice B and D have more to do with the "roles" or "characters" the actors play, rather than their true selves. Choice C, "self-images," is better, but too neutral - it doesn't carry the same conflict-causing "egotistical" (meaning self-centered, absorbed in oneself) connotations of the word "ego."

17. B - Key words are "offended" and "ignoring attempts to apologize." We can use the word "frigid" to indicate a behavior or attitude of "coldness" towards someone else - it means "showing no friendliness; stiff in behavior." Choice A, "freezing," and Choice C, "sub-zero," are generally used in a more literal sense to refer to temperatures, not to behaviors or attitudes. Choice D, "rigid," could be used to describe a person's behavior, but lacks the key connotation of *unfriendliness*, and merely captures the meaning of someone "unable or unwilling to change."

LESSON 13
Redundancy & Wordiness

We're on to another of my favorite topics: Redundancy & Wordiness! I like this topic because students usually aren't aware of its existence, but once they learn to recognize it, this can be a fun and easy source of points on the SAT & ACT Grammar sections. Once you've learned to look for these type of questions, they aren't hard to find. You'll wonder how you ever used to miss them!

"Redundancy" means "the use of words that could be removed without loss of meaning; unnecessary repetition." That's exactly what we're looking for in this lesson: the unnecessary repetition of information that could be removed without harming the clarity or meaning of the sentence.

When a word is unnecessarily defined, repeated or rephrased into a nearly-identical synonym within the same sentence, there is a strong chance that the question is focused on Wordiness and Redundancy.

For example, if a sentence includes the word "contemporary," it should not also include the phrase "these days" in that sentence - because "contemporary" and "these days" both mean exactly the same thing.

> **Redundant and BAD:** "*Contemporary* movies produced *these days* often use an excessive amount of computerized special effects. "

Notice the redundancy of pairing "contemporary" with "these days" in the same sentence - they have identical meanings.

For another example, the tests might try the following sentence on you:

> **Redundant and BAD:** "The rare fish had blue (the color) and red stripes down its tail fins. "

Notice the inclusion of completely redundant information: "blue (the color)". Of *course* blue is a color; there's no room for misinterpretation here. This is another example of a Redundancy error, and the best solution is to completely remove the words "the color" from the sentence. No loss of meaning or clarity will occur. (Believe it or not, there are actually Redundancy & Wordiness choices like this on the SAT and ACT!)

Here's a third example of a Redundancy error:

> **Redundant and BAD:** "The company *annually* recycles a million tons of paper *each and every year.*"

"Annually" already means "each year," so keep "annually" and remove "each and every year."

> **With Redundancy Eliminated:** "The company recycles a million tons of paper annually."

"Redundancy" vs. "Wordiness"

So, is there a difference between "Redundancy" and "Wordiness"? Yes: the two concepts are similar, but there are a few useful differences to be aware of.

As we've already seen, the concept of a *Redundancy* mistake is based on unnecessary *repetition* that could be removed without harming the meaning or clarity of the sentence.

On the other hand, *Wordiness* is the mistake of using an excessive amount of words when a simpler, more direct phrase is available.

Here is a rather basic example of Wordiness:

> **Wordy and BAD:** "He walked along the path, and he was being accompanied by a friend."

To make the same point in about half the words, we could have said:

> **Less wordy and BETTER:** "He walked along the path, accompanied by a friend."

Notice we've removed the entire wordy phrase "and he was being," without harming the clarity or meaning.

The Word "Being" is a Common Giveaway of Wordiness

Any time the word "being" shows up in a SAT or ACT Grammar question, you should immediately consider the possibility of a Wordiness error. There's almost always a more concise and direct way to rewrite the sentence without use of the word "being."

As a rule of thumb, the SAT & ACT tests don't like the word "being" - mostly because it tends to create wordy, "passive" sentences. (We'll examine the *Passive Voice* more in a moment).

Here's an example of the dangers of the word "being," taken from the Pretest:

The Vauxhall <u>automobile, being designed</u> to be economical, has recently regained popularity among car collectors.

   (A) [NO CHANGE]

   (B) automobile being designed

   (C) automobile, designed

   (D) automobile, a car designed

Notice how when you remove the word "being," the sentence's meaning loses absolutely nothing, and is just a little bit shorter and more direct? That eliminates Choices A and B. **The correct answer is Choice C.** This is a "Wordiness" mistake.

Also, notice the Redundancy error of restating "a car" after "automobile" in Choice D - these two words have the same definitions, and nothing meaningful is lost if we remove one of them from the sentence.

Always remember this simple rule: the SAT and ACT Grammar tests dislike choices that use the word "being" in them.

Hey, Shakespeare's famous words were "To be or not to be," not "*Being* to be or *being* not to be," right?

Passive Voice vs. Active Voice

"Passive Voice" vs "Active Voice" is a grammar topic that fits nicely into this lesson on Wordiness.

What do "Active" and "Passive" mean in the context of grammar? Well, when someone *does something*, that's Active Voice. But, when someone has something *done to* them, that's Passive Voice. In English, we generally prefer the Active Voice - it's typically more direct and concise - and avoid the Passive Voice when possible.

This concept may be a unclear, so I've included some examples of Active vs. Passive Voice below. Which versions seem better (clearer, more direct) to you?

Active: He drove the school bus.

Passive Voice: The school bus was being driven by him.

Passive Voice: Deer and rabbits being hunted with her bow and arrow was liked by her. (LOL! So wordy!)

Active Voice: She liked to hunt deer and rabbits with her bow and arrow.

Active Voice: The subway traveled through many tunnels.

Passive Voice: Many tunnels were being traveled through by the subway.

Now let's look at another example of Passive Voice and Wordiness from the Pretest:

<u>Unethical political decisions are able to be protested by concerned American citizens.</u>

(A) [NO CHANGE]

(B) Unethical political decisions have the ability to be protested by concerned American citizens.

(C) Concerned American citizens are able to protest unethical political decisions made by politicians.

(D) Concerned American citizens are able to protest unethical political decisions.

As written, this sentence is in the Passive Voice: "Decisions *are able* to be *protested by*..." Just think about how poorly this idea is expressed: saying "decisions are able to..." makes it sound like decisions have *agency* (the ability to decide and act independently). Instead, it should be the *citizens* that have the agency and independent action.

Choice D fits our Active Voice improvement. Now the *"citizens are able* to protest," and a related (positive) side effect is that the sentence is shorter and less wordy. Also notice the Redundancy in Choice C: it's unnecessary to remind the reader that "political decisions" are made by "politicians."

So, let's sum this lesson up and make a simple point of strategy very clear: on the SAT and ACT Grammar tests, if picking between two choices that have no major grammar errors from the previous lessons, you should always pick the shortest, most concise, most active and direct answer that is offered to you. If there are two choices that seem free of errors, but one choice is less wordy, then *pick the less wordy option!*

The *shortest, clearest,* and *most direct answer* wins – as long as there are no other grammar errors in the sentence, of course. And, remember to always avoid the use of the word "being" whenever possible.

Redundancy & Wordiness Quick Reference

- Start looking for Redundancy & Wordiness. It's easier to notice when you're already looking for it.

- When choosing between two error-free answers, always favor the shortest, clearest, most Active-Voiced answer that is available.

- "Redundancy" is the mistake of including repetitious information that can be removed without harming the meaning or clarity of a sentence.

- It's redundant to define a word twice in a sentence - for example, "annually each year," or "contemporary movies these days."

- "Wordiness" is the use of long-winded phrasing that could be made simpler and more direct.

- The word "being" is a common red flag for Passive Voice and Wordiness. Avoid use of the word "being" whenever possible.

- Active Voice is when the noun does the verb. Passive Voice is when a noun has a verb done *to* them. In English, the Active Voice is typically preferred over the Passive Voice.

Redundancy & Wordiness
Practice Questions

1. Although <u>initial success can be rewarding, the feeling of satisfaction can promptly</u> wear off quickly.

   (A) [NO CHANGE]
   (B) the first initial success can be rewarding, the feeling of satisfaction can
   (C) initial success can be rewarding, the feeling of satisfaction can rapidly
   (D) initial success can be rewarding, the feeling of satisfaction can

2. <u>The safety of bridges, keeping them from becoming dangerous, is overseen by government departments, but</u> unfortunately, the spans occasionally suffer abrupt structural failure and collapse.

   (A) [NO CHANGE]
   (B) Government departments oversee bridge safety, but
   (C) Bridge safety, being overseen by government departments, is crucial, but
   (D) The safety of bridges is being overseen by government departments, but

3. <u>This fine wool sweater was once being knitted by my grandmother, and it</u> has always been among my favorite articles of clothing.

   (A) [NO CHANGE]
   (B) My grandmother knitted this fine wool sweater, and it
   (C) This fine wool sweater was knitted by my grandmother, and she
   (D) This fine wool sweater was knitted and made by my grandmother, and it

4. There was an immediate and <u>massive and tremendous public outcry against the dictator's proclamation.</u>

   (A) [NO CHANGE]
   (B) massive public outcry and popular complaint against the dictator's proclamation.
   (C) ferocious public outcry against the dictator's proclamation.
   (D) tremendous public outcry against the dictator's proclamation when he declared it.

5. <u>The teacher taught a lesson that</u> cleared up any misconceptions about the nature of space travel.

(A) [NO CHANGE]
(B) Being taught by the teacher, a lesson
(C) A lesson was taught by the teacher that
(D) The teacher taught and instructed the class in a lesson that

6. When <u>a budget is stuck to by you, you</u> will find yourself with more money left in your pocket at the end of each month.

(A) [NO CHANGE]
(B) a budget is being stuck to, you
(C) you stick to a budget, you
(D) you stick to a financial budget, you

7. Sangita Santosham, a respected vocalist, <u>has multiple genres of singing that are known by her.</u>

(A) [NO CHANGE]
(B) can sing in multiple genres.
(C) has the ability to sing in multiple different genres.
(D) knows how to sing in multiple genres and categories of singing.

8. Perhaps some superstitions arose from the belief that after <u>a disaster first occurred, it would repeat itself</u> under similar circumstances.

(A) [NO CHANGE]
(B) a disaster first occurred, it would repeat itself again
(C) an initial disaster first occurred, it would repeat itself
(D) a troublesome disaster first occurred, it would repeat itself

9. <u>The bicycle was pedaled by him furiously as he tried to catch up to the bus that had left without him.</u>

(A) [NO CHANGE]
(B) Being pedaled furiously, the bicycle he rode was trying to catch up to the bus that had left without him.
(C) The bus, leaving without him, was trying to be caught up to by him as he pedaled the bicycle furiously.
(D) He pedaled his bike furiously as he tried to catch up to the bus that had left without him.

10. The <u>World Cup is a famous and well-known</u> soccer (or football) championship with fans around the world.

(A) [NO CHANGE]

(B) World Cup is a famous and commonly-known

(C) well-known World Cup is a famous

(D) World Cup is a famous

11. <u>The art and artifacts of ancient American cultures were intended to be represented by the artist.</u>

(A) [NO CHANGE]

(B) The artist intended to represent the art and artifacts of ancient American cultures.

(C) The artist's intention was to represent the art and artifacts of early ancient American cultures.

(D) The artist intended to represent and portray the art and artifacts of ancient early American cultures.

12. <u>A thrifty investor may buy diverse assets in order to make a fortune.</u>

(A) [NO CHANGE]

(B) To make a fortune, diverse assets may be bought by a thrifty investor.

(C) A thrifty investor may buy many different diverse assets in order to make a fortune.

(D) Many different diverse assets may be bought by a thrifty investor in order to make a fortune.

13. Gustav Holst, though known mainly for his orchestral suites, <u>also has several operas composed by him.</u>

(A) [NO CHANGE]

(B) also composed and wrote several operas.

(C) also composed several operas.

(D) also composed several operas that he wrote.

14. The Olympic runner was legendary for winning the marathon <u>and also</u> the 100-meter dash in the same week.

(A) [NO CHANGE]

(B) and the

(C) and additionally the

(D) and, furthermore, the

15. The unique structural-support <u>beams, specifically built and intended for this particular use, were</u> both artistic and technical marvels.

(A) [NO CHANGE]

(B) beams, built for this function, were

(C) beams were

(D) beams, constructed and intended for this particular use, were

16. Some love songs <u>are written for a specific romantic interest; others are composed about more general ideals.</u>

   (A) [NO CHANGE]
   (B) are written and created for a specific romantic interest; others are composed about more general ideals or principles.
   (C) are written for a specific romantic or love interest; others are composed about more general ideals.
   (D) or tunes are written for a particular and specific romantic interest; others are composed about more general ideals or principles.

17. The masterful fresco <u>painting, unmatched by any other artwork in its genre, was extremely unique.</u>

   (A) [NO CHANGE]
   (B) painting was extremely unique.
   (C) painting, unmatched by any other artwork in its genre, was one-of-a-kind.
   (D) painting was unique

Redundancy & Wordiness Answers

1. D
2. B
3. B
4. C
5. A
6. C
7. B
8. A
9. D
10. D
11. B
12. A
13. C
14. B
15. C
16. A
17. D

Redundancy & Wordiness Explanations

1. D - In the original version, notice the Redundancy of "*promptly* wear off *quickly*." It's a classic tip-off to a Wordiness-focused question. Same goes for Choice C: "can *rapidly* wear off *quickly*." And, Choice B is redundant with a different pair of words: "the *first initial* success." That leaves Choice D, which avoids any paired-synonym redundancies.

2. B – As written, the sentence is redundant and wordy: "keeping them from becoming dangerous" adds nothing to the sentence that the single word "safety" doesn't already convey. It also uses the Passive Voice: "The safety is overseen by..." Choices C and D both use the word "being," a classic no-no for the SAT and ACT if any other option is available. Choice D also uses the Passive Voice again: "Bridge safety is overseen by..."

Only Choice B presents an option that avoids redundancy, doesn't use the word "being," and is in the Active Voice: "Departments oversee safety...."

3. B - As written, the sentence uses the no-no word "being" and uses the Passive Voice ("This sweater was knitted by...") Choice D features a redundant pairing of "*knitted* and *made*" - the word "knitted" already covers the meaning of the word "made." Choice B is clear, direct Active Voice, has no Redundancies, and avoids use of the word "being." Did you notice the **Misplaced Modifier** error (Lesson 11) in Choice C? With the details removed, this version would read: "*My grandmother* has always been among my favorite articles of clothing!"

4. C - As written, there is a significant bit of Redundancy: "*massive* and *tremendous*" step on each others' toes with nearly-identical meanings. Choice B has a similar problem: "public outcry" and "popular complaint" have identical meanings, and there's no need to use both phrases at once.

Choice D has another, more subtle Redundancy, because part of the Redundancy error comes from outside the underlined portion: "*immediate... when he declared it.*" Note that "immediate" and "when he declared it" are synonymous and therefore redundant. Choice C is the best option because it avoids all the Redundancies of the other answer choices.

5. A – NO CHANGE. Although "The teacher taught a lesson" might seem like it has a bit of Redundancy, it's probably safe - not only do "teacher," "taught," and "lesson" all serve different grammatical functions, there's also not much of an easier way available to express this concept.

Furthermore, Choices B through D are all worse. Choice B uses the no-no word "being" and uses the Passive Voice (by implying the *lesson* carried out the action, rather than the *teacher* who taught it.) Choice C is passive as well. Choice D features an unacceptable Redundancy: "*taught* and *instructed the class in.*"

6. C – The original is Passive and Wordy: "When a budget is stuck to by you" makes the *budget* out to be the subject or main actor of the sentence, rather than "*you*" acting as the subject - the idea behind Active Voice is that it just makes more sense to phrase this sentence as if the *person* did the action, rather than the *budget* doing the action. Choice B has similar Passive issues; it also uses the no-no word "being." Choice D features the amusing Redundancy of "a *financial* budget," which is surely overkill in a sentence that's clearly about saving money.

7. B – As written, the phrasing "has multiple genres that are known by her" is awfully Wordy and Passive. Choice B is by far the clearest, most direct, Active-Voiced option - it's also the most concise.

Compared to this option, Choice C pointlessly expands the concise single word "can" to the wordy phrase "has the ability to," and "multiple *different* genres" adds nothing that "multiple genres" doesn't already express, so that's even more Redundancy. Choice D has a similar problem, but possibly even worse, with the phrase "multiple genres *and* categories of singing" providing an obvious Redundancy and Wordiness error.

8. A - NO CHANGE. There are no Redundancy, Wordiness, or Passive Voice errors in the original sentence. Notice in Choice B the Redundancy of "*repeat* itself *again*." Choice C has the Redundancy of "*initial* disaster *first* occurred." Choice D features an amusing Redundancy as well: "a *troublesome* disaster." What other kind of disaster could there be, exactly?

9. D – In the original version, "the bicycle was pedaled by him" is a ridiculously Passive way of saying "He pedaled his bike." Notice how the original Passive form forces "the bicycle" to be the subject / "do-er" of action, while the improved Active Voice form puts "he" in the role of the subject and main character - this is more direct, clearer, and just plain better in English speech and writing. Choices B and C are just more variations on similar Passive Voice issues. Only Choice D simplifies and clarifies matters with an appropriate Active Voice version of the sentence.

10. D - Some obvious Redundancy errors present themselves in Choice A ("famous and well-known"), Choice B ("famous and commonly-known"), and Choice C ("well-known... famous"). Only Choice D eliminates these Redundancy errors. Easy, once you're aware of the Redundancy error!

11. B - The original version features a Passive Voice error: "The art and artifacts... were intended to be represented by the artist" is a long-winded, passive way of expressing the central idea, and puts the "art and artifacts" in the central action position as subject of the sentence. In English, it's much better to make this *artist* the "do-er" of action - the subject - rather than the *art*. Choices C and D include some juicy Redundancy errors, such as "early ancient" and "represent and portray." Choice B is best because it avoids these Redundancies and is in the Active Voice ("The artist intended...")

12. A – NO CHANGE. Choices B and D are both in the undesirable Passive Voice: "Assets may be bought by..." Choices C and D also feature a small, but undesirable Redundancy error: "many *different diverse* assets."

13. C – In the original version, we should improve the Passive Voice ("has operas *written by him*") with the Active version, "*he wrote* several operas," conveniently provided in Choice C. Choices B and D feature Redundancy errors: "composed and wrote" both mean the same thing in this context, so it's overkill to use both of them - especially when a more concise (but equally-clear) option is available in Choice C.

14. B – There is a common Redundancy error in most of these options - one you may even commit in your own writing or speech: "and also" is Redundant because *and* and *also* have identical meanings. Once you realize this, the Redundancy errors of Choice C ("and additionally") and Choice D ("and, furthermore") are also obvious.

15. C - By this point, you will hopefully recognize the Redundancy and Wordiness right away in the phrase "specifically built and intended for this particular use." Remember, one way of defining the Redundancy and Wordiness error is when you can remove one or more words in a sentence without losing any clarity or meaning whatsoever; this is such a case. Choices B and D commit essentially the same mistake as the original version. Notice how much more *concise* Choice C is than all the other options - without sacrificing any meaning or clarity.

16. A – NO CHANGE. Choices B through D all feature various Redundancies. In Choice B we have *"written* and *created* for," as well as *"ideals* and *principles."* Perhaps this isn't the *most* terrible case of Redundancy we've ever seen; at the same time, it's hard to argue against simply trimming those redundant phrases down a bit. Choice C uses *"romantic* or *love* interest," and Choice D goes for *"particular* and *specific"* and *"songs* or *tunes"* as well as duplicating the "ideals and principles" Redundancy we already saw in Choice B.

17. D - You may not know this, but the word "unique" cannot be made any more intense than it already is - by definition, "unique" means "one-of-a-kind." That's why Choice B, "extremely unique," is Redundant: you can't possibly be any *more* unique than the word "unique" already conveys. From this perspective, Choices A and C are obviously redundant as well. The shortest answer, Choice D, wins again! (Of course, this "shortest is best" rule of thumb only applies to questions that you've confidently identified as "Wordiness and Redundancy.")

LESSON 14
Objective Questions

What is an Objective Question?

An Objective Question is my personal name for a very particular and interesting type of question we will see on both the SAT & ACT tests. These types of questions are *instantly recognizable* once you learn to identify them, yet each Objective Question also has the potential to be *completely unique*.

Consider the majority of questions you face on the SAT & ACT Grammar sections, and you may notice something interesting: most grammar questions *do not actually give you any instructions*.

Instead, most grammar questions simply present you with an underlined portion of a sentence - with no instructions - then give you four answer choices to correct any possible grammar mistakes in the underlined portion. Notice that no instructions are provided (and none are necessary) because if you recognize and understand the appropriate rule(s) of grammar that the question is testing, that will be enough information for you to arrive at a correct conclusion.

In contrast, Objective Questions *require* a set of instructions in order to be answered correctly. These are questions that, without sufficiently clear directions, could not have a definitive "right answer."

For example, the following questions require specific instructions. Without these instructions, our task would be unclear, and the single best answer choice would remain uncertain:

"Which choice *best introduces the argument* in the following sentence?"

"Which choice provides the most *relevant and vivid sensory details*?"

"Which choice most *effectively combines* the underlined sentences?"

To put this another way, Objective Questions assign you a specific writing task in their instructions, and the correct answer choice is the one that best accomplishes those specific instructions. Think about this, as you read a few more examples of possible Objective Questions:

"Which choice best *summarizes the author's central argument* in the preceding paragraph?"

"Which of the following placements for the underlined portion *makes it most clear that the business was continuing to expand its operations*?"

"Suppose the writer's goal had been to write a brief essay *explaining the rise and fall of an ancient culture in South America*. Would this essay accomplish that goal?"

Because they have specific instructions, you can see that each Objective Question has the potential to be unique. In practice, many types of Objective Questions will reoccur in similar forms across different tests. However, the possibility *always* exists to see a brand-new type of Objective Question that you have never encountered before.

Furthermore, it takes a lot of testing experience to start encountering and recognizing "repeated" Objective Questions. For these reasons (and more), I find it easier to simply treat each and every Objective Question as its own unique experience, rather than trying to generalize them all into a single inflexible approach.

Clearly, we must read the detailed instructions for each of our Objective Questions very carefully, and avoid making any foolish assumptions about the nature of our task, or we will get many of them wrong.

Why Do I Call Them "Objective Questions"?

Think about the name itself. **Objective**: *a thing aimed at or sought, a goal. A mission, a specific task to accomplish*.

Doesn't this perfectly describe the type of question we've just seen? We're given a specific goal, a mission, a set of instructions to follow.

I had to make up a name for this type of question, and I thought "Objective Questions" captured the essence pretty nicely. Feel free to make up your own name for them, if you prefer, and email it to me at **Help@LovetheSAT.com**!

Another Definition of "Objective"

There's also a useful alternative meaning for the word "Objective": *not influenced by personal feelings or opinions*.

Contrast this against its antonym (opposite word), "Subjective," meaning "based on personal feelings, tastes, or opinions."

This is another reason I like the name "Objective Questions," because we must follow the instructions we're given, and must not be influenced by our own preferences, opinions, or assumptions.

Objective Questions: A Research-Based Approach

I've conducted painstaking exclusive research into the details of Objective Questions to make this lesson more informative, accurate, and useful. Below are some of the key takeaways I've discovered. These secrets are not common knowledge, even among SAT and ACT prep tutors.

Amount of Objective Questions per Grammar Test

On the SAT Grammar test, there are an average of 9 Objective Questions per 44-question Grammar test. This makes Objective Questions about 20% of all SAT Grammar questions - a sizeable percentage of your final score. On some tests, this can drop as low as 15% or rise as high as 30%.

It seems that the ACT has a slightly lower percentage of Objective Questions on average - about 13 out of 75 questions, or 17% of all questions, with a minimum of about 12% and a maximum of about 20% per test. Still, they make a significant contribution to your final ACT Grammar score. The ACT Objective Questions are also slightly less predictable and contain a higher percentage of "unique" Objective Questions (see next page).

Most Common Types of Objective Questions by Test

According to my personal research, here are the most common types of Objective Questions by test, with their approximate percentage of all Objective Questions listed after each type:

The SAT's 8 Most Common Types of Objective Questions:

1. Most effectively combines the two sentences (20%)
2. Supports main point of paragraph or gives relevant / supporting details or examples for paragraph (18%)
3. Sets up or supports the information, examples, or argument that precedes or follows (15%)
4. Accurately and effectively represents relevant info in a graph, table, or figure (12%)
5. Very specific, unique instructions (12%)
6. Provides best introduction or conclusion to a sentence, paragraph, or passage (10%)
7. Matching the existing style and/or tone (8%)
8. Transition between paragraphs, sentences, or the ideas within a sentence (4%)

The ACT's 6 Most Common Types of Objective Questions:

1. Very specific, unique instructions (24%)
2. Provides relevant / specific supporting information (22%)
3. "Suppose the writer's goal had been to write about [X topic]. Would this essay accomplish that goal? (19%)
4. Introducing or concluding the topic of a passage, paragraph, or sentence (14%)
5. Transitioning between sentences or paragraphs (11%)
6. If [specific sentence] were deleted, the paragraph would primarily lose... (11%)

Objective Questions Can Overlap with Other Grammar Topics

Note that some Objective Questions overlap with the other Grammar rules presented in the lessons of this book.

For example (and as you can see in the lists above), a common type of Objective Question will focus on creating an effective *transition*; this can be between sentences, paragraphs, or even two halves of the same sentence. These questions can essentially be seen as variations on **Conjunctions and Transitions** questions (Lesson 7), but may also involve **Punctuation Marks** (Lesson 8), **Sentence Structure** (Lesson 9), **Parallelism** (Lesson 10), **Misplaced Modifiers** (Lesson 11), **Wordiness** (Lesson 13) or any other Grammar topic we have covered in the preceding lessons.

Preview of Lessons 15 & 16:
Common Subcategories of Objective Questions

For the moment, we're most interested in the varieties of Objective Questions that have "special instructions," as in the lists of common question types shown above.

However, there are two common "subcategories" that we will study in the next two lessons of this book. These subcategories are called "**Adding or Removing Sentences**" (Lesson 15) and "**Moving Sentences and Paragraphs**" (Lesson 16). I have *not* included these subcategories within the lists above, because the next two chapters will cover them in more detail.

These two common subcategories of Objective Questions occur frequently enough that I eventually broke them out of this lesson and into their own special chapters with specific techniques and strategies to deal with them.

Look for these two subcategories of Objective Questions in the following two lessons. For now, we'll continue to focus on techniques for the more "unique" varieties of Objective Questions that we will find within the SAT & ACT tests.

Strategies for Answering Objective Questions

The most effective workflow for Objective Questions is flexible enough to adapt to multiple different situations and question types, and looks something like this:

1. Recognize Objective Questions on sight.
2. Read them carefully.
3. Underline the most important keywords and instructions.
4. Eliminate the 2 worst answers first.
5. Double-check the instructions again.
6. Make your final choice based on the instructions.
7. Remain "objective." Give what *they* ask for, not what *you* think would be best.

Try these strategies out on the following Pretest question.

"The Cloisters" is a museum in New York City that is constructed of four covered walkways from Europe - <u>named the Cuxa, Bonnefont, Trie, and Saint-Guilhem, respectively</u> - that were disassembled and transported to American soil between 1934 and 1939.

Which of the following choices provides the most relevant and useful supporting details for the sentence?

(A) [NO CHANGE]

(B) a continent located in the Northern Hemisphere of the globe

(C) "cloisters" is another word for "covered walkways"

(D) moved from their places of origin

Let's try following the steps I've given in the strategy above. First, we can easily recognize that this is an Objective Question by the specific instructions that are provided beneath the sentence. Let's read them carefully. It seems that the most important instructions are "relevant and useful supporting details."

On that basis, let's eliminate two of the worst choices. This would probably be Choice B (because the main sentence is neither focused on the continent of Europe nor on giving geographical details about its location) and Choice D (this information is **Redundant** (see Lesson 13) because the rest of the sentence already makes clear that the walkways were removed from their places of origin).

Check the instructions one more time, to be safe. Right - we're looking for "relevant and useful supporting details." Choice C is *relevant* but not *useful*, because it simply defines the word "cloisters" as "covered walkways" - and the sentence has already provided that information, so it's also a case of more Redundancy.

Would Choice A, "No Change", be acceptable? Yes - it provides the specific names of the four walkways, which is new info (therefore "useful") and relevant to the topic as well. **Choice A is the best answer.**

Objective Questions Quick Reference

- Objective Questions are those that give *specific directions* within the question.

- The instructions for these questions can be unique, although many will fall into common categories.

- Always underline the most important parts of the instructions before working on the answer choices.

- Follow the instructions *exactly*. Never assume you already know what they want, or you will occasionally misread and lose valuable points.

- Objective Questions can also include elements of other grammar topics within them. It's up to you to notice and recognize the other grammar rules from this book - as always, the tests will not tell you.

- Use patient elimination to narrow down your answer choices first. Don't rush to pick an answer.

- Always double-check the instructions before giving your final answer.

Let's look at another Pretest question:

James Scawen was a British politician in the mid-1700s who was once pressured by a large mob to reveal how he had voted in an important election, <u>and his father inherited a large estate near London.</u>

Which of the following choices provides the most relevant conclusion to the preceding sentence?

(A) [NO CHANGE]

(B) but he declined to share this information, stating that he must keep his vote secret in order to remain "an independent man."

(C) and in his later years, he developed Carshalton Park with improvements like canals, mills, and grottoes.

(D) and he lived from 1734 to 1801.

Again, let's apply the steps of the Objective Question strategy. It's clear this is an Objective Question because it has a set of specific instructions provided along with the question. Reading the instructions carefully, we should underline the most important directions: to provide the "most relevant conclusion" to the preceding sentence.

With that in mind, we can eliminate anything that doesn't seem like a "conclusion" to the "politics" and "mob pressure" that the sentence highlights. I'd get rid of Choice A, which is about Scawen's father, not Scawen himself. Next I would drop Choice C, which changes topic from politics to the development of a park many years later.

Now, for safety's sake, double-check the instructions: *"most relevant* conclusion." Although discussing his year of death ("1801") is a form of conclusion, it's not nearly as relevant to the political topic of the sentence as Choice B is, which concludes the story of the mob's pressure to reveal his vote with Scawen's response to the mob. That's why **Choice B is the best answer**.

Objective Questions
Practice Questions

1. Which of the following choices provides the most relevant introduction to the sentence that follows?

   Considered one of the most popular Western songs of all time, "Bury Me Not on the Lone Prairie" is actually an adaptation of an old sea song called "The Sailor's Grave."

   (A) [NO CHANGE]

   (B) A favorite song of mine,

   (C) Often recorded by radio artists,

   (D) Although a watery origin may seem strange for a Western song,

2. Which of the following choices most effectively combines the two underlined sentences below?

   Alan Dinehart was an American actor and director who initially studied to be a priest. He entered the film industry and eventually appeared in over eighty-eight films.

   (A) Alan Dinehart was an American actor and director who initially studied to be a priest, who entered the film industry, and eventually appeared in over eight-eight films.

   (B) Alan Dinehart was an American actor and director who initially studied to be a priest, but entered the film industry instead, eventually appearing in over eighty-eight films.

   (C) Entering the film industry, Alan Dinehart was an American actor and director who initially studied to be a priest, and eventually appeared in over eighty-eight films.

   (D) Alan Dinehart, entering the film industry, an American actor and director, initially studied to be a priest, and eventually appeared in over eight-eight films.

3. Which of the following choices provides the most relevant and specific supporting examples for the following sentence?

A "rake angle" is a measurement used to describe the sharpness or dullness of edges or points when making tools <u>that have cutting edges or chiseling points</u>.

(A) [NO CHANGE]

(B) to use in various applications

(C) such as chisels, blades, and saws

(D) for industrial purposes

4. Which of the following choices provides the most relevant and vivid sensory details for the following sentence?

The mountains of northern Scotland, while often cold and dangerous for inexperienced hikers, are also filled with <u>sweeping sunlit glens and the sweet smell of native wildflowers.</u>

(A) [NO CHANGE]

(B) interesting areas, charming weather, and beautiful sights.

(C) many native plants and animals to observe.

(D) excellent places to hike alone or in a group.

5. Which of the following choices most effectively transitions between the two underlined sentences below?

<u>Debra Sina is a monastery located in the highlands of Eritrea, a country in the Horn of Africa. This monastery is the site of an annual pilgrimage in June of each year.</u>

(A) Debra Sina, located in Eritrea, a country in the Horn of Africa, in the highlands, is the site of an annual pilgrimage in June of each year, and is a monastery.

(B) Located in the highlands of Eritrea, a country in the Horn of Africa, Debra Sina is a monastery and the site of an annual pilgrimage in June of each year.

(C) The monastery Debra Sina, the site of an annual pilgrimage each June, is located in the highlands of a country in the Horn of Africa, which is Eritrea.

(D) Debra Sina is a monastery located in the highlands of Eritrea, a country in the Horn of Africa, and is the site of an annual pilgrimage each June.

6. Which of the following choices provides the most relevant and effective conclusion to the following sentence?

Romania is perhaps the only former Soviet country that is attempting to remedy the illegal appropriation of factories, homes, and business through the foundation of a national joint-stock company that <u>helps reimburse the original owners for their stolen property.</u>

(A) [NO CHANGE]

(B) was founded in 2005 and is called "Fondul Proprietetea."

(C) has more than 150,000 individual shareholders across the nation.

(D) is unprecedented among nations that were once held under Communist governments.

7. Which of the following choices provides the most specific and vivid description of the colors of the Hawaiian sunset in the following sentence?

The Hawaiian sunset is famed for its colors, <u>which are generally quite vivid,</u> and has been commemorated in song by no less a luminary than Elvis Presley himself.

(A) [NO CHANGE]

(B) which range from azure blue to ripe-lemon yellow

(C) which can be spectacularly amazing

(D) which contain a variety of hues due to rare trace elements in the atmosphere

8. Which of the following choices provides the most effective and specific supporting details for the following sentence?

So-called "Grid computing" is a computer network in which each computer shares its <u>resources, rather than keeping each computer isolated from</u> every other computer in the system.

(A) [NO CHANGE]

(B) resources and links with

(C) resources - such as processing power, data storage, and memory - with

(D) resources - any physical or virtual component of limited availability - with

Objective Questions Answers

1. D
2. B
3. C
4. A
5. D
6. A
7. B
8. C

Objective Questions Explanations

1. D - This Objective Question specifically asks for "the most *relevant introduction* to the sentence." So, what's the topic of the sentence? It's about the history and origin of a Western song that originally came from a sea song. That's what makes Choice D ("a watery origin") the best answer to their specific question. Also notice the nice pairing this creates between "although" and "actually." Choices A, B, and C all focus on various aspects of the song's *popularity*, not its *history*, which makes them less relevant in comparison to Choice D.

2. B - This Objective Question is one of the most common types on the SAT and ACT: "effectively combining" two sentences. These questions can combine a variety of grammar subtopics, such as **Punctuation Marks** (Lesson 8), **Sentence Structure** (Lesson 9), **Misplaced Modifiers** (Lesson 11), **Redundancy and Wordiness** (Lesson 13), and more.

Let's look for ways to eliminate and narrow things down. Choice A commits a **Parallelism** error (Lesson 10) - there is a list of three items, and two start with "who," but the third item does *not* maintain the pattern of beginning with "who." The timeline of Choice C is a bit questionable - "entering the film industry" (a present or ongoing action) clashes with "[he] *was* an actor and director" (which implies that he already *was* in the industry). Choice D has a similar problem, along with some questionable **Sentence Structure** (Lesson 9) - notice the back-to-back Parenthetical Clauses "entering the film industry" and "an American actor and director," which feel clunky and disorganized.

Choice B avoids any grammar mistakes and has a clear timeline. The Sentence Structure is the simplest, most direct option available. It's our best choice.

3. C - This Objective Question calls for "the most relevant and specific supporting examples." Let's get rid of Choice B right away, because "various applications" is very vague (not *specific*, which is what we were asked to give). Choice D has a similar problem - "industrial purposes" is vague and abstract compared to our other two choices.

Choice A seems decent, but if you think about it, "tools that have cutting edges or chiseling points" is not only a bit repetitive (this answer repeats "edges" and "points" from earlier in the sentence), it's also less *specific* than the right answer, Choice C, which includes the specific examples "chisels, blades, and saws."

Note that the "chiseling points" and "cutting edges" that we liked in Choice A are in fact covered by "chisels, blades, and saws" in Choice C, but this latter example is even more *specific* with its supporting examples, which is exactly what the instructions told us to find.

4. A - NO CHANGE. This Objective Question calls for "the most relevant and vivid sensory details." Keep in mind the meaning of the word "sensory," which means "relating to the physical senses" - for example, hearing, sight, sound, smell, touch, and taste.

Choices C and D, while relevant to "the mountains of Scotland," lack the *sensory* details we're looking for. Choice B is a bit better ("beautiful sights" at least has to do with the sense of sight) - although that is the only "sensory" part of the answer. Even worse, it's far from *vivid*; consider, for example, the blandness of "interesting areas" in Choice B. That leaves us with Choice A, which is both sense-based (using sight and smell) and quite vivid ("sweeping sunlit glens" and "the sweet smell of native wildflowers.")

5. D - First, notice the **Redundancy** (Lesson 13) in Choice A ("annual... each year.") We can often find such Redundancy when trying to merge two sentences. Choice B has a subtle **Misplaced Modifier** (Lesson 11) error at the beginning of the sentence: notice that it describes the *highlands* of Eritrea as "a country." We can still understand the meaning, so this choice *might* be acceptable without any other issues, but notice there's also the "annual... each year" Redundancy issue again.

Choice C isn't too bad until the end, where it uses an awkward phrasing that's also another Misplaced Modifier error, since "which is Eritrea" appears to modify "the Horn of Africa" itself, rather than a country located *in* the Horn of Africa. That leaves us with Choice D, which avoids any Misplaced Modifier or Redundancy errors, and is clear and free of other mistakes as well. The winner by default! It reminds us how unpredictable Objective Questions can be...

6. A - NO CHANGE. This Objective Question instructs us to find "the most relevant and effective conclusion" to the sentence. What is the topic of that sentence? It has to do with remedying the theft of businesses and homes stolen by the former Soviet government.

Choice B offers little in the way of an "effective conclusion," merely stating two relevant facts: the name of the company and the year it was founded. Choice C has a similar problem - the information is relevant, but merely adds another data point of related information; it doesn't form a particularly-effective *conclusion* to the sentence. Choice D is a more interesting option; unfortunately it is somewhat **Redundant** (Lesson 13), since "unprecedented" means "it's never happened before" (which is already covered by "perhaps the only country" earlier in the sentence) and "nations once held under Communist governments" is essentially covered by "former Soviet country," since the Soviets are historically known for holding nations under a Communist government.

Choice A is best of all: it is *relevant* because it explains the work the national company does; it avoids direct repetition and redundancy; and it *concludes* the story of the theft of private property by counterbalancing with the return of financial value to the original owners.

7. B - This Objective Question asks for "the most vivid and specific description of the colors" of the Hawaiian sunset. Shouldn't be too hard, now that we know what we're looking for! Get rid of Choice C, because "spectacularly amazing" is neither vivid nor specific. Same with Choice A - just because it uses the word "vivid" doesn't actually make this choice a vivid or specific description.

That leaves Choices B and D. Choice D is specific in its description of the *source* of the colors in the sunset, but not in its description of the colors themselves. That makes Choice B the best answer - "azure blue" and "ripe-lemon yellow" are certainly "vivid and specific descriptions of colors"!

8. C - This Objective Question calls for "the most effective and specific supporting examples" for the sentence. So what is the sentence about? It describes a type of "computer network" before focusing in on the sharing of resources between computers in the network.

Choice A is **Redundant** (Lesson 13) compared to other choices; ("shares... rather than keeping isolated") simply rewords the concept of a shared computer network without providing any specific examples. Choice B is not specific, especially compared to other choices; all it tells us is that the computers "link" into a network, which is also somewhat redundant.

Choice D is better - it defines what "resources" are in this context - but still, doesn't provide any *specific* supporting examples. Choice C is best: there's no redundancy, and best of all, it gives the specific supporting examples ("processing power, data storage, and memory") that we were instructed to find.

LESSON 15
Adding or Removing Information

What are Adding or Removing Information Questions?

"Adding or Removing Information" questions are a commonly-seen subcategory of **Objective Questions** (see Lesson 14) that follow a particular and recognizable format. The general idea behind these questions is that the writer is trying to decide if a particular sentence (or shorter phrase) should be *added* or *deleted* from the passage. The answer choices will always present two "Keep" options and two "Remove" options, and each of the four choices will provide specific *reasons* and *justifications* to either keep or delete the sentence from the passage.

These questions are easy to identify, and with a little patience can be an easy source of points without needing to master any of the more technical rules of Grammar. Adding or Removing Information questions are intermediate in difficulty: the concept is easy to understand and recognize, but the finer details of each problem take some time and patience, or you'll miss key details and get more questions wrong than you should.

How to Recognize Adding or Removing Information Questions

There are two ways to recognize Adding or Removing Information: The *question* format and the *answer choices* format.

The *questions* follow a pattern something like this:

> At this point, the writer is considering adding the following true statement: "[Statement X]". Should the writer make this addition here?

The *answers* follow a pattern something like this:

> (A) Yes, because [Reason A].
>
> (B) Yes, because [Reason B].
>
> (C) No, because [Reason C].
>
> (D) No, because [Reason D].

Note that these questions are *not* about "*where*" to put a sentence - that is a topic covered in the next lesson, **Moving Sentences & Paragraphs**. Instead, Adding or Removing Information questions follow a very specific pattern, and will never allow you to *move* a sentence, only decide whether to include it or remove it. The answer choices always contain the "Yes, Yes, No, No" or "Keep, Keep, Delete, Delete" pattern.

If this pattern is not met, it is *not* an "Adding or Removing Information" question, but rather something else - most likely either a **Moving Sentences & Paragraphs** question or possibly another type of **Objective Question**.

Examples of the Most Common Questions

Here are some examples of the most common types of Adding or Removing Information questions on the SAT & ACT Tests.

SAT Questions:

- The writer is considering deleting the underlined sentence. Should the sentence be kept or deleted?
- The writer is considering adding the following sentence: [New sentence]. Should the writer make this addition here?
- The writer is considering adding the following information: [new information]. Should the writer do this?
- The writer is considering adding the following graph: [graph/chart]. Should the writer make this addition here?
- The writer is considering *revising* the underlined portion of the sentence to read: [Revised sentence]. Should the writer make this change?

ACT Questions:

- At this point, the writer is considering adding the following true statement: [new statement]. Should the writer make this addition here?
- The writer is considering deleting the preceding sentence. Should the sentence be kept or deleted?
- The writer is considering deleting the underlined portion of the sentence. Should the underlined portion be kept or deleted?

Minor Variations to the Question Style

As you may notice in the lists above, there are several minor variations to these questions that you may encounter. One variation is to consider adding or deleting *phrases* within a sentence, instead of a complete sentence:

> At this point, the writer is considering deleting the underlined *portion* of the sentence...

Or, sometimes you'll be asked to consider adding a phrase to the beginning or end of a sentence:

> The writer is considering adding the following phrase to the *end* of the sentence...

Or, about starting or ending the essay with a new statement:

> The writer is considering *beginning the essay* with the following true statement...

Finally, there is a rare variation about adding charts or graphs (in my experience, it is only the SAT test that will ask about adding or removing a chart or graph):

> The writer is considering adding the following *[chart/graph]* at this point in the passage...

Despite these small changes to the wording or the question, all other elements are the same - particularly the answer choices, which will continue to follow the characteristic pattern of:

> (A) Yes, because [Reason A].
>
> (B) Yes, because [Reason B].
>
> (C) No, because [Reason C].
>
> (D) No, because [Reason D].

In other words, despite some minor stylistic differences, the basic concept of all these question variations is exactly the same as every other Adding or Removing Information question.

Examples of Common Answer Choices

Take a look at this list of common reasons for choosing "Keep" or "Delete" on Adding or Removing Information questions. You don't need to memorize this list - it's just to give you a clearer idea of the incredible variety of specific reasons to either "Keep" or "Delete" information on the SAT & ACT tests. Always remember, the little details matter a lot to the right answer!

- Delete, because the sentence interrupts the flow of the paragraph.

- Delete, because the sentence repeats unnecessary information.

- Delete, because the sentence is not related to the main topic of the passage.

- Keep, because the sentence provides useful examples.

- Delete, because the sentence introduces irrelevant information to the paragraph.

- Keep, because the sentence provides relevant supporting info to the paragraph.

- Keep, because the sentence sheds light on the main topic of the passage.

- Delete, because the sentence does not provide an accurate interpretation of the data in the graph.

- Keep, because the sentence provides additional support for the main topic of the paragraph.

-Keep, because the sentence serves as an effective counterargument to a claim expressed in the passage.

- Keep, because the sentence reinforces the passage's main point.

- Delete, because the sentence undermines the passage's claims.

- Delete, because the sentence blurs the paragraph's focus.

- Keep, because the sentence elaborates on a specific topic in the paragraph.

- Delete, because the sentence restates what has already been said.

- Keep, because the sentence introduces an idea that becomes the focus for the rest of the essay.

- Delete, because the sentence uses negative terms such as *lonely* and *forlorn* to describe the narrator's experience.

- Delete, because the sentence provides a level of detail that is inconsistent with the level of detail in the rest of the essay.

- Keep, because the sentence establishes a correlation that is significant to the rest of the essay.

- Keep, because the sentence provides evidence to support a relevant claim.

- Delete, because the sentence contradicts a central idea in the passage.

- Delete, because the sentence makes an informal observation that is not consistent with the essay's tone.

- Keep, because the sentence elaborates on the preceding sentence's point.

Similarities & Differences Between the SAT & ACT

In regards to "Adding or Removing Information" questions, there is little noticeable difference between the SAT and the ACT tests. The styles of questions and answer choices are almost indistinguishable between the two tests - even the most highly-trained tutor would have a hard time telling if one of these questions came from the SAT or the ACT.

The percentage of these questions is also similar on the two tests: between about 4% and 8% of the Grammar test. So, for all test-takers, these questions make a small, but noticeable, contribution to your final score.

Essential Strategies For These Questions

The most important thing to remember when confronting these types of questions is that *the details of the answer choices matter a lot!* Even a single wrong word in an answer choice is enough to make the whole answer wrong.

Also, these questions are much more focused on content and context, and much less focused on the rules of grammar - which makes them more similar to "Critical Reading" questions than to "Grammar" questions. In fact, almost none of these questions have anything to do with actual grammar rules. So,focus your attention on content, context, and meaning.

It's very hard to "read the test's mind" on these questions and jump straight to the correct answer. So, I recommend against trying to find the right answer directly. Instead, strategic Elimination is key. Don't try to "pick" the right answer to these questions; rather, narrow down your options by identifying weak or questionable points in each answer choice and crossing them out. If any part of an answer choice is wrong, then the whole answer is wrong.

When searching for these weak points, use both broad strokes of "keep or delete" along with the finer details buried within the answer choices. Often, one of these approaches will help more than the other on a given question, but this will often change from question to question. Remain flexible in the order you attack the answer choices, attend carefully to small details of context, and proceed carefully by elimination.

If you've narrowed down as much as you can, but run out of ideas to finish the question off, then take a final look and try to avoid any needless repetition or review of previous information. Speaking broadly, both the SAT and ACT prefer to avoid repeating information that has already been given, as we've seen in Lesson 13 on **Redundancy & Wordiness**.

Adding or Removing Information Quick Reference

- These types of questions can be easily recognized by their wording ("The writer is considering adding the following information" and similar variations) and their answer choices ("Keep / Keep / Delete / Delete" and similar variations).

- These questions have almost nothing to do with "grammar rules" and are usually not very hard for careful and patient readers, but they *do* take patience and attention to the fine details of the answer choices.

- Eliminate some answer choices before making your decision. Don't leap to a final answer before you eliminate most of your other options.

- Don't decide your answer exclusively on the basis of "Keep/Delete" or "Add/Remove." You may be occasionally surprised what the SAT & ACT think about this. Be sure to investigate the *details* of the answer choices and proceed by careful, steady elimination.

Let's try a pair of Pretest questions based on the following paragraph:

[1] Of these, polyethylene is the most common type of plastic, accounting for 34% of the world's total plastics market. It has a startlingly-wide range of applications; for example, ultra-high-density polyethylene is used in hip joint replacements, industrial shipping, and ice-skating rinks. [2] <u>On the other end of the spectrum, low-density polyethylene is often used for plastic wraps, tubing, and food storage.</u> In between these "high-density" and "low-density" uses, polyethylene can also be found in film applications, water plumbing, milk jugs, garbage containers, and children's toys.

1. The writer is considering adding the following sentence as an introduction to the paragraph.

Plastics are one of the most common and useful construction materials in modern global industry, and are produced in a wide range of varieties.

Should the writer make this addition here?

(A) Yes, because the sentence provides an essential supporting example to the paragraph.

(B) Yes, because the sentence effectively introduces the main topic of the paragraph.

(C) No, because the sentence contradicts a central point made within the paragraph.

(D) No, because the following sentence ("Of these, polyethylene is...") already provides a more effective introduction to the paragraph.

2. At this point, the writer is considering deleting the underlined sentence. Should the writer make this change here?

(A) Yes, because it provides an excessive list of examples for a term that has already been defined.

(B) Yes, because it interrupts the overall flow of the paragraph.

(C) No, because it provides effective support for an essential counterargument within the paragraph.

(D) No, because it provides examples that are used as a key point for a comparison within the paragraph.

Here are explanations for the two questions.

Question 1 Explanation

Would this sentence provide an effective introduction to the paragraph? Perhaps. Let's analyze our options.

At a minimum, the new sentence is *related* to the topic of "polyethylene plastic" and doesn't contradict any central points within the paragraph. That eliminates Choice C. On the other hand, it would be a stretch to call this new sentence a "supporting example," so let's eliminate Choice A.

Choice B and Choice D offer two possible views on the same idea: either this sentence *is* an effective introduction to the paragraph, or the following sentence is already a better introduction. However, the original first sentence ("Of these, polyethylene is…") makes an unclear reference to whatever "these" are - a **Pronoun-Antecedent Clarity** error (see Lesson 4).

The new sentence *would* provide an effective introduction to the paragraph by providing the antecedent "a wide range of varieties [of plastics]" leading into "of *these*, polyethylene is…" Therefore, **Choice B is the correct answer** because the new sentence provides a clear pronoun antecedent and an effective introduction to the next sentence and the paragraph as a whole.

Question 2 Explanation

In this question, we're considering whether we should keep or delete the underlined sentence. First, let's take a close look at that sentence. It describes "the other end of the spectrum," and gives several specific examples of "low-density polyethylene."

There is a good argument for *keeping* this sentence, because there is indeed a "spectrum" from "high-density" to "low-density," which this sentence helps clarify. Furthermore, the next sentence focuses on examples between these "high-density" and "low-density" options, and again refers to "low-density" - all of which would suddenly make less sense if we deleted the underlined sentence.

Choices A and B are already looking pretty weak, because they propose sentence deletion. Let's take a closer final look to be sure: Choice A criticizes the "excessive list of examples" for a term "that has already been defined." The term in question must be "low-density polyethylene," which has *not* been defined elsewhere, and the list of examples is no more excessive than the other lists of examples given in the paragraph for high-density polyethylene or the "in-between" examples in the final sentence. Let's eliminate Choice A.

Choice B claims the underlined sentence "interrupts the flow of the paragraph," but it's simply not true: the sentence finishes the prior thought about the "startlingly-wide range" of "high-density" and "low-density" polyethylene, before transitioning to the next sentence about the mid-range of density. So, let's eliminate Choice B.

Between the two "Keep" options, Choices C and D, we can see that Choice C refers to a "counterargument" within the paragraph. But, there's no *counterargument* - simply a spectrum of options from high-density to low-density. On that basis, let's eliminate Choice C and choose **the correct answer, Choice D**, which hits the nail on the head: the underlined sentence provides examples ("plastic wraps, tubing, and food storage") that are used as a key point for a comparison (the "spectrum" between "high-density" and "low-density" polyethylene).

Final Words

Remember, these questions can be easy if you treat them more like "Reading Comprehension" questions. Details in the answer choices are key, so slow down and use an Elimination-based strategy.

Don't be afraid of these types of questions! They are easy to recognize, and, although they often take a bit of extra time to answer, they can give you a nice break from the more "technical" grammar questions.

Adding or Removing Information
Practice Questions

The nature reserve, owned and operated by the Royal Society, is located in Minsmere, Suffolk. Intended primarily to aid in bird conservation, the environment is favorable for bird nesting and breeding, and includes a diverse variety of habitats such as marshes, grasslands, and forest areas. [1] Guests of the reserve can access a visitor center and spot many species of birds on an extensive network of footpaths and trails. [2]

1. At Point [1], the writer is considering adding the following sentence:

Over 15,000 curious bird-lovers travel to the reserve each month during birding season.

Should the writer make this addition here?

(A) Yes, because it provides both relevant information and a transition to the following sentence.

(B) Yes, because the sentence reinforces the paragraph's main point.

(C) No, because it blurs the paragraph's focus by adding irrelevant information.

(D) No, because it includes information that has already been stated elsewhere in the paragraph.

2. The writer is considering concluding this paragraph with the following sentence:

Many bird conservation sites around the world are experiencing funding problems due to lack of public support and private donations.

Should the writer make this addition here?

(A) Yes, because the sentence provides a satisfactory conclusion to the preceding paragraph.

(B) Yes, because the sentence provides evidence to support a relevant claim.

(C) No, because the sentence provides a level of detail that is inconsistent with the rest of the paragraph.

(D) No, because the sentence introduces irrelevant information to the paragraph.

Edgar Rice Burroughs, who lived from 1875 to 1950, was an American writer known for his works in the adventure and science-fiction genres. While many of his stories and characters have faded into obscurity over the past century, he will probably always remain in the public eye as the creator of Tarzan, the famous "man raised by apes" who became a cultural icon. [3] <u>Though many literary critics of the past and present have not exactly respected Burroughs' work for its stylistic merits</u>, there can be no doubt that his adventures have had a great impact upon popular culture at large, and on a smaller scale, upon the imaginations of his readers, both young and old. [4]

3. The writer is considering deleting the underlined portion of Sentence 3. Should the writer make this change?

(A) Yes, because it interrupts the flow of the paragraph.

(B) Yes, because it contains a negative tone that is not consistent with the rest of the paragraph.

(C) No, because it offers an effective and informative counterpoint to the rest of the sentence.

(D) No, because introduces a relevant supporting example.

4. The writer is considering concluding this paragraph with the following sentence:

> After a long and successful life, Burroughs' final resting place was his ranch in California, fittingly named "Tarzana," which has since become a residential neighborhood in the city of Los Angeles.

Should the writer make this addition here?

(A) Yes, because it provides evidence that supports a relevant claim within the paragraph.

(B) Yes, because it provides an interesting conclusion to Burroughs' life story that ties back to information presented earlier in the paragraph.

(C) No, because it fails to provide evidence for the paragraph's central claim.

(D) No, because it does not fit with the style and tone of the preceding paragraph.

[5] <u>The International Space Station ("ISS"), launched into orbit in 1998, has been continuously inhabited since November 2000</u>. This astonishing technological achievement represents one of humanity's largest and most ambitious leaps into outer space. Largely powered by massive solar arrays, the ISS provides a completely self-contained living environment, although its continued functioning depends upon regular supply runs and crew replacements. [6] If all goes well, the ISS is expected to serve until at least the year 2028.

5. The writer is considering deleting the underlined sentence. Should this sentence be kept or deleted?

(A) Kept, because it offers an effective introduction to the paragraph and defines a key acronym.

(B) Kept, because provides a relevant example that supports the paragraph's main point.

(C) Deleted, because it distracts from the primary focus of the paragraph.

(D) Deleted, because it does not provide an effective introduction to the paragraph.

6. At Point [6], the writer is considering adding the following sentence to the paragraph:

The station's research laboratories provide an invaluable environment for experiments in micro-gravity in fields that range from biology and physics to astronomy and meteorology.

Should the writer add this sentence here?

(A) Yes, because this sentence maintains the informal and conversational tone of the paragraph.

(B) Yes, because this sentence adds relevant information about the purpose of the ISS.

(C) No, because this sentence does not provide an effective counterargument to the previous sentence.

(D) No, because this sentence blurs the main focus of the paragraph with irrelevant information.

[7] In the United States, warrantless searches are restricted by the Fourth Amendment. This was partially a product of the British Empire's treatment of colonists, whose homes soldiers could search without warning for evidence of revolutionary activities. [8] <u>The First Amendment also protects an important freedom of citizens by guaranteeing freedom of religion, speech, and press.</u> During certain periods in history (for example, during wartime) or under specific circumstances (such as fears of domestic terrorism or foreign spying), there have been exceptions to this restriction. The topic of warrants and related search-and-seizure laws in the United States continues to be hotly debated in a new era of communications technology and social media.

7. The writer is considering adding the following sentence as an introduction to the paragraph:

A "warrantless search" is a search or seizure of personal property conducted without a documented court order to justify the intrusion on a citizen's privacy.

Should the writer add this sentence here?

(A) Yes, because this sentence provides a useful example that will be explored in the paragraph.

(B) Yes, because this sentence provides a useful definition of a key term explored in the paragraph.

(C) No, because this sentence provides an unnecessary amount of detail about a single term.

(D) No, because this sentence fails to introduce the main topic of the paragraph.

8. The writer is considering deleting the underlined sentence. Should this sentence be kept or deleted?

(A) Kept, because the sentence expands upon a relevant topic.

(B) Kept, because the sentence provides an additional supporting example for the paragraph.

(C) Deleted, because the sentence distracts from the main topic of the paragraph.

(D) Deleted, because the sentence undermines the primary claims of the paragraph.

Adding or Removing Information Answers

1. A
2. D
3. C
4. B
5. A
6. B
7. B
8. C

Adding or Removing Information Explanations

1. A - This question asks us to consider adding a new sentence in the middle of the paragraph. It's safe to eliminate Choice C, because the new information is not "irrelevant" - it provides visitor statistics for the nature reserve under discussion, and also transitions into the next sentence, which describes what visitors can do at the reserve. In fact, this is why Choice A is the best answer.

Choice B is not as good as Choice A, because the new sentence doesn't particularly reinforce the "main point" of the paragraph; rather it develops and transitions by adding new information. Choice D is also not good, because these visitor statistics are *new* information that has not been included elsewhere.

2. D - This sentence should *not* be added, because it adds completely new information about *other* bird reserves and their funding problems; this opens an entirely new line of reasoning and fails to conclude the paragraph, which has been focused on a single nature reserve - and no mention of funding or finances has been raised until this point. This eliminates Choices A and B. Furthermore, Choice C can be eliminated: the problem is that the sentence veers off-topic, failing to effectively conclude the paragraph; furthermore, there's no problem with the "level of detail" in the new sentence, because the it maintains a similar level of detail to the rest of the paragraph.

3. C - Should we delete this portion of the sentence? As we know, the details of our answer choices will make a major difference to our final selection. Let's eliminate Choice B: this portion of the sentence does have some "negatives," but they aren't out of place in a paragraph that analyzes both the ups and downs of Burroughs' writing and career. We can also eliminate Choice D, because this portion of the sentence doesn't contain any specific "example."

Our final issue is whether this portion of the sentence "interrupts the flow of the paragraph" [delete] or "offers an effective and informative counterpoint" [keep] to the sentence. Note that this underlined portion is certainly "informative," since it provides new information about how critics saw Burroughs in his own time. Furthermore, the underlined portion offers an effective *negative counterpoint* to the rest of the sentence, which goes on to describes the *positive* impact of Burroughs' writing on culture and imagination. This underlined portion doesn't disturb the flow of the paragraph; instead it adds relevant information and an interesting counterpoint. Therefore, Choice C is better than Choice A.

4. B - Will this new sentence provide an effective conclusion to the paragraph? Personally, my instincts say "yes," because the focus of the new sentence remains on relevant topics: Burroughs, his life, career, impact, and his final resting place. Still, let's examine our choices. I don't feel that Choice A is the best option, because this sentence provides *new* information, not "supporting evidence" for any particular claim within the paragraph. Choice D seems wrong - the "style and tone" of the new sentence are closely matched to the main paragraph (a "book report" type of tone that is informative, fairly neutral and academic).

Next, I'll eliminate Choice C - not only because I'd rather add the sentence than remove it, but also because I think Choice B is a much better answer when you look at the details: this new sentence *does* provide "an interesting conclusion" to Burroughs' life that also ties back to previous information (e.g. that Burroughs created Tarzan, and then named his ranch "Tarzana" before it became a neighborhood in Los Angeles.)

5. A - Right off the bat, I feel strongly that this sentence should *not* be deleted. First of all, it provides a perfect introduction to the paragraph. Secondly, it defines the key acronym "ISS" - and the underlined sentence is the only place where this abbreviation is defined, so if we remove it, the whole paragraph becomes more difficult to understand. Finally, the next sentence begins with "this astonishing technological achievement," which would come out of nowhere and would have no **Pronoun-Antecedent Clarity** (Lesson 4) without the presence of the first sentence. All of this points me directly towards the correct answer, Choice A, and away from Choices B, C, and D.

6. B - This sentence almost certainly belongs amid the rest of this paragraph, which provides an overview of the International Space Station. The new sentence adds additional information about the *purpose* of the ISS and what sort of research is done aboard it. Let's eliminate Choice D, since the new information *is* relevant. Also, Choice C doesn't make sense, because there's no particular reason to introduce a "counterargument" within a purely informative paragraph.

Choice A is wrong, since neither the new sentence nor the existing paragraph have an "informal" or "conversational" tone - the tone is more "informative" or "academic." This leaves Choice B as the correct answer, and indeed, "relevant information" about "the purpose of the ISS" is exactly what makes the new sentence a valuable addition to the paragraph.

7. B - Should we add this sentence as an introduction to the paragraph? There's a very good reason to do so: this new sentence clearly defines "warrantless searches," a key term that readers may be unfamiliar with that also forms a core idea of the paragraph. That's what makes Choice B the correct answer.

Choice A isn't so good; even though it adds the new introductory sentence, it's for the wrong reasons (the new introduction provides a *definition*, not an *example*). Choice C is wrong, because the level of detail in the new sentence is neither unnecessary nor dissimilar to that of the paragraph, and Choice D is wrong, because this new sentence does an excellent job of introducing the upcoming paragraph with a clear definition of a key term.

8. C - Should the underlined sentence be deleted? Look carefully and you'll notice that the underlined sentence introduces a new concept (the *First* Amendment), which is different from what is currently under discussion (the *Fourth* Amendment). We should probably delete the underlined sentence. It's not an "additional supporting topic" (Choice B) but rather a complete diversion into a different set of laws and rules. The underlined sentence also doesn't "expand upon a relevant topic" (Choice A) since it's veering far off topic to a completely-different amendment.

When it comes to choosing between our two remaining "Delete" answers, the problem isn't that this sentence "undermines" the claims of the sentence (Choice D), but that it blurs and confuses the central focus on warrantless searches. That makes Choice C the correct answer.

LESSON 16
Moving Sentences & Paragraphs

What are "Moving Sentences & Paragraphs" Questions?

Now we move on to the third and final subcategory of **Objective Questions** (introduced in Lesson 14).

These new types of questions are called **Moving Sentences & Paragraphs**. They ask you to consider moving a particular sentence (or paragraph) to a different spot in the passage.

Although the concept is easy to explain and identify, these remain some of my least-favorite questions to do *as a test-taker*. Why? Even in the best of circumstances, they are time-consuming and include a lot of information to consider - there is NO "quick and easy" way to confidently and consistently answer these questions correctly.

In other words, compared to most other types of grammar questions, these take far longer to answer correctly. Still, there's no use burying our heads in the sand. Let's take a careful look at Moving Sentences and Paragraphs.

How to Recognize Moving Sentences & Paragraphs

"Moving Sentences and Paragraphs" have a very distinctive format for both the questions and their answer choices.

Here's some good news: the style of these questions for both the SAT and ACT tests is virtually identical. If you can recognize them on one test, it's quite simple to find them on the other test as well.

Remember, these questions are all about *moving* an existing sentence or paragraph elsewhere. Or, you may be adding a new sentence, but selecting *where* should it go in the passage.

The questions are quite distinctive - and we'll take a look at them in a second - but their *most* instantly-recognizable feature is their *answer choices*.

If you're moving a single sentence within a paragraph, the answer choices look something like this:

> (A) where it is now.
> (B) before sentence 1.
> (C) after sentence 3.
> (D) after sentence 6.

If you're moving an entire paragraph to a new location within the passage, then the answer choices will look something like this:

> (A) where it is now.
> (B) after paragraph 1.
> (C) after paragraph 2.
> (D) after paragraph 4.

You may also be given the opportunity to move a sentence to a new spot throughout the *passage*, not just within a single *paragraph*, in which case the answer choice variations will look something like this:

> (A) Point A in paragraph 1.
> (B) Point B in paragraph 2.
> (C) Point C in paragraph 3.
> **(D)** Point D in paragraph 4.

Variations and Styles of Question

Both the SAT and ACT tests share two *types* of "Moving Sentences & Paragraphs" questions:

Type 1: Move an *existing* sentence (or paragraph) to another location.
Type 2: Add a *new* sentence - but *where* will it be added?

Notice that Type 2 is noticeably different from **Adding or Removing Sentences** questions (Lesson 15), because you are not given a *choice* of whether or not to include the new sentence. Instead, the sentence *will* be added no matter what, and you just decide *where* it belongs. All of these type of questions are about the *placement* of information in the paragraph or passage.

As I've mentioned earlier, these questions are virtually identical between the SAT & ACT tests. In fact, I was hard-pressed to find any significant differences in my research.

Here are the exact phrasings the SAT and ACT tests use for these questions. You don't need to memorize these lists, but it's good to be familiar with the question formats:

SAT Questions

SAT Type 1 ("Moving") Questions

- To make this paragraph most logical, Sentence X should be placed...

- For the sake of logic and cohesion of the paragraph, Sentence X should be placed...

- Think about the previous passage as a whole as you answer question #. To make the passage most logical, Paragraph X should be placed...

SAT Type 2 ("Adding") Questions

- The writer wants to add the following sentence to the paragraph: [New Sentence.] The best placement for this sentence is...

- Where is the most logical place in this paragraph to add the following sentence? [New Sentence.]

- To improve the cohesion and flow of this paragraph, the writer wants to add the following sentence. [New Sentence.] The sentence would most logically be placed...

ACT Questions

ACT Type 1 ("Moving") Questions

- For the sake of logic and cohesion, the best placement for [Sentence / Paragraph X] would be...

ACT Type 2 ("Adding") Questions

- Question # asks about the preceding passage as a whole. The writer wants to add the following sentence to the essay: [New Sentence.] This sentence would most logically be placed at...

- The writer wants to add the following sentence to the paragraph: [New Sentence.] The sentence would most logically be placed at...

Frequency of Appearance

In terms of frequency, these questions show up as an average of 4% of all Grammar-section questions on both the SAT and the ACT, or "1 per 25 questions." So, they make a small, but important, contribution to your score.

The ACT has a minimum of 2 "Moving Sentences & Paragraphs" per 75 questions, or about 3% of all questions. It has a maximum of 5 per 75 questions, almost 7%. As mentioned, the average is 4%.

The SAT has a minimum of 1 "Moving Sentences & Paragraphs" per 44 questions, or about 2%. There is a max of 3 questions, which is about 7%. Again, the average is 4%.

Essential Strategies for Moving Sentences & Paragraphs

The number-one strategy on these questions is *patience*. PATIENCE! If you think you'll be able to quickly identify the right answer 100% of the time, you are *very* wrong. Even the most experienced tutors require extra time to analyze the possibilities, eliminate answer choices, and draw a confident conclusion. Never rush. You don't have some special skill or intuition that allows you to get these questions right faster than everyone else - I *promise*. Because no one does.

I like to start by analyzing the sentence that is being moved. Often I break that sentence down into two halves: "how it starts" and then "where it goes next." Then I write a short summary of each half. In other words, I split the sentence into two halves and create a simple written summary of each half. Use this opportunity to look for clues (keywords, a timeline, transition words, etc) that may help explain where the sentence should (or should *not*) go.

The next step is to skim and analyze the entire paragraph for good places to put the sentence, while eliminating a few of the obviously wrong answers. In this step, I'm trying to *predict* where the sentence *might* go, while I eliminate a few bad answer choices along the way.

The only thing I can do next is to try moving the sentence to each of the remaining possible locations. Make sure that, wherever you put it, the end of the previous sentence leads into the moved sentence, and that the start of the *next* sentence after it is a good followup to the moved sentence.

One of the most common mistakes I see students make is rushing and failing to give enough *context* - they don't consider the entire paragraph, only small portions of it. It's not unusual to have to reread the entire paragraph, from the first word to the last word, to fully grasp the context. I have had many good students express shock when they realize "Oh, wow, I really needed to go back *that far* and re-read the whole darn thing?"

A Note on Time Management

Because of the necessary time commitment, it's wise to leave Moving Sentences & Paragraphs questions for *last* on your timed tests. They are a *low* percentage of points (about 4% of your score), but a *high* consumption of your time (often taking 3x-5x longer than a typical grammar question). Circle back around to these questions when you are finished with all the other questions in the section.

Let's try out these strategies on the following Pretest question...

Think about the paragraph below as you answer the following question:

[1] The Japanese battleship *Nagato* was built in 1920 as the most powerful capital ship in the Imperial Japanese Navy. [2] Her earliest noteworthy service was carrying supplies for the survivors of the Great Kanto earthquake in 1923. [3] *Nagato* then participated in the Second Sino-Japanese War of 1937. [4] Now, the wreck of the *Nagato* is considered one of the top ten shipwreck-diving spots in the world. [5] She remained in service during World War 2 and was involved in the surprise attack on Pearl Harbor as the flagship of Admiral Isoroku Yamamoto. [6] Impressively, *Nagato* was the only Japanese battleship to survive the entirety of World War 2. [7] In 1946, the massive vessel was destroyed (with no sailors on board) in the American nuclear weapons tests named "Operation Crossroads" held at Bikini Atoll.

1. To make this paragraph most logical, sentence 4 should be placed

   (A) where it is now.

   (B) before sentence 1.

   (C) after sentence 5.

   (D) after sentence 7.

Explanation: Luckily, this question gives us a relatively easy example of a "Moving Sentences & Paragraphs" question. What makes it easy? Well, the clear sequence of years and events in a historical timeline makes our job of re-positioning the sentence much easier. It's logical to follow a timeline.

Let's consider the sentence we're moving, sentence 4:

> "Now, the wreck of the *Nagato* is considered one of the top ten shipwreck diving spots in the world."

This sentence starts with a first half, "Now." This is indicates that it comes *after* some other information from the past, not before. It implies a timeline. It finishes with a second half that tells us the *Nagato* is now a shipwreck. That gives us more context: we should look for a spot in the paragraph *after* the ship has been sunk or destroyed.

Considering our options, Choice B makes very little sense. Putting this sentence at the very beginning of the paragraph would ruin destroy the timeline by putting the sinking of the ship as the *first* event of the story. Choice A isn't great either: it interrupts two periods of operational service, during two separate wars, to discuss the wreck of the ship. The sequence is illogical.

What about Choice C? Nope - it's illogical - and goes against the timeline - to follow up a description of the "wreck" of the *Nagato* with the sentence about "surviving" all of World War 2.

That leaves Choice D as the best answer. As the last sentence of the paragraph, it creates an effective timeline and concluding sentence that "ends the life" of the ship. It's also logical to follow up on the ship's destruction in sentence 7 with a description of its new status as a popular diving attraction.

Moving Sentences & Paragraphs Quick References

- These questions are easy to recognize. The questions are distinctive on their own, but the answer choices in particular make this type of question very easy to spot at a glance.

- They are a low percentage of questions, but they are very time-consuming. Leave them for last, but don't forget about them.

- There's no quick and dirty strategy that always works. It takes a lot of patience, analysis, and elimination, even for pro tutors. You may have to test the sentence in each of the four possible locations.

- My favorite strategy is to break the sentence in half and write a quick summary of both the first half and second half. This helps me make an educated decision about where the sentence belongs.

- Even experienced tutors don't love these questions. Don't expect perfection from yourself, and don't get frustrated. Just stay *patient* and practice as many of these as you can find.

Final Thoughts

These questions are usually very time-consuming, and they aren't easy either. As a tutor, I see a lot of frustration around these question types. Many students express the feeling that they are "taking too long" to answer them. This is probably what causes so many students to rush through them, not considering and analyzing all the available options, and the contents of the entire paragraph itself.

It's unfortunately true that there is no super-secret strategy to ace 100% of these Moving Sentences & Paragraphs questions. Patient analysis and practice is the only way. Stay calm and leave them for last. At least these questions are easy to identify and avoid until the time is right to tackle them!

Moving Sentences & Paragraphs
Practice Questions

[1] Laurence Olivier, born in 1907, was a respected English actor and director who rose to become one of the most famous men in cinema and stagecraft. [2] Although his family had no connections to the theater, Olivier studied at a drama school in London as a boy and achieved his first success in the theater in his early 20s. [3] By the 1940s, he was an established star, and co-directed at the Old Vic, one of the most important theaters in London. [4] His final major role was as King Lear, and critics glowed over his realistic, natural portrayal of the grieving old king. [5] Some of his most famous roles were as Shakespearean leads, but he displayed a great versatility in portraying a wide variety of characters over the course of his career. [6] For his vast critical and popular success, Olivier was honored with a knighthood and other national decorations during his lifetime. [7] He died at the age of 82 after a prolonged period of ill health, although he continued to work throughout his illnesses.

1. To make this paragraph most logical, sentence 4 should be placed

    (A) where it is now.
    (B) after sentence 1.
    (C) after sentence 5.
    (D) after sentence 7.

[1] "Techno" is a form of electronic dance music that was pioneered in Detroit, Michigan in the mid-1980s. [2] The style and sounds of Techno emerged as a response to a variety of stimuli and pressures. [3] For one thing, the young musicians who created this style often had little disposable income with which to purchase expensive music gear, which is part of the reason for the stripped-down, minimal style of early techno. [4] Furthermore, the gear itself had many limitations. [5] For example, many of the drum machines and synthesizers only had enough "memory" to program short, repeating sections of music called "loops." [6] Most early techno tracks were built out of several electronic loops played over each other; traditionally, a drum machine, bass synthesizer, and lead synthesizer would form the core of the sound. [7] A third major influence was the sound of the city of Detroit itself. [8] Known for its industrial character and filled with machinery, Detroit can be seen in many ways as a physical embodiment of the "Techno sound."

2. To make this paragraph most logical, sentence 5 should be placed

    (A) where it is now.
    (B) after sentence 1.
    (C) after sentence 3.
    (D) after sentence 6.

[1] The comics simply would not be the same without Stan Lee. [2] Born in 1922, Lee was a comic book author, editor, and publisher who rose to lead industry juggernaut Marvel Comics for twenty years. [3] His cultural impact was enormous: he co-created famous superheroes such as Spider-Man and the X-Men, forced needed change upon the outdated regulations of the Comics Code Authority, and helped revolutionize the very essence and style of modern comic books. [4] Known as a generous, creative soul and revered by comic fans around the world, Stan Lee never failed to receive thunderous applause at all of his public appearances. [5] Although the world lost Stan Lee in 2018, he will never be forgotten as long as his colorful heroes still spring off the silver screen and the printed page.

3. The writer wants to add the following sentence to the paragraph:

> In his later years, blockbuster movies based on his characters hit the theaters, and Lee was ever-popular for the cameo roles he made in many of these films.

The best placement for this sentence is

(A) after sentence 1.

(B) after sentence 2.

(C) after sentence 3.

(D) after sentence 5.

[1] The act of bending one knee to the ground is properly called "genuflecting," though in conversation it may be called simply "kneeling." [2] Traditionally considered a sign of deepest respect, this gesture is common in many cultures, religions, and ceremonies around the world and throughout history. [3] Alexander the Great was known for requiring genuflection in his court etiquette, and in medieval Europe, commoners were typically required to genuflect before kings and other high-ranking members of the noble class. [4] However, elderly people, pregnant women, or people in poor physical condition are often exempted from mandatory genuflection. [5] Instances of genuflecting in the modern era are seen in the traditional marriage proposal, in the Roman Catholic Church, and in presentations of a folded flag to the family members of a fallen veteran. [6] A failure to genuflect at the required moment may be interpreted as a sign of disrespect and dishonor.

4.   To make this paragraph most logical, sentence 4 should be placed

   (A) where it is now.
   (B) after sentence 1.
   (C) after sentence 5.
   (D) after sentence 6.

A list of the richest Americans in history will be filled largely with self-made entrepreneurs, although there will also be some appearances from heirs and heiresses to family fortunes. And, because of America's preeminence among the world's economy, the richest members of American society are frequently among the richest men and women in the entire world. [A] John D. Rockefeller may have been the wealthiest American in history by percentage of the nation's total wealth (or "GDP") in his time. [B] His staggering fortune may have been worth as much as 2% of the entire country's national production at the time. [C] In 2018, Jeff Bezos, founder of Amazon.com, became the richest man in modern history, with an eye-popping net worth estimated at over 150 billion dollars. If there's one major lesson the list can teach, it's that if you want to reach the pinnacle of financial fortunes, it pays to either create an industry yourself, or to dominate one that already exists. [D]

5.   The writer wants to add the following sentence to the paragraph:

> Other noteworthy "richest Americans" include Andrew Carnegie, Cornelius Vanderbilt, Bill Gates, and Henry Ford.

The sentence would most logically be placed at:

(A) Point A.
(B) Point B.
(C) Point C.
(D) Point D.

[1] The role of a navel architect is to handle the engineering and design of marine vessels and structures. [2] This can include working on a range of projects, from deep-sea oil platforms to the smallest of sailboats. [3] A seagoing vessel may be described as having a "fair" shape, which, in essence, means a shape that is "right for the job." [4] Required knowledge for a professional naval architect includes hydrodynamics, materials properties, and construction techniques. [5] Somewhere between an art and a science, the field of naval architecture still finds it difficult to quantify its principles into simple rules. [6] Given the continued importance of well-built vessels for both industrial and pleasure purposes, and the lack of well-quantified design principles, it seems likely that job prospects for talented young naval architects will remain relatively strong.

6.   For the sake of logic and cohesion, the best placement for Sentence 3 would be

   (A) after sentence 1.
   (B) after sentence 5.
   (C) after sentence 6.
   (D) where is is now.

Moving Sentences & Paragraphs Answers

1. C
2. A
3. C
4. D
5. C
6. B

Moving Sentences & Paragraphs Explanations

1. C - It's usually best to start with a close look at the sentence we're moving. Sentence 4 mentions Olivier's "final role." Since it's his "final role," it makes the most logical sense to put this sentence near the end of the paragraph, somewhere close to the end of his life and career. That eliminates Choice B, which would put this "end of career" sentence near the very beginning of the paragraph, before Olivier has even started studying to become an actor. Choice A, "where it is now," also seems a bit premature: the paragraph hasn't yet touched upon the actor's roles in the prime of his career, so the coverage of his "final role" is still arriving too early.

On the other hand, waiting until *after* Olivier's death to cover his final role makes less logical sense than including that information in chronological sequence. In other words, Choice C makes the most sense chronologically: first we'll cover his most famous roles in the middle of his career, then mention and explore his "final role" as King Lear, before moving onto the awards he won for "his life's work" and his death as a conclusion to the timeline. This also provides a stronger, closer link between "critics [glowing]" over his portrayal of King Lear and his "vast critical and popular success."

2. A - As usual, let's examine the sentence we're moving. Sentence 5 begins with the transition words "For example," and then mentions the limited memory of the synthesizers and drum machines before introducing a new key term, "loops." These clues give us quite a lot to work with. First of all, "for example" seems to provide a strong connection back to the previous sentence about the "limitations" of the "gear itself." Does our current sentence explore limitations of the music gear? Yes, that's exactly what it does: describing the "limited memory" of the electronic instruments would match perfectly.

Now, let's look at the key term, "loops." Notice that our Sentence 5 introduces the term in quotation marks, and is the first place in the paragraph that this term has been used or defined. The following Sentence 6 then elaborates further on the use of loops in Techno music production, *without* the quote marks. This is a clue that Sentence 5 (where the term is explained) should come *before* Sentence 6 (where the term is used as if it should already be familiar to the reader). For these reasons, it's best to leave the sentence where it is now.

3. C - Let's start by exploring the sentence we're moving. In this case, we've been given a brand-new sentence, and we must decide *where* in the paragraph it would best fit. The new sentence mentions Lee's "later years" and movies "based on his characters." Right away, we can safely assume this sentence will fit better near the *end* of the timeline than at the beginning. On this basis, we can easily eliminate Choices A and B. However, placing it after sentence 5 is *too* late in the paragraph, because now Lee's life and career have already ended. Our sentence fits best after sentence 3, where it ties in as a followup example of the impact of his career and his popularity, before leading into more descriptions of his popular acclaim and finally, his death.

4. D - As usual, let's start by examining the sentence we're moving. Sentence 4 begins with a useful transition word, "however," before introducing a group of people who are exempt from "mandatory genuflection." So, here's a possible approach to the question: start by looking for sentences in the paragraph that describe "mandatory" acts of genuflection.

Actually, "where it is now" *does* provide an example of mandatory genuflection, in the court of Alexander the Great, and also for the nobles of Medieval Europe. However, the **Verb Tenses** (Lesson 2) show a disconnect. Our sentence focuses on the *present tense*, but those examples are firmly placed in the *past*.

Instead, take a look at sentence 6: "A failure to genuflect at the *required* moment..." Notice that this is another case of "mandatory genuflection" because of the word "required." Could our sentence fit after sentence 6? Yes, indeed: Now the two sentences combine - both in present tense, conveniently - to inform us that it's crucial to genuflect at the proper moment; *however*, those people who are physically unable to do so may form an exception to this rule.

5. C - Let's take a close look at the sentence we're moving. It begins with the phrase "*other* noteworthy 'richest Americans',*" which provides a clear link to the topic of the sentence before it. Then it includes a simple list of four names, without any further explanation of their accomplishments. This seems like a supplemental sentence that could be the follow up to a description of a specific "richest American."

That really only leaves two possibilities, because the only other "richest Americans" mentioned in the paragraph are John D. Rockefeller and Jeff Bezos. However, there is no answer choice giving us the option to follow Bezos's example directly with the sentence we're moving. Furthermore, the list of names in our sentence is composed entirely of *historical* "rich" figures, so it makes perfect sense to choose Point C, where our sentence will provide a followup to the in-depth description of the historical figure and legendary "rich American" John D. Rockefeller. The final sentence of this paragraph is already an effective conclusion ("if there's one lesson the list can teach..."), which is another good reason *not* to place the new sentence after it and to favor Choice C over Choice D.

6. B - Let's take a close look at the sentence we're moving. The main focus of the sentence is on a "fair" shape, which (somewhat circularly) means a "good" shape, according to the paragraph. A bit confusing, perhaps, but it also seems that the author's intention is to show the reader that it's difficult to clearly define exactly what a "fair shape" is. In that case, the sentence would fit perfectly after sentence 5, which admits that it is "difficult to quantify" exactly what good naval design looks like, and fits with the idea that the field is "both *art* and science."

LESSON 17
Idioms & Prepositions

Introduction

Here we are - the final lesson of this book. By this point you should understand and recognize a vast amount of rules and common grammar situations. What you know from the first sixteen chapters would be enough to earn you a stellar score on the SAT or ACT Grammar section - quite possibly in the top 1% of test-takers around the world.

I highly recommend you master the first sixteen rules before you worry about this final chapter. As you will soon see, the rules of **Idioms & Prepositions** are unpredictable, frustrating, and impossible to fully prepare for.

Compared to this lesson, the other sixteen are far more logical - and more useful towards a high SAT & ACT score. So be sure you've mastered the other sixteen rules first and left this lesson for last.

What are "Idioms?"

Let's start with a definition of the word "Idiom":

> An idiom is a group of words that have a specific meaning - which is established by common usage - that can *not* be understood by analyzing the individual words one at a time.

In other words, an idiom is "a phrase we say the way we say it, because that's the way we say it." Pretty circular reasoning, but that's what happens when a phrase develops its own unique meaning through common usage over time.

For example, "it's raining cats and dogs" is an example of a well-known idiom. Obviously it doesn't *literally* have anything to do with the animals "cats and dogs"; it's just a phrase we've established in English, through common usage, to mean "it's raining *very hard*."

Every language has its own idioms. These are often challenging to learn if it's not your first language. If a French exchange student asked you to explain exactly *why* "raining cats and dogs" means "it's raining very hard," then you might realize that there's no obvious explanation - it's just "the way we say it," or "that's just what it means."

Even worse, if you make a change to the idiom - no matter how small - it usually won't work any more. Test for yourself: "it's raining horses and goats"? Even a subtle change will ruin the idiom: "It's raining dogs and cats?" Try saying it out loud - it will sound "weird" to you because the familiar, established order of the phrase has been reversed. This is another reason these idioms are so difficult for most people to learn in a foreign language.

More Examples of Idioms

Here are a few more common idioms.

"Beat around the bush" = Avoid saying what you mean

"Get out of hand" = Get out of control

"Hit the sack" = Go to sleep

"Under the weather" = Sick

There are hundreds more. Your goal should not be to memorize them, but to start becoming aware of them. Mastery of idioms comes through experience - typically, through reading and conversation.

Prepositions: A Quick Review

Now, before we go further on Idioms, it may be helpful to head back to the Prelesson A on **Parts of Speech**, but for now I'll summarize the key information about that part of speech we call *prepositions*.

Prepositions are "position" words. To name a few examples, these are words like:

- on	- above	- from
- under	- below	- behind
- around	- in	- among
- between	- of	- with

You may also recall the "Squirrel Test" for prepositions:

The squirrel runs *up* the tree.

The squirrel runs *behind* the tree.

The squirrel runs *[preposition]* the tree.

How do Idioms and Prepositions Relate?

So you may be thinking, "Great, I understood prepositions already, but what do those have to do with *Idioms*?" The connection may not be clear.

However, many idioms are based on specific prepositions. For example, consider the idiom "*look it up* in a dictionary." Notice the preposition *up*, which forms an essential part of the idiomatic phrase. Now imagine replacing *up* with *down*: "look it *down* in a dictionary."

The idiom doesn't work anymore, right? But why is that? I mean, there's no logic to it: you don't look *upwards* at anything when you use a dictionary. If anything, you look more *downwards* at the pages of the book. Still, you have to say "look it *up*" or the idiom doesn't sound right.

See, that's why Idioms questions are so frustrating to teach. There's almost never any *logical* reason for them to be said the way they're said… they just *are*. Using the wrong preposition (like "down" instead of "up") may completely invalidate the meaning of the idiom.

In other cases, using one preposition with the idiom may have one meaning, but using a different preposition may create an entirely different meaning.

For example, if you say a house is *on* fire, that means it's aflame. If you say a house is *with* fire, it sounds wrong - we just don't say it like that. The phrase "*with* fire" just isn't a "thing."

But wait - what if we change the preposition to "the house is *under* fire"? That has a completely different meaning - the idiom "under fire" means that the house *is being shot at*.

All we've done is tried changing out a few different prepositions in the same idiomatic phrase, but we've created dramatically different meanings. One preposition means one thing ("*on* fire" = "aflame"), one means nothing ("*with* fire" = not how we say it), and a third means something else entirely ("*under* fire" = "being shot at").

I'm sure you can already start to see how these Idioms & Prepositions can get a *little annoying* on a standardized test…

Recognizing Idioms & Prepositions Questions

It can be tough to know when you're dealing with an Idioms & Prepositions question. One possible approach is to master the first sixteen grammar rules, and then if the question doesn't fit into one of those sixteen rules, it may be an idiom.

Even better: if the answer choices are playing with prepositions (for example, swapping the words *for*, *into*, *around* and *on*) then it is probably an Idioms & Prepositions question. But, not all idioms are based on prepositions - although many are.

Sometimes, when I know the right answer to a grammar question, but can't come up with a good *logical* explanation for it - and this is *very* rare, probably less than 1 in 200 questions - I will just throw my hands up and declare it an "idiom": the answer is just the answer because "that's how we say it."

Examples of Idioms & Prepositions Questions

Below, I've included a partial list of actual Idioms and Prepositions questions and answer choices that I've found on real SAT and ACT tests. You do NOT need to memorize this list - I just want you to browse through some examples. Also, I'll warn you now: expect this list to seem "random." Idioms are a pretty bizarre topic with a huge variety.

I've *italicized* many of the prepositions in these idioms to call your attention to them.

- months *of* witnessing / months as if witnessing / months when witnessing / months then witnessing

- *in* this regard / *in* which this regard / ones that / which

- chances *of* surviving / chances *to* survive

- famous *for* making / famous when he would make / famous as he made / famous and made

- stripped away all *in* its path / stripped away all *on* its path

- one side *of* them / their one side

- far better / farther, better / far more of a better / a far, better

- had gone *out of* style / had went *out of* style / had went *from* style / had gone *from* style

- cuts crossed / cut *through*

- would *of* / would have

- age-old / aging or older / old age / aging old

- serves to be / serves as / serves like / serves for

- read *into* / read *about* / read *upon* / read *for*

- practice *by* which / practice *at* which / practice *from* which / practice so that

- means *through* / means *of* / means *from*

- in order *to* / in order *for*

- go so far / go as far / go as far and / go so far as

- both *of* which / *of* which both / both *of* them / both

- subject *to* / subjected *to* / subjected *from* / subject *for*

Frequency of Appearance

Although these questions can be frustrating, there's a silver lining: they are relatively uncommon.

On the SAT, you will only see about 1 Idiom question per 44-question Grammar test. That's less than 3% of your entire score. Sometimes, an SAT test won't have a single Idioms question on it. At a maximum, I have seen 3 of them on a single SAT - but it's rare to have so many.

On the ACT, these questions are only slightly more common. The average is about 4 Idioms questions per 75-question Grammar test, or about 5% of your score. In my research I saw a minimum of 3 Idioms questions per ACT, and a maximum of 5.

Since it's impossible to fully prepare for these questions, it's definitely good news that they are one of the least-common question types on both the SAT & the ACT grammar tests.

Essential Strategies for Idioms & Prepositions

I'm going to be completely honest - there's no way to be 100% prepared for these Idioms questions. There are too many and their "rules" are just too random and illogical. So what can you do to improve your chances?

First of all, read more! The more time you spend reading, the more familiar you'll be with the appearance and sound of common Idioms and Prepositions (plus this will help your SAT & ACT Reading-section scores).

You can also be more active: search for lists of idioms on Google, print them off, hand-make flashcards, or take written notes. Make your own lists of surprising idioms you've never seen before and what they mean. You can even start working these new Idioms into your own writing. Focus particularly on Idioms that depend on specific prepositions.

Review your **Parts of Speech** (Prelesson A) and know exactly how to recognize *prepositions*, so you can immediately notice when the answer choices to a Grammar question are playing around with prepositions.

In the bigger picture, remember to leave this entire topic for LAST. Only bother with Idioms when you're already 100% in control of every other rule in this book. In fact, you should be scoring an average of 95%+ accuracy on your SAT or ACT Grammar tests before you even *consider* worrying about Idioms. These are the single-most unpredictable questions on the grammar tests. While every other topic can be completely prepared for and mastered, the Idioms & Prepositions questions are vastly more unpredictable, and not subject to the normal, logical rules of grammar.

Let's try out one of our Pretest questions...

> During his college interview, Jose was <u>confused by</u> several questions,
> including one about his favorite types of animals, and another that asked,
> "if you were a flavor of ice cream, what flavor would you be?"
>
> (A) [NO CHANGE]
> (B) confused at
> (C) confused with
> (D) confused for

Explanation: We can tell that this is probably a Prepositions and Idioms question by a quick glance at the answer choices. Notice that they all change the preposition being used - from *by* to *at*, *with* or *for*. This is exactly how most Idioms & Prepositions answer choices will appear.

It's great that we've recognized the question type, but from here, it just comes down to our knowledge, experience, and intuition. **The answer is Choice A**, No Change, because "confused by" is just the way we say this phrase in English. You may say you're "confused *by* the question," but never "confused *at* the question," for example.

Hopefully, Choice A "sounds right" to you - because there's no deeper explanation than that. And that's an Idioms question for you!

Idioms & Prepositions Quick Reference

- Master all other 16 Rules of Grammar first. Don't even bother to study Idioms until you can consistently hit 95%+ accuracy on any SAT or ACT Grammar section.

- Read more. Keep an eye out for Idioms in your reading.

- If you're really ambitious and have the other rules locked down, search up a list of English idioms on Google. Make handwritten notes or flashcards for idioms that are new to you.

- Start becoming aware of Idioms in your own writing, reading, and conversations. Try to use more of them in your own essays and writing assignments.

- Review *prepositions*. Recognize this **Part of Speech** (Prelesson A) on sight. When the answer choices play with different prepositions, this is a tip-off that the topic is probably Idioms.

- Don't worry if you're not getting these questions 100% correct. Focus on what *is* more under your control: the other 16 Rules of Grammar.

Let's try our luck on one more Pretest question...

Darla's apartment was often difficult to fall asleep in, because it was <u>adjacent with</u> a room of rowdy party animals who loved to stay up late and blast their stereo system at maximum volume.

(A) [NO CHANGE]

(B) adjacent to

(C) adjacent at

(D) adjacent into

Explanation: Just like our previous question, we can tell it's probably an Idioms & Prepositions question because the four answer choices all play with different prepositions: *with*, *to*, *at*, and *into*. From here's just a matter of experience, intuition, and "what sounds right." The correct answer is **Choice B**, "adjacent to" - not for any specific reason, just because the preposition "to" is what we pair with the word "adjacent" in English. And that's just the way it is!

Idioms & Prepositions
Practice Questions

1. India - a diverse country containing a mix of cultures and customs within its borders - is <u>famous in</u> its warm hospitality, its spicy rice dishes, and its embrace of many different spiritualities.

   (A) [NO CHANGE]
   (B) famous to
   (C) famous for
   (D) famous on

2. James decide to become a mechanic, for he had always been <u>curious on</u> the inner workings of machinery and engines.

   (A) [NO CHANGE]
   (B) curious for
   (C) curious into
   (D) curious about

3. Though most domesticated dogs are not <u>capable of</u> caring for themselves for extended periods of time, in some cities there are packs of roaming feral dogs who are able to scavenge and survive on their own without any human support whatsoever.

   (A) [NO CHANGE]
   (B) capable to
   (C) capable in
   (D) capable with

4. Galileo Galilei was a profound thinker, influential in many fields, but particularly known for his theories and research in astronomy, and for his <u>rebellion from</u> religious authority through his insightful assertion that the Earth revolved around the Sun.

   (A) [NO CHANGE]
   (B) rebellion against
   (C) rebellion under
   (D) rebellion from

5. Although visiting relatives in another city can be fun, you must be careful not to <u>impose on</u> their hospitality for too long, lest you become a burden.

(A) [NO CHANGE]

(B) impose to

(C) impose for

(D) impose around

6. "Asymmetrical warfare" is another name for guerrilla-style tactics, when a smaller force must engage a much larger <u>force to</u> battle.

(A) [NO CHANGE]

(B) force for

(C) force in

(D) force with

7. Before a recording artist <u>enters through</u> a contract with a record label, he or she should have the deal examined by at least one independent lawyer with expertise in the fields of entertainment and contract law.

(A) [NO CHANGE]

(B) enters by

(C) enters towards

(D) enters into

8. Austin, Texas is <u>regarded in</u> some residents and music journalists as "the Live Music Capital of the World," although one must admit that there are many other cities that could contend for the honor.

(A) [NO CHANGE]

(B) regarded by

(C) regarded between

(D) regarded upon

9. <u>In keeping with</u> the era of its design, the old hotel maintains a complete set of antique furnishings, and all the art on its walls are original works.

(A) [NO CHANGE]

(B) As keeping to

(C) By keeping with

(D) In keeping to

10. Leonardo da Vinci is <u>celebrated for</u> one of humanity's foremost geniuses: his creative insights into painting, anatomy, and mechanical design can stun a contemporary audience even five centuries after his death.

(A) [NO CHANGE]

(B) celebrated within

(C) celebrated as

(D) celebrated upon

Idioms & Prepositions Answers

1. C
2. D
3. A
4. B
5. A
6. C
7. D
8. B
9. A
10. C

Idioms & Prepositions Explanations

NOTE: Unfortunately, there is not much to "explain" about the answers to this chapter. When it comes to Idioms & Prepositions, the answers are right because "that's just the way we say it!"

1. C - The correct preposition is "for," as in "India is *famous for*…"

2. D - The correct preposition is "about," as in "James had always been *curious about*…"

3. A - NO CHANGE. The correct preposition is "of," as in "Most dogs are not *capable of*…"

4. B - The correct preposition is "against," as in "Galileo was known for his *rebellion against*…"

5. A - NO CHANGE. The correct preposition is "on," as in "You must be careful not to *impose on*…"

6. C - The correct preposition is "in," as in "A smaller force must *engage in* battle."

7. D - The correct preposition is "into," as in "Before an artist *enters into* a contract…"

8. B - The correct preposition is "by," as in "Austin is *regarded by* some as…"

9. A - NO CHANGE. The correct idiom is "In keeping with," which means "in harmony or conformity with."

10. C - The correct idiom is "celebrated as," which means "greatly admired for being…"

Conclusion

My goal in writing this book was to improve your SAT and ACT grammar scores - plain and simple - with three supporting objectives underneath:

1. To thoroughly evaluate your understanding of the rules of English grammar.
2. To teach you - in easily-understandable terms - the grammar mistakes you were already making.
3. To provide extra practice on each essential SAT and ACT grammar topic.

This book was originally intended to be written in under three weeks (what was I thinking?) In the end, it took me over *seven months* to finish. It was quite a long journey, but looking back, I think that I have succeeded.

I think this book is an excellent guide to the SAT and ACT grammar sections. In fact, I think this book has become an excellent resource for *anyone* who wants to master the laws of English grammar - even if they don't plan to take the SAT or ACT tests. If you agree, please find this book on **Amazon.com** and leave a detailed review of your experience using and studying with it. If you disagree, please e-mail me at **Help@LovetheSAT.com** to give me your personal feedback.

So, have you:

1. Tested your grammar basics on the Pretest?
2. Thoroughly studied the chapters covering each mistake you made on the Pretest?
3. Done all of the practice questions on each topic that you studied?

If so, you should be ready to pass the upcoming Posttest with flying colors. This Posttest is just like the Pretest. You will be tested multiple times on each basic grammar topic. When you check the test, you will again be able to identify any of the 17 grammar topics that you need to continue studying.

Remember to apply the twin strategies of **Eliminating Details** and **Rearranging Sentences** on all grammar questions throughout this book and on the real SAT and ACT grammar tests.

If you've worked through all the practice questions and you're still making a lot of mistakes, then *wait* a couple of weeks, *forget* all about this book for a while, and then come back to *review* those topics again. You can use the time in between to prep for other SAT and ACT sections. Give your brain some space to relax and then try again.

Practice makes perfect. No one is born understanding this stuff automatically. And I want you to know that I support you 100% on your journey towards higher scores on the SAT and ACT tests,

- Christian, Founder of Love the SAT Test Prep

Posttest

37 Questions

17 Topics

Answers and Explanations follow the Posttest

1. The group of people, walking through the prestigious museum <u>collection, were talking loudly</u>, while others concealed their irritation.

(A) [NO CHANGE]
(B) collection, was talking loudly
(C) collection and talking loudly
(D) collection, are talking loudly

2. <u>To build city bridges and roads and laying pipes is the job</u> of some construction workers, but competent workers can be found building other industrial projects as well.

(A) [NO CHANGE]
(B) To build city bridges and roads and to lay pipes are the jobs
(C) Building city bridges and roads and to lay pipes are the jobs
(D) To build city bridges and roads and to lay pipes is the job

3. The study of <u>law, which may lead to a well-respected career, but you</u> must also consider the extremely high cost of attending law school.

(A) [NO CHANGE]
(B) law may lead to a well-respected career, but you
(C) law, leading to a well-respected career, but you
(D) law, may lead to a well-respected career, but you

4. Though <u>it is comprehended by</u> only a few, the theories postulated by the famous physicist could be of the utmost importance to society.

(A) [NO CHANGE]
(B) they comprehend
(C) it was comprehended by
(D) they are comprehended by

5. In the Swedish town of Gavle, a giant wood-and-straw statue of a traditional Christmas goat <u>will be damaged</u> by deliberate arson a total of 37 times since 1966.

(A) [NO CHANGE]
(B) is damaged
(C) has been damaged
(D) once was damaged

6. <u>Chewing loudly and talking endlessly at the table</u> are frowned upon within many social circles.

(A) [NO CHANGE]
(B) Chewing loud and endless talking
(C) Chewing loudly and talking endless
(D) Chewing loud and talking endlessly

7. The executives at the record company agreed that <u>the new band must be listened to by them before the company considered promoting</u> its self-recorded album.

(A) [NO CHANGE]

(B) only after they listened to the new band would the company consider promoting

(C) only after the new band was listened to by them would they consider promoting

(D) they must listen to the new band before they considered promoting the album the band made on its own,

8. Although life is short, passing briefly before our eyes, <u>yet</u> we may choose to make the most of it, since we are aware of our mortality.

(A) [NO CHANGE]

(B) so

(C) and

(D) [DELETE the underlined portion]

9. A *Pinkernes* was an official cup-bearer - always male - for the Byzantine emperor, who had an extensive staff that responded to <u>his</u> every whim and command.

(A) [NO CHANGE]

(B) him at

(C) the *pinkernes's*

(D) that man's

Consider the passage below as you answer the following question, Question 10.

[1] The 1980 Summer Olympics were held in Moscow, in the Soviet Union (now Russia). [2] These were the first Olympic Games ever held in a socialist country, which may have been part of what caused these Games to be so controversial on an international scale. [3] Only 80 countries were represented at the 1980 Olympics; over sixty countries boycotted the entire competition because of the Soviet invasion of Afghanistan. [4] These 1980 Olympics were also controversial for another reason: steroids, blood doping, and other illegal performance-enhancing drugs were widespread among the athletes. [5] Surprisingly, there was a greater variety of events held than at any previous Olympics, a total of 203 different fields of competition. [6] It's also of note that some athletes from boycotting countries still participated in the Games under the Olympic Flag, since they were prevented from representing their home countries by the international tensions. [7] Nearly 10 years later, a report from the Australian Senate would claim that "the Moscow Games might well have been called the Chemists' Games." [8] The ramifications of these troubled Olympic Games - from political tensions to drug usage - have continued to reverberate through the modern era.

10. For the sake of logic and cohesion, the best placement for sentence 4 would be

(A) where it is now.

(B) before sentence 3.

(C) after sentence 5.

(D) before sentence 7.

11. Albert Einstein is considered by many to be the <u>preeminent</u> theoretical physicist of all time for his astonishing insights into the nature of the universe.

    (A) [NO CHANGE]
    (B) preceding
    (C) premature
    (D) permanent

12. <u>As it shook violently and spun in circles, Jimmy watched the carnival ride go</u> from an amusing diversion to a dangerous piece of rogue machinery.

    (A) [NO CHANGE]

    (B) Shaking violently and spinning in circles, Jimmy watched the carnival ride go

    (C) Jimmy, as it shook violently and spun in circles, watched the carnival ride go

    (D) As it shook violently and spun in circles, the carnival ride that Jimmy watched went

Consider the sentence below as you answer the question that follows, Question 13.

The Lotus 25 was a revolutionary design for a Formula One race car, and within a year of its debut, driver Jim Clark <u>won the World Championship with it.</u>

13. Which choice provides the most relevant and vivid sensory details to the previous sentence?

(A) [NO CHANGE]

(B) sped to a World Championship victory in the roar of its engine.

(C) proved that its design was exceptional with a World Championship victory.

(D) demonstrated its speed and power with a World Championship victory.

14. I prefer <u>the way that Frank Gehry designs buildings to</u> Frank Lloyd Wright's buildings.

    (A) [NO CHANGE]
    (B) Frank Gehry's designs to
    (C) Frank Gehry to
    (D) Frank Gehry's designs more than

15. The trial lawyer found herself increasingly troubled by the number of convicted felons who had never <u>admitted of</u> their crimes, despite the evidence being strongly in favor of their guilt.

(A) [NO CHANGE]

(B) admitted for

(C) admitted to

(D) admitted that

16. <u>John was debating the finer merits of interplanetary exploration, but Sarah was rebutting</u> his argument with excellent points about world hunger.

(A) [NO CHANGE]

(B) John, debating the finer merits of interplanetary exploration, but Sarah was rebutting

(C) John debated the finer merits of interplanetary exploration, Sarah rebutted

(D) John was debating the finer merits of interplanetary exploration; but Sarah was rebutting

17. <u>Her trainer and her, surprisingly, both</u> preferred to practice in the pouring rain, and agreed that if one could ride a horse in a storm, one could ride a horse in any conditions.

(A) [NO CHANGE]

(B) Surprisingly, both her and her trainer

(C) She and her trainer, surprisingly, both

(D) Both her and her trainer, surprisingly,

Consider the passage below as you answer the following questions, Question 18 and 19.

[1] Just outside of the major metropolis of Chengdu, China, lies the world's foremost Giant Panda breeding facility. [2] The facility, founded in 1987 and known officially as the "Chengdu Research Base of Giant Panda Breeding," is a non-profit research center and internationally-recognized tourism destination. [3] The research base spreads over dozens of acres and is home to over 80 pandas of all ages - from tiny newborn infants to rambunctious, playful adolescents to fully-grown giant bears who seem calm and contemplative as they munch bamboo shoots. [4] Here, the pandas are kept safe and happy in large enclosures that mimic their natural environments and provide plenty of space to climb, play, sleep, and eat. [5] Although the Giant Pandas are the main attraction, there is also a large pen dedicated to the fox-like Red Pandas. [6] Both Giant Pandas and Red Pandas are endangered after years of poaching, pollution, and habitat loss. [7] Thus, the Chengdu Panda Base is not only an extraordinarily interesting place for nature-lovers to visit, but also a crucial force in the battle to keep these magnificent animals from going extinct forever.

18. The author is considering deleting sentence 6. Should the author make this change?

(A) Yes, because the sentence distracts from the primary topic of the paragraph.

(B) Yes, because the negative tone of this sentence is not consistent with the rest of the paragraph.

(C) No, because the sentence includes useful information that relates to the conclusion of the paragraph.

(D) No, because the sentence provides a relevant example to the paragraph.

19. At Point [5], the author is considering adding the following sentence to the paragraph:

Tourists enjoy watching the bears' daily activities so much that the Giant Pandas even have their own live video stream, which is broadcast around the world via the internet.

Should the writer add this sentence here?

(A) Yes, because this sentence provides additional relevant information to the paragraph.

(B) Yes, because this sentence provides an effective supporting argument to the paragraph.

(C) No, because this sentence introduces unrelated information to the paragraph.

(D) No, because this sentence repeats information that has already been provided elsewhere.

20. In contrast to the purpose of typical audio equipment, which is to provide a pleasant sound, "reference" speakers are designed to reproduce sound exactly as it was recorded.

(A) [NO CHANGE]

(B) "reference" speakers are designed for reproducing

(C) the purpose of "reference" speakers is to reproduce

(D) the purpose of "reference" speakers is reproducing

21. Grateful for avoiding the perils of war, my thoughts were that a military draft should never again be reinstated in a civilized country.

(A) [NO CHANGE]

(B) Grateful for avoiding the perils of war, I thought that

(C) My thoughts were, grateful for avoiding the perils of war, that

(D) My thoughts, grateful for avoiding the perils of war, were that

22. The Baron Tyrawley was born Charles O'Hara: who rose through the ranks to become the Commander-in-Chief of the Royal Irish Army in the early 1700s.

(A) [NO CHANGE]

(B) Charles O'Hara who

(C) Charles O'Hara; who

(D) Charles O'Hara, who

23. Hanging on the wall in my room are one acoustic guitar, which I won in a music competition, and two electric bass guitars.

(A) [NO CHANGE]

(B) Hanging on the wall in my room is one acoustic guitar, which were won

(C) On the wall in my room is hanging one acoustic guitar, which I won

(D) Hanging on the wall in my room are one acoustic guitar, which were won

24. The *Sixpenny Library* was a complete set of reference books (almost two hundred in total) that was published in the late 1920s and earned praise for its high quality and affordable price.

(A) [NO CHANGE]

(B) high quality, level of excellence, and its affordable price.

(C) high quality, low cost, and affordable price.

(D) affordability, high quality, and inexpensive price.

25. Tara and Philippe liked their new patio, which <u>they constructed themselves, it was built out of recycled plastic and reclaimed timber.</u>

(A) [NO CHANGE]

(B) they constructed themselves out of recycled plastic and reclaimed timber.

(C) out of recycled plastic and reclaimed timber, they had constructed it.

(D) they constructed themselves, the patio was built out of recycled plastic and reclaimed timber.

26. With little time left to spare before the plane's arrival, <u>my parents and me rushed</u> to the international airport to pick up my little brother.

(A) [NO CHANGE]

(B) me and my parents are rushing

(C) my parents and I rushed

(D) my parents and myself rushed

27. The citizens and government of the costal city of Alicante, Spain, have ensured their port is integrated with the coastline through local planning <u>laws; they prohibit</u> the construction of high buildings, with the exception of specialized situations such as construction cranes.

(A) [NO CHANGE]

(B) laws, prohibit

(C) laws; it prohibits

(D) laws; these laws prohibit

28. The beans of the petai <u>tree - known for</u> their peculiar smell and distinctive, powerful flavor - are used in the cuisine of many Southeast Asian countries such as Indonesia, Malaysia, and Thailand.

(A) [NO CHANGE]

(B) tree (known for

(C) tree, known for

(D) tree; known for

29. When attending a stand-up comedy show, remember that the comedian's jokes aren't <u>meant to</u> hurt your feelings, although he or she may make fun of specific people in the audience - including you!

(A) [NO CHANGE]

(B) meant for

(C) meant by

(D) meant that

30. A "luge" is a tiny, minimalist sled for one or two people often used in high-speed downhill competitions; luging <u>originates</u> as a winter pastime in the town of St. Moritz, Switzerland in the 1800s, but has since evolved into a thriving Olympic-level sport.

(A) [NO CHANGE]

(B) originated

(C) originating

(D) has originated

31. Whether <u>studying weeks in advance or you cram at the last second</u> on the way to school, the final exam will inevitably be challenging.

(A) [NO CHANGE]

(B) you study weeks in advance or cramming at the last second

(C) you study weeks in advance or cram at the last second

(D) you studied weeks in advance or it's a last-second cram

32. Anyone hoping to become a professional athlete must make sure that <u>they are constantly practicing</u> the fundamental skills of the sport.

(A) [NO CHANGE]

(B) they constantly practice

(C) these constantly practice

(D) he or she is constantly practicing

33. Ground squirrels are adept at hiding many <u>nuts, but</u> frequently not so talented at remembering where they place their caches.

(A) [NO CHANGE]

(B) nuts; yet

(C) nuts; consequently, they are

(D) nuts, for they are

34. The eruption of Mount St. Helens in 1980 was a <u>misadventure</u> of epic proportions that destroyed 250 homes and killed fifty-seven people.

(A) [NO CHANGE]

(B) catalyst

(C) affliction

(D) calamity

35. I was too embarrassed to tell my little brother, who is a professional picture-hanger, that <u>the picture hung crooked on the wall.</u>

(A) [NO CHANGE]

(B) on the wall, the picture hung crooked.

(C) the picture on the wall hung crookedly.

(D) the picture, hung crookedly on the wall.

<u>A large bridge in France,</u> the Millau Viaduct is currently the tallest bridge in the world - 23 meters taller than the Eiffel Tower - and it saves tens of thousands of hours of driving time for French citizens and tourists each year.

36. Which choice provides the most effective introduction to the preceding sentence?

(A) [NO CHANGE]

(B) Although it was constructed at great expense,

(C) Consistently ranked as one of the greatest engineering successes of all time,

(D) When compared to other bridges,

37. <u>Bad drivers, always a source of mystery and amusement to me, though they</u> are dangerous to others on the road.

 (A) [NO CHANGE]

 (B) Bad drivers, though amusing and mystifying to me, they

 (C) To my mystification and amusement, bad drivers, they

 (D) Bad drivers are always a source of mystery and amusement to me, though they

Posttest Answers

1. B, Subject-Verb Agreement (Lesson 1)
2. B, Parallelism & Comparisons (Lesson 10)
3. B, Sentence Structure (Lesson 9)
4. D, Pronoun-Antecedent Agreement (Lesson 5)
5. C, Verb Tense & Form (Lesson 2)
6. A, Adjectives & Adverbs (Lesson 3)
7. B, Redundancy & Wordiness (Lesson 13)
8. D, Conjunctions & Transitions (Lesson 7)
9. C, Pronoun-Antecedent Clarity (Lesson 4)
10. D, Moving Sentences & Paragraphs (Lesson 16)
11. A, Vocab Word Choice (Lesson 12)
12. D, Misplaced Modifiers (Lesson 11)
13. B, Objective Questions (Lesson 14)
14. B, Parallelism & Comparisons (Lesson 10)
15. C, Idioms & Prepositions (Lesson 17)
16. A, Sentence Structure (Lesson 9)
17. C, Pronoun Case (Lesson 6)
18. C, Adding or Removing Information (Lesson 15)
19. A, Adding or Removing Information (Lesson 15)
20. C, Parallelism & Comparisons (Lesson 10)
21. B, Misplaced Modifiers (Lesson 11)
22. D, Punctuation Marks (Lesson 8)
23. A, Subject-Verb Agreement (Lesson 1)
24. A, Redundancy & Wordiness (Lesson 13)
25. B, Sentence Structure (Lesson 9)
26. C, Pronoun Case (Lesson 6)
27. D, Pronoun-Antecedent Clarity (Lesson 4)
28. A, Punctuation Marks (Lesson 8)
29. A, Idioms & Prepositions (Lesson 17)
30. B, Verb Tense & Form (Lesson 2)
31. C, Parallelism & Comparisons (Lesson 10)
32. D, Pronoun-Antecedent Agreement (Lesson 5)
33. A, Conjunctions & Transitions (Lesson 7)
34. D, Vocab Word Choice (Lesson 12)
35. C, Adjectives & Adverbs (Lesson 3)
36. C, Objective Questions (Lesson 14)
37. D, Sentence Structure (Lesson 9)

Posttest Explanations

1. B - The original sentence incorrectly uses the plural verb "*were* talking" in reference to a sneaky singular subject: "The group." It's just one *singular group*, so we should use the singular verb "*was* talking" (Lesson 1, **Subject-Verb Agreement**). Choice D correctly uses the plural verb "*are* talking," but causes a verb tense conflict between the present tense "are talking" and the past tense "others concealed" (see Lesson 2, **Verb Tense & Form**). Choice C creates a Sentence Fragment (see Lesson 9, **Sentence Structure**).

2. B - The original sentence contains a **Parallelism** mistake (see Lesson 10). There is a list with two items in it: "*To build* city bridges and roads" and "*laying* pipes." (It may seem like three items at first, but there are really only two: "to build" and "laying".) Regardless, there's a Parallelism mistake because the two items don't match their forms - the first item uses the infinitive form "to build," and the second uses the -ing form "laying." This also eliminates Choice C for the same reason. Choice D follows correct Parallelism, but unfortunately it contains a **Subject-Verb Agreement** error (Lesson 1) by matching the two *plural* jobs ("to build" and "to lay") with the *singular* verb and noun, "*is the job*." Only Choice B follows correct Parallelism without making a singular-plural mistake.

3. B - The original sentence contains a Sentence Fragment error (see Lesson 9, **Sentence Structure**). Use the **Eliminating Details** tactic (Prelesson B), particularly to remove the Parenthetical Clause ("which...career") in the middle. This will leave you with "The study of law, but you must also consider the cost." Notice that the second clause is a Dependent Clause - and that's just fine - but the first clause is *not* a complete Independent Clause - it's just a subject ("study") without a main verb. That means the underlying Sentence Structure contains a Sentence Fragment. If you analyze Choices C and D, you'll find that they have a similar problem. Only Choice B correctly matches a complete Independent Clause in the first half of the sentence with a Dependent Clause in the second half.

4. D - The original sentence incorrectly uses the *singular* pronoun "it" to refer to a *plural* antecedent noun, "theories," which are comprehended by only a few people (see Lesson 5, **Pronoun-Antecedent Agreement**). Choice C commits the same mistake. Although Choice B correctly uses the plural antecedent "they," it bungles the meaning of the sentence by saying that the theories *comprehend*, rather than the theories *are comprehended*. That leaves the correct answer, Choice D, which matches a plural pronoun "they" to a plural antecedent, "theories."

5. C - The original sentence contains an illogical use of the *future tense*, "will be damaged," to refer to a *past event* that has already occurred many times since 1966 (see Lesson 2, **Verb Tense & Form**). Choice B uses the *present tense*, which also doesn't work for a past event. Choices C and D are both forms of past tense, but Choice D incorrectly implies that the event happened "once" in the past, when we know it has happened "37 times." That leaves us with Choice C as the best possible answer.

6. A - NO CHANGE. The original sentence is the best choice for two reasons: First, it correctly uses the adverbs "loudly" and "endlessly" to describe the actions of "chewing" and "talking" (see Lesson 3, **Adjectives & Adverbs**, and Prelesson A, **Parts of Speech**). Secondly, it follows correct parallel structure (see Lesson 10, **Parallelism**). The other answer choices either break Parallelism or incorrectly use an *adjective* (like "loud" or "endless") to modify a verb (like "chewing" or "talking.") *Adjectives* can only modify *nouns*, never verbs; we must always use *adverbs* (which usually end in "-ly") to modify verbs.

7. B - The original sentence is wordy as a result of being in the passive voice (see Lesson 13, **Redundancy & Wordiness**). Rather than saying "the new band must be listened to by them," it's more active and less wordy to say "they listened to the new band," as in the correct answer, Choice B. Also note the Redundancy in Choice D: "the album the band made on its own" is redundant when the sentence also states it's a "self-recorded album" - these two phrases have identical meanings, so it's redundant to use both of them together.

8. D - The original sentence uses *two* conjunctions ("although" and "yet") to connect between a single pair of ideas. We should know this isn't allowed; only *one* conjunction is used to link between two ideas (see Lesson 7, **Conjunctions & Transitions**). Our only choice is to DELETE the conjunction "yet," leaving us with a single conjunction at the beginning of the sentence ("although") to establish the connection between the two clauses. Notice that the sentence begins with a Dependent Clause, and ends with an Independent Clause, which is a bit less common than the reverse of Independent-Dependent, but still completely acceptable - as long as there's only *one* conjunction linking the two clauses.

9. C - The original sentence contains a **Pronoun-Antecedent Clarity** problem (Lesson 4). The singular masculine pronoun "his" could easily refer to *either* the "pinkernes" or the "emperor." In other words, we have a pronoun ("his") without a crystal-clear antecedent for it to refer to. This is one of the major risks of using pronouns in writing and speech, and we should always be on the lookout for this mistake. Most of our other options, particularly Choices B and D, don't do anything to make this problem any better. Only Choice C actually specifies that we're referring to the *pinkernes*; we resolve the Pronoun Clarity issue by simply removing the pronoun completely and restating the person we're referring to instead.

10. D - When dealing with a **Moving Sentences & Paragraphs** question, it's a smart strategy to begin by analyzing the sentence you're moving (see Lesson 16). Sentence 4's first half says these Olympics were "*also* controversial for *another* reason," indicating that this sentence should follow a prior example of a controversy. The second half of the sentence introduces the idea that "steroids" and "other performance-enhancing drugs" were used by the athletes. The easiest way to proceed is to find a place to put this sentence which is *preceded* by a controversy and *followed* by more discussion of steroid usage. Choice D is perfect - now our sentence is preceded by a section about political boycotts (a "controversy") and followed by a report about "the Chemists' Games," which could be a followup to the illegal steroids introduced in our sentence.

11. A - NO CHANGE. This is a standard **Vocab Word Choice** question (see Lesson 12). These questions are easiest when you know the meaning, connotations, and common contexts of each word choice. In this case, we need a word that represents Einstein's great skill as a physicist ("astonishing insights"). However, Choice B means "coming before," Choice C means "too early," and Choice D means "lasting forever." None of these convey the correct meaning as well as Choice A, which means "best and most famous."

12. D - The original sentence contains an amusing **Misplaced Modifier** error (see Lesson 11): the introductory descriptive phrase ("as it shook violently and spun in circles") is currently attaching itself to the nearest noun, "Jimmy". That implies that *Jimmy* is shaking violently and spinning in circles! From the details of the sentence, it's clear that the *ride* should be shaking and spinning, not *Jimmy*. Choices B and C repeat the same error in different forms; only Choice D correctly places the modifying phrase next to what it's actually meant to describe, which is "the carnival ride."

13. B - This is an **Objective Question** (see Lesson 14), which we can quickly recognize by the set of specific instructions we're given ("provides the most relevant and vivid sensory details"). Let's give them exactly what they want. "Sensory details" are words that evoke our senses (like sound, motion, smell, or sight). Choice A completely fails to use any sensory descriptions; same with Choice C. It's possible that Choice D has a bit of sensory detail ("speed and power" might *just barely* qualify as "sensory") - but Choice B is *much* better: "*sped* to victory in the *roar* of its engine" evokes our senses of both hearing and kinetic motion.

14. B - Notice the comparison of two items: "the *way* that Frank Gehry designs" vs. "Frank Lloyd Wright's *buildings*." This is classic **Parallelism & Comparison** territory (see Lesson 10). The two items are not the same: a *way* of designing cannot be compared to actual *buildings*. Choice C contains an amusing variation on this same mistake, comparing the *man* "Frank Gehry" to the *buildings* of Frank Lloyd Wright. Choice D correctly fixes the Comparison error (comparing the two similar nouns "designs" and "buildings"), but unfortunately contains a subtle **Idioms & Prepositions** error (see Lesson 17) because we don't say "prefer [A] *more than* [B]," but rather "prefer [A] *to* [B]." Only Choice B is acceptable (and yes, it's acceptable to compare one architect's "designs" to another architect's "buildings," since these two nouns can have nearly identical meanings in this context).

15. C - Notice how the answer choices swap out different prepositions (see Prelesson A, **Parts of Speech**) *of, for,* and *to*, all paired with the same base word "admitted." For better or for worse, this is an **Idioms & Prepositions** error (see Lesson 17), which means you just have to know the right answer because "that's the way we say it." In this case, the proper phrasing is "admitted *to* their crimes."

16. A - NO CHANGE. The original sentence is fine, both in terms of **Parallelism** (Lesson 10) and **Sentence Structure** (Lesson 9). Our other choices all create Sentence Structure mistakes, which are easier to spot if you apply Prelesson B on **Eliminating Details**. Choice B contains a Sentence Fragment - the first half reduces to simply "John," a subject without a main verb. Choice C is a Comma Splice, because the first half and second half are both Independent Clauses. Choice D can also be seen as a **Punctuation Marks** mistake (Lesson 8) because it incorrectly uses a semicolon without an Independent Clause on either side of it (remember that semicolons are essentially the same as periods). There's an Independent Clause on the left side of the semicolon, which is great, but unfortunately there's a Dependent Clause on the right side ("but Sarah was...") which is unacceptable.

17. C - The original sentence contains a **Pronoun Case** error (Lesson 6), which is easier to notice if you remove the "trainer" from the sentence. That leaves you with *"Her* preferred to practice." Sounds awfully weird, doesn't it? Try changing the Pronoun Case from *objective form* ("her") to *subjective form* ("she"): *"She* preferred to practice." Sounds much better, right? To get technical for a moment, that's because a *subjective* pronoun like "she" can *do* something like "prefer to practice." However, an *objective* form like "her" is meant to have things done *to* her (you could "throw to ball *to her*," for example). In our original sentence, *she* is *doing* something; she is the *subject*; "she" is "preferring," all of which is why the subjective form "she" sounds so much better to you - your ear knows this stuff already, as long as you remember to look for it and remove distracting details. Choices B and D repeat the same Pronoun Case error as the original sentence.

18. C - It's easy to recognize this **Adding or Removing Information** question (Lesson 15) by the phrasing: "The author is considering deleting sentence 6." The answer choices ("Yes / Yes / No / No") are also distinctive to this type of question. Are there any answer choices we can quickly eliminate? How about Choice A, because this sentence stays focused on the pandas - certainly not a "distraction" from the primary topic of the paragraph, which is also about pandas. Let's also eliminate Choice B: although the pandas being "endangered" is definitely a "negative," it's not as if this sentence suddenly switches into a deep, dark tone that conflicts with the positive tone of the rest of the paragraph; no, sentence 6 simply provides some relevant, factual information that just happens to be on the negative side, but the *tone* of the sentence stays relatively neutral and informative. It seems that we'll be "keeping" sentence 6, since our only remaining choices are C and D. However, sentence 6 doesn't provide an "example" - it just gives us additional information that relates to the concluding final sentence, which calls the Chengdu Panda Base a "crucial force in the battle to keep these animals from going extinct."

19. A - This is another **Adding or Removing Information** question (Lesson 15), as we can see from the wording "Should the writer add this sentence here" and the answer choices "Yes / Yes / No / No." Are there any answer choices we can eliminate? We can definitely get rid of Choice D, because this information about internet video streaming has *not* been given anywhere else in the paragraph. Also, let's eliminate Choice C ("unrelated information"), since the new sentence remains closely focused on the pandas, their daily activities, and the tourists and visitors who enjoy watching the pandas. That means we *are* going to be adding the sentence, since our only remaining choices are A and B. However, this new sentence does not function as a "supporting argument," since the purpose of the sentence is neutral and *informative*, not *persuasive* or *argumentative*. Therefore, let's go with Choice A - this new sentence *should* be added, because it provides "additional relevant information."

20. C - Choices A and B both contain **Illogical Comparisons** (Lesson 10). The original sentence is not comparing *speakers* to speakers; the first item in the comparison is about the *purpose* of some speakers and the second item is the *speakers* themselves. This is an Illogical Comparison. Choices C and D both correctly swap the second item to "the *purpose* of speakers," but Choice D contains a **Parallelism** mistake (also Lesson 10) because the first item uses the infinitive form "to provide" but the second item switches to "-ing" form ("reproducing"). Only Choice C makes a correct, logical comparison between "purpose" and "purpose," while also maintaining Parallelism by using two infinitive forms, "to provide" and "to reproduce."

21. B - The original sentence contains a **Misplaced Modifier** error (Lesson 11). "Grateful for avoiding the perils of war" is the descriptive modifying phrase that starts off the sentence, but we are waiting to hear *who* this description is attached to - and then we get "my thoughts," instead. A *person* would be grateful for avoiding a war, not their *thoughts*. In other words, the descriptive phrase at the beginning ("grateful for avoiding the perils of war") is currently applying to the closest noun, "my thoughts," which is incorrect - the "grateful" phrase should apply to the *person* thinking, not to their *thoughts*. That's why Choice B is best: now the modifying phrase of gratefulness is applying directly to "*I*," since "I" is someone who can be grateful for avoiding the "perils of war."

22. D - This question is about **Punctuation Marks** (Lesson 8). You can tell by the differences in the answer choices - the only thing that changes is the punctuation mark between "O'Hara" and "who." Let's go down the list. We can't use a colon (:) - remember the two criteria for using a colon correctly are "the colon is preceded by a *complete sentence*" (it is) and "the colon *introduces* one or more *examples* or a *definition*" (it doesn't). We can't use a semicolon, as in Choice C, because that requires a complete sentence on both sides, and the second half of the sentence ("who rose...") can't stand on its own, because it's a Parenthetical Clause (refer to **Sentence Structure**, Lesson 9). Between Choices B and D, the only difference is a comma between the Independent Clause (ending with "O'Hara") and the Parenthetical Clause ("beginning with "who..."). Commas are used to separate clauses from each other (except when they are both Independent Clauses), so let's use one now - which gives us Choice D as the best answer.

23. A - NO CHANGE. This sentence is based on **Subject-Verb Agreement** (Lesson 1) and uses a *compound-plural subject* that's tricky to spot because of the unusual way the sentence is structured. Ask yourself, what is hanging on the wall? At first, it seems like just "one acoustic guitar," but reading the complete sentence to the end informs us that two more electric bass guitars are *also* hanging on the wall. That means the subject of the sentence (three total guitars) is *plural*, so we must use a plural main verb like "*are* hanging," not a singular like "*is* hanging." That eliminates Choices B and C, which both use the singular verb "is hanging." As for Choice D, it fixes the original singular-plural issue, but then commits a new mistake - the one acoustic guitar (singular) *was* won (singular), not *were* won (plural). Only the original version correctly handles all the singular-plural Subject Verb Agreements.

24. A - NO CHANGE. This is a simple case of **Redundancy** (Lesson 13). Note that Choice B mentions "high quality" *and* "level of excellence," which are essentially duplicates of each other; Choice C mentions "low cost" *and* "affordable price," which also have duplicate meanings; Choice D mentions "affordability" *and* "inexpensive price" - same problem. When you notice this sort of redundant, repetitive situation, it's usually safe to assume the SAT or ACT wants the shortest, least repetitive answer - which is Choice A.

25. B - The central issue in this sentence is a question of **Sentence Structure** (Lesson 9). The original sentence contains a Comma Splice, because there are two complete Independent Clauses joined only by a comma, without a subordinating conjunction to make one half "Dependent". Take a look: the first half, "Tara and Philippe liked their new patio" can stand alone; so can the second half, "It was built out of recycled plastic." Choice C and D commit the same Comma Splice error with a couple of creative variations on the original sentence. Still, they both contain two Independent Clauses, connected only by a comma (you can also review **Punctuation Marks**, Lesson 8, for more practice). Choice B is correct, and results in an Independent Clause at the start, followed by a comma and a subordinate Parenthetical Clause ("which they constructed...") that connects to that Independent Clause.

26. C - You can identify this **Pronoun Case** (Lesson 6) question by the switches between "me" and "I" in the answer choices (other common giveaway words could be "he" vs. "him", "she" vs. "her", "us" vs. "we", "they" vs. "them", etc). The standard tactic is to read the pronoun by itself - in this case, ignore "my parents" and just read "*Me* rushed to the airport." Now trust your ear. When you change "me" to "I," it sounds much better: "*I* rushed to the airport." Only the correct answer, Choice C, gives us the objective form, "I." You can also compare this to the explanation of Posttest Question 17 for more technical details, and be sure to refer back to Lesson 6 if you're still confused.

27. D - Notice the underlined pronoun "they" (**Parts of Speech**, Prelesson A). What is the antecedent of this pronoun? To be honest, it's not clear. "They" could refer to "the citizens," "the government," "the laws," or possibly something else. That makes this a textbook **Pronoun Clarity** mistake (Lesson 4). Often, the easiest way to solve this sort of problem is to completely remove the pronoun and/or replace it with the specific noun it's meant to replace. That's exactly what Choice D does, which clarifies "who" or "what" is prohibiting this construction. Choice B avoids the Pronoun Clarity error, but has a **Sentence Structure** problem (Lesson 9) because there are two main verbs in the clause ("have ensured" and "prohibit") both competing for one plural subject ("citizens and government").

28. A - NO CHANGE. This is clearly a **Punctuation Marks** question (Lesson 8) because the only thing changing in the answers are the punctuation marks between "tree" and "known." This question is easy: read ahead in the sentence to notice the dash mark (-) between "flavor" and "are used." One common use of dash marks is as a substitute for parentheses, surrounding a Parenthetical Clause (review **Sentence Structure**, Lesson 9). That's exactly what's going on here. We can't use the open parentheses "(" in Choice B, because the sentence doesn't contain a close parentheses ")". We can't use a semicolon ";" as in Choice D, because there isn't an Independent Clause on either side (think, "could we use a period here?" Definitely not - and the same rules apply for a semicolon). Choice C, the comma, could work to surround a Parenthetical Clause - except that would require the dash mark after "flavor" to *also* be a comma. Instead we're just going to leave the sentence the way it is: a pair of dash marks will surround the Parenthetical Clause "known for... flavor" to mark it out as separate from the rest of the main sentence.

29. A - NO CHANGE. The answer choices reveal that this is an **Idioms & Prepositions** (Lesson 17) question because of the changes from "to," "for," and "by." The answer is A, because in English we would pair the words "meant" and "to," as in: "he *meant to* hurt your feelings." That's just how it is. As always with these Idiom questions, "that's just the way we say it."

30. B - Notice that the only thing changing in the answer choices is **Verb Tense & Form** (Lesson 2). Usually, that makes our job pretty easy - just track down the timeline of the sentence and establish what tense we should use. In this case, we need a *past-tense verb* because of the historical context - this sport was created "in the 1800s." That eliminates the present tense Choice A. We also can't use Choice C, because the form "originating" would create a Parenthetical Clause (**Sentence Structure**, Lesson 9) instead of acting as a main verb for the Independent Clause that must come after the semicolon (**Punctuation Marks**, Lesson 8). Both Choices B and D are forms of the past tense, but we want the simple past tense "originated," because the action of originating has already been *completed* in the past, instead than the present perfect tense, "has originated," which implies that the action of originating may still be *ongoing.*

31. C - Here's another example of one of our favorite errors, **Parallelism & Comparisons** (Lesson 10). There is a list or comparison between two items: "studying weeks in advance" or "you cram at the last second." Several Parallelism mistakes are present, so let's remember that we want the **Parts of Speech** (Prelesson A) and **Verb Forms** (Lesson 2) to match as closely as pssible. For example, in the original sentence, one problem is that "studying" is an "-ing" form, but "cram" is a present tense form. A similar problem exists in Choice B. Choice D uses a verb in the first half ("you studied") against a noun in the second half of the comparison ("a last-second cram"). All of these are forms of Parallelism mistakes; only Choice C uses two verbs in the same forms and same tenses ("study" and "cram"). They also match in their finer details of time periods, which offers further confirmation that the Parallelism pattern-following is on point: notice "study [in time period]" vs "cram" [in time period]".

32. D - The original sentence contains a sly **Pronoun Agreement** error (Lesson 5). "Anyone" is a *singular* pronoun (makes sense, right, because it says "any *one*?") However, the underlined portion uses the *plural* pronoun "they" to refer to the same hopeful athlete. We don't know if it's a male or female athlete, so we use the *singular* pronoun construction "he or she" provided by Choice D. This reasoning also eliminates Choices B and C, which use more plural pronouns, "they" and "these."

33. A - NO CHANGE. The answer choices to this question are mostly based on **Conjunction & Transition** errors (Lesson 7). The first and second halves of the sentence contain two *contradicting* ideas (first idea: squirrels are skilled at hiding nuts; second idea: squirrels are also *unskilled* at finding those nuts again). Therefore the *continuing* conjunctions like "consequently" or "for" are illogical, which eliminates Choices C and D. We need a word like "but" or "yet" that indicates the two ideas in this sentence are *contradicting* each other. However, Choice B contains a **Sentence Structure** mistake (Lesson 9) - or it could be a **Punctuation Marks** mistake (Lesson 8), depending on how you look at it. Either way, Choice B incorrectly uses a semicolon without having an Independent Clause on both sides; the second half of Choice B is a Dependent Clause, so we must use a *comma* instead of a *semicolon*. That leaves us with the original version of the sentence, Choice A, as our only option.

34. D - This is a **Vocab Word Choice** question (Lesson 12). These rely on the meanings, connotations, and contexts of the four word choices. In this sentence, we see a massive, deadly natural disaster - clearly a serious, negative event. A "misadventure" has a more lighthearted or humorous tone to it; it's not the most appropriate choice for the seriousness of this disaster. A "catalyst" (Choice B) doesn't have the correct meaning - it essentially means a "stimulus" or something that "increases the rate" at which something else happened. Doesn't fit the required meaning. An "affliction" (Choice C) is something that causes pain or suffering, but is more commonly used in the context of an illness or ill health. Choice D, "calamity," is the best option - it means "a disaster; a sudden event that causes great damage," and it has the appropriate negative connotation and fits the context of a volcanic eruption.

35. C - The original sentence incorrectly uses an adjective (**Parts of Speech**, Prelesson A), "crooked," to describe *how* a picture "hung." "Hung" is a verb, but adjectives can *only* describe nouns (see Lesson 3, **Adjectives & Adverbs**). Use the adverb form, "crooked*ly*," and you'll be fine here. Choice D contains a **Sentence Structure** mistake (Lesson 9) because the verb "hung" doesn't have a subject - it's become incorrectly separated from the main clause by a comma.

36. C - This is an **Objective Question** (Lesson 14) - we can tell by the specific instructions to "provide the most effective introduction" to the sentence. Take note of the sentence's focus: the "tallest bridge in the world," it "saves tens of thousands of hours" for the people who use it. Get rid of Choice B, because the sentence doesn't focus on any aspect of cost; also, it doesn't make sense use a contradicting **Conjunction** (Lesson 7) to say "it's the tallest bridge *although* it was expensive." Also, remove Choice D, which is **Redundant** (Lesson 13): obviously it can only be the tallest bridge "when compared to other bridges." Between Choice A and Choice C, both have some useful information; however, Choice C emphasizes the context and tone of a massive, spectacular, and successful bridge while offering new information ("ranked one of the greatest engineering successes of all time"). On the other hand, Choice A is underwhelming by comparison, simply offering "a large bridge in France" - surely a bit of an understatement for "the tallest bridge in the world," and one that we can already easily deduce is in France by the context clue of "French citizens."

37. D - The original sentence contains a Sentence Fragment error (**Sentence Structure**, Lesson 9). Use the **Eliminating Details** tactic (Prelesson B) and you're left with the fragment "Drivers, though they are dangerous." This lacks a main verb. Choices B and C have similar problems that become evident by Eliminating Details. That leaves Choice D, which follows excellent sentence structure: there is an Independent Clause to begin ("Bad drivers are...") followed by a comma, a subordinating conjunction ("though"), and then a Dependent Clause.

What To Do Next

You may have just finished this book, and you may be feeling great about your grammar scores, but there are many other major sections of the tests still to tackle. Don't stop preparing for higher SAT & ACT scores now!

The next step is to contact us directly at **Help@LovetheSAT.com** for a FREE personalized consultation on SAT & ACT prep. We want to hear from *you* and help you on a 1-to-1 basis, so please get in touch today, before you forget in the midst of your busy high school lifestyle.

Also visit our website at **www.LovetheSAT.com** for free articles and more valuable information about getting ready for - and getting *into* - your top-choice college. While you're there, subscribe to our SAT & ACT email list at **https://bit.ly/2FLG1m7** for more score-improving tips and incredibly-useful secrets from a team of veteran SAT & ACT tutors.

There is simply so much that you can do to control and improve your SAT and ACT test scores! From reviewing this book to studying 1-on-1 with one of our staff tutors... from increasing your amount of daily personal reading to doing timed practice SAT & ACT tests under pressure... the key is to take consistent daily action towards your long-term goals.

Please contact us with the details of your current situation and we'll keep you moving towards new high scores!

About the Author

Christian Heath is a veteran SAT & ACT prep tutor with over 10 years of teaching experience focused exclusively on SAT & ACT testing. He is the founder and lead tutor of Love the SAT Test Prep, the highest-rated SAT & ACT prep center in Austin, TX, where he lives and works.

As a thought leader in the SAT & ACT prep industry, he has been invited to teach at Chengdu International School in China on three occasions. He maintains perfect scores on both the SAT and ACT tests.

Don't forget to check out his other book for teens, *Ultimate Time Management for Teens and Students*, available on Amazon.com at https://amzn.to/2SxWPj8 or through www.LovetheSAT.com/store. You can read more of his writings at www.LovetheSAT.com/blog.

Also by Christian Heath

Ultimate Time Management for Teens and Students

If there's one thing that unites every high school student, it's that they never have enough time or energy to get everything done. It's time for that to change.

This book contains an arsenal of tips, tricks, and strategies from a veteran SAT & ACT tutor and elite-college graduate that will work for every high school student at any point in their high school career.

Get better grades, have more fun, reduce your anxiety, enjoy life more, win more scholarships, and get into a better college! Available on Amazon at https://amzn.to/2SxWPj8.

Personalized SAT & ACT Tutoring

Get higher SAT & ACT scores with a fun & friendly 1-on-1 personal tutor! Our staff of experienced SAT & ACT prep tutors can work with any high school student to reach new high scores, build confidence, eliminate testing anxiety, and have fun along the way. Contact us today by emailing **Help@LovetheSAT.com** or call **1-800-653-8994** for a FREE, personalized consultation and lesson plans custom-tailored to your needs, goals, and busy schedule.

Made in the USA
Monee, IL
25 February 2020